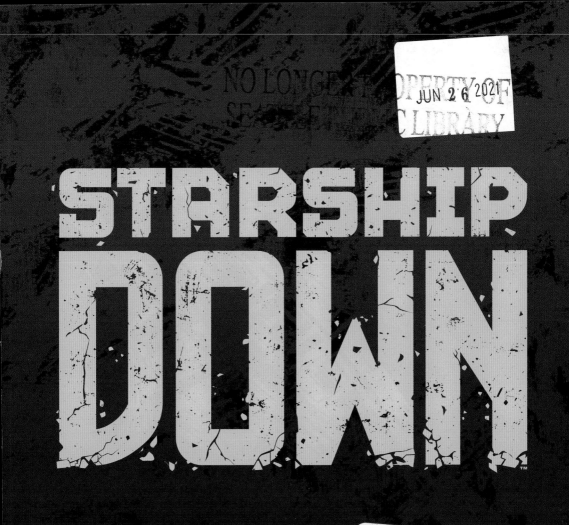

STARSHIP
DOWN™

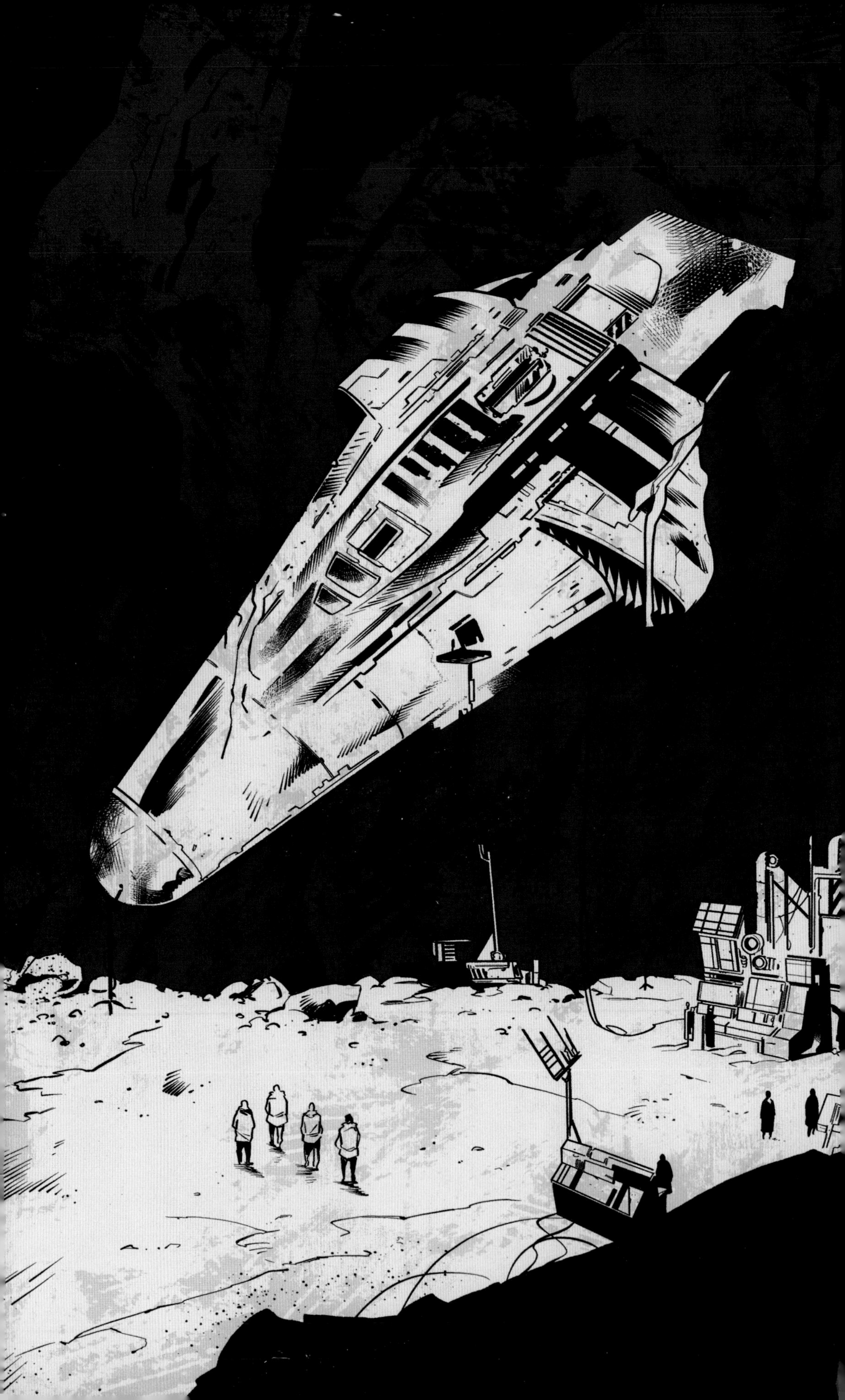

STARSHIP DOWN

STORY BY
JUSTIN GIAMPAOLI

ART BY
ANDREA MUTTI

COLORS BY
VLADIMIR POPOV

LETTERS BY
SAL CIPRIANO

DARK HORSE BOOKS

PRESIDENT & PUBLISHER
MIKE RICHARDSON

EDITOR
SPENCER CUSHING

ASSISTANT EDITOR
KONNER KNUDSEN

DESIGNER
SKYLER WEISSENFLUH

DIGITAL ART TECHNICIAN
ADAM PRUETT

Advertising Sales: (503) 905-2315 | ComicShopLocator.com

Published by Dark Horse Books
A division of Dark Horse Comics LLC
10956 SE Main Street
Milwaukie, OR 97222

DarkHorse.com

First edition: October 2020
eBook ISBN 978-1-50670-484-5
Trade Paperback ISBN 978-1-50670-485-2

10 9 8 7 6 5 4 3 2 1
Printed in China

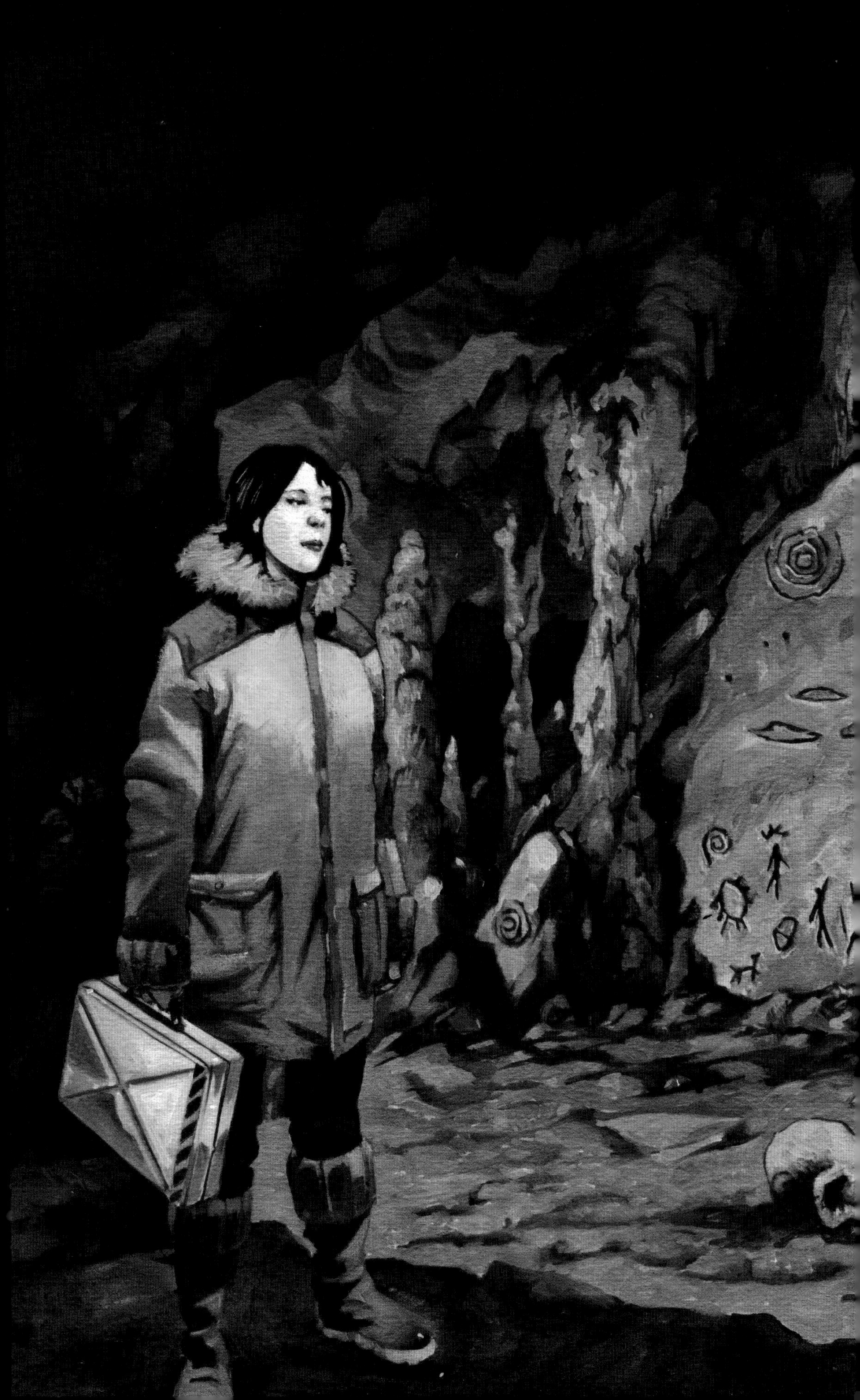

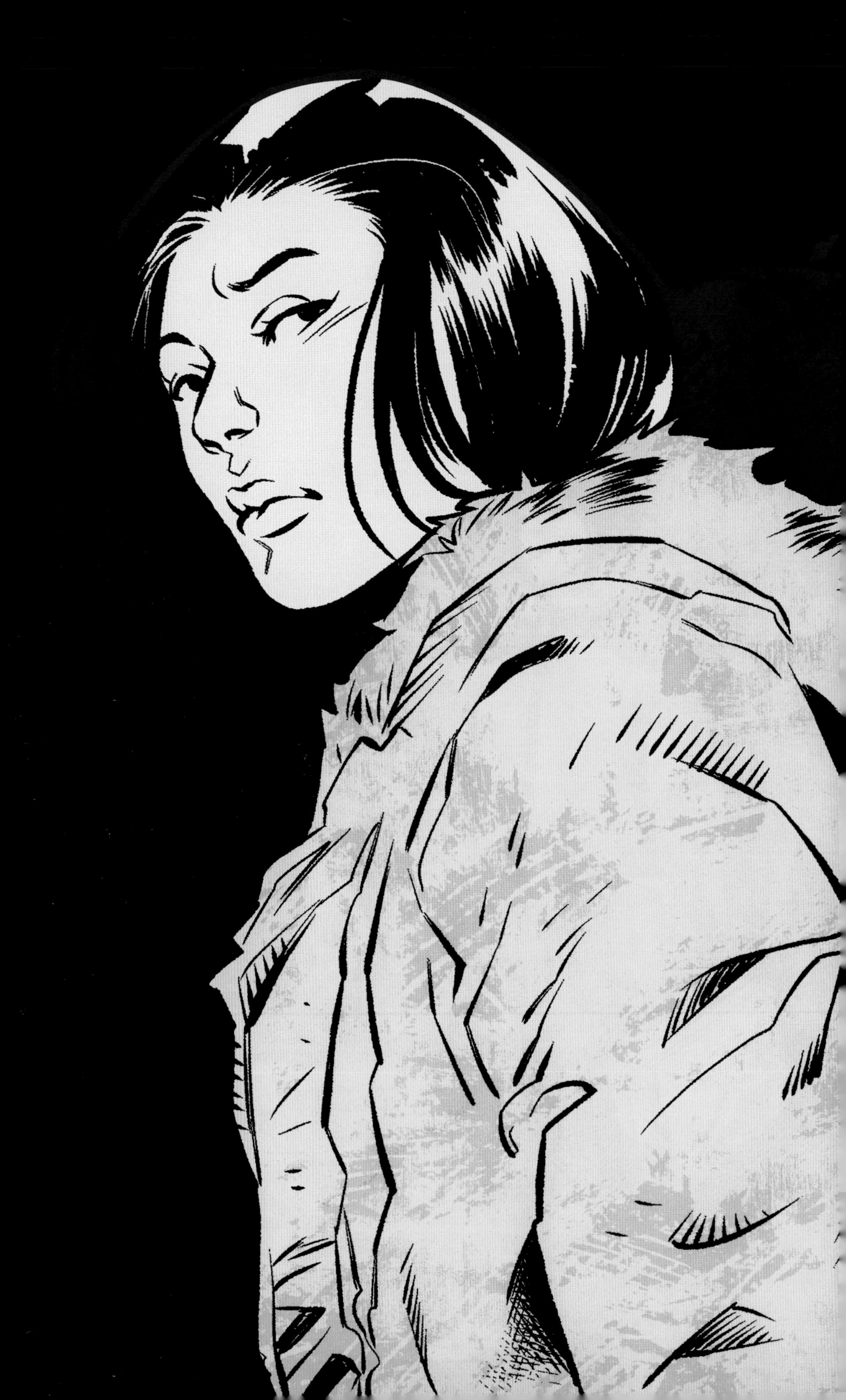

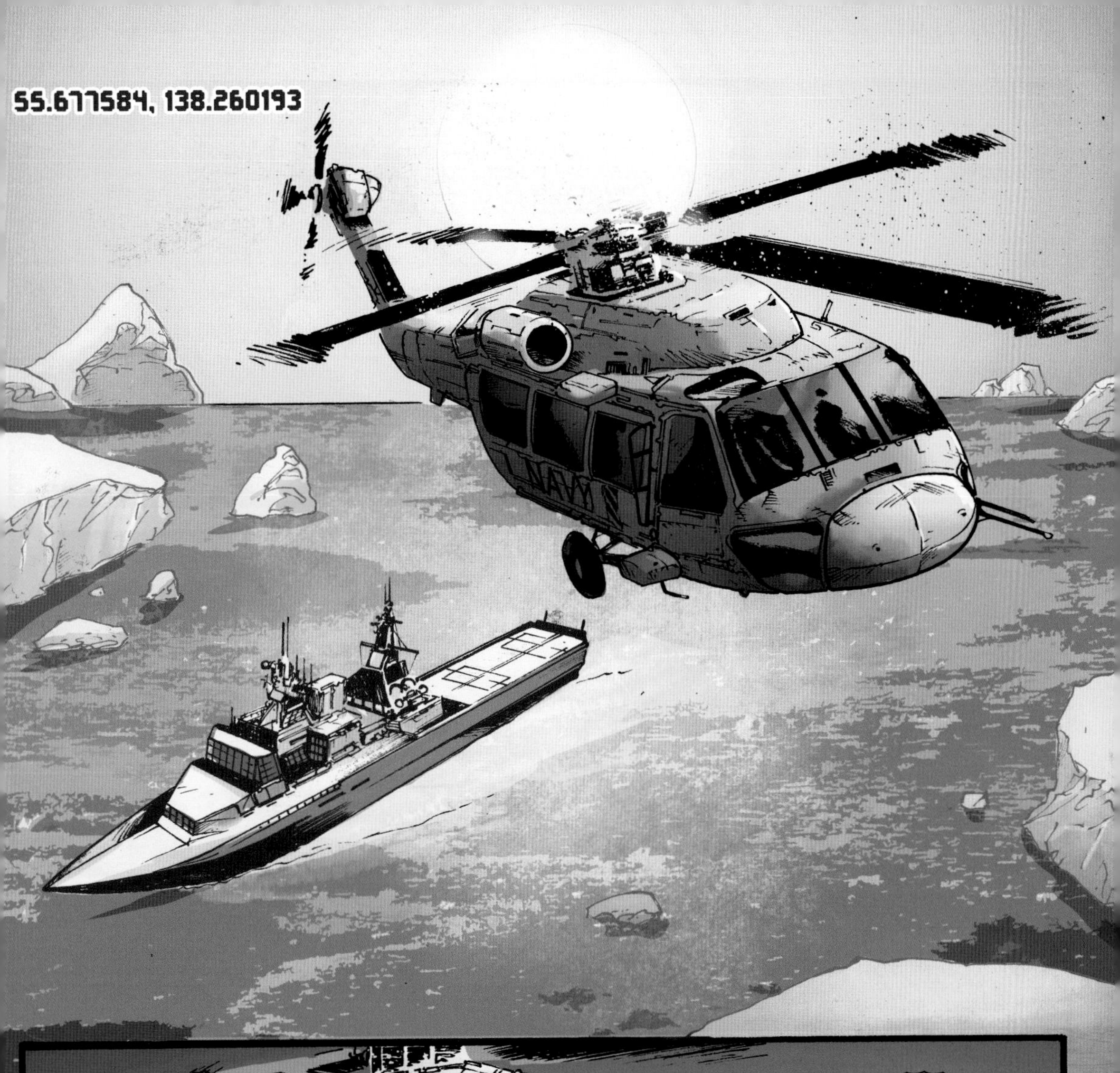
55.677584, 138.260193

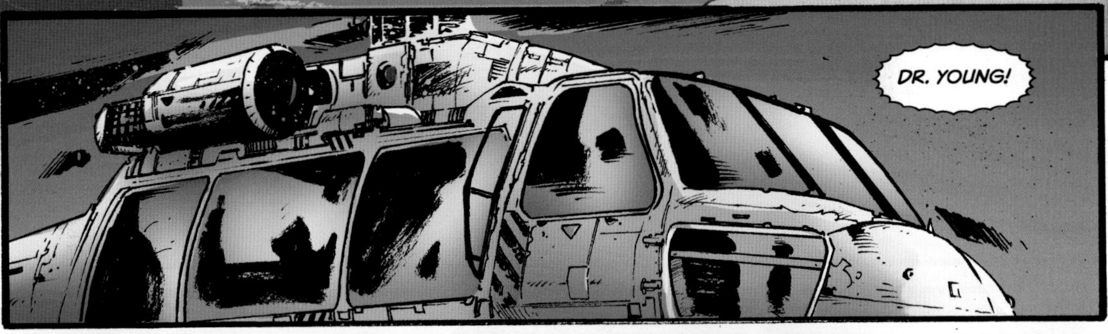
DR. YOUNG!

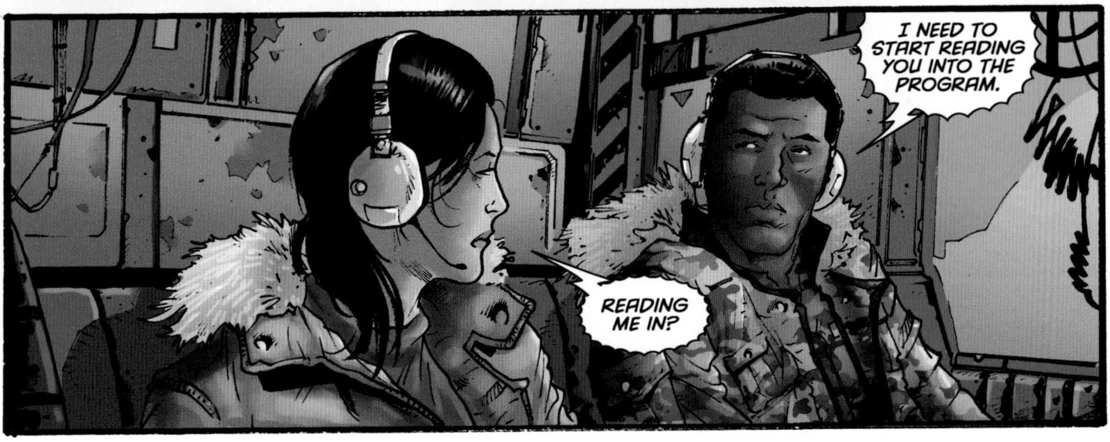
I NEED TO START READING YOU INTO THE PROGRAM.
READING ME IN?

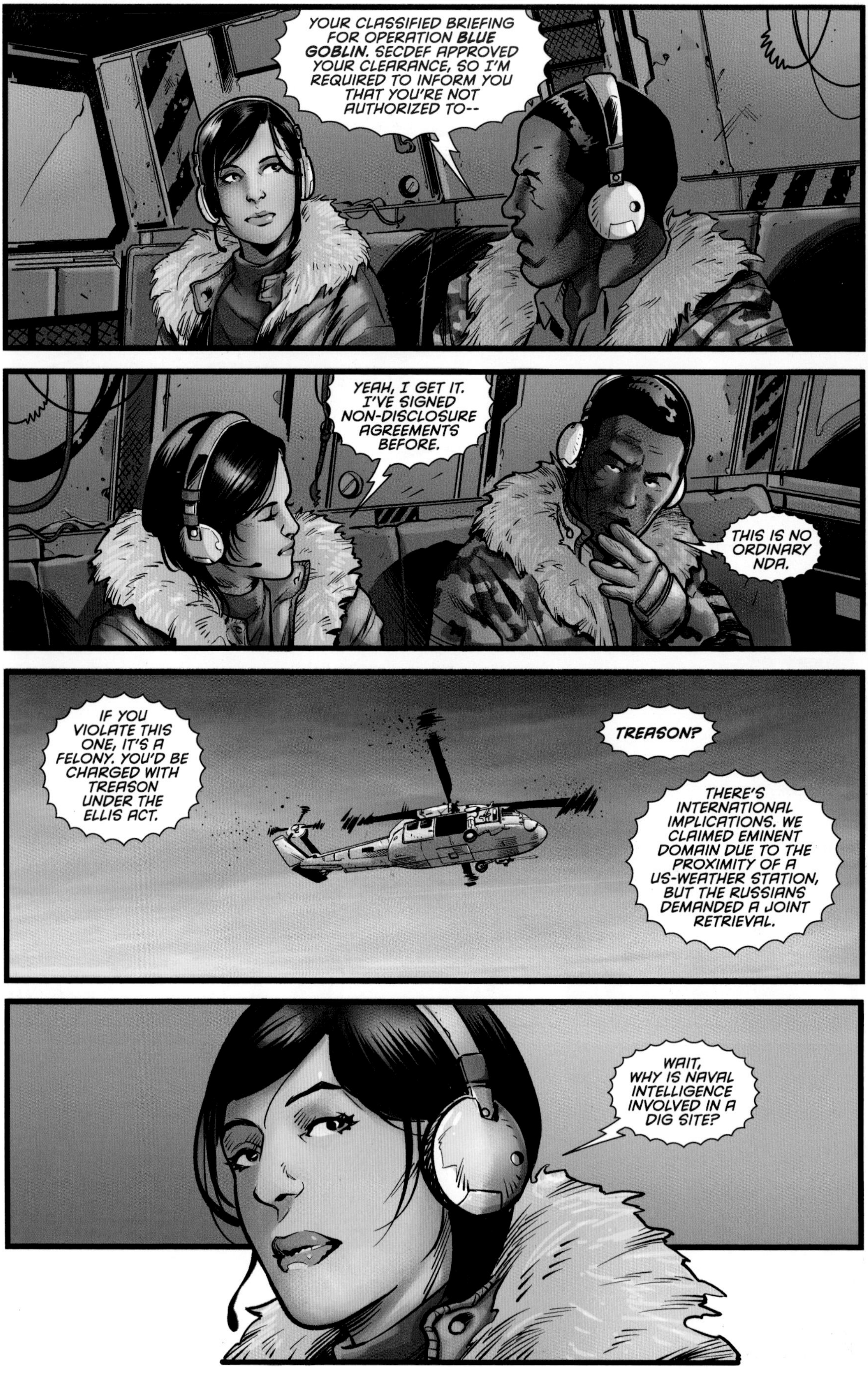

YOUR CLASSIFIED BRIEFING FOR OPERATION **BLUE GOBLIN**. SECDEF APPROVED YOUR CLEARANCE, SO I'M REQUIRED TO INFORM YOU THAT YOU'RE NOT AUTHORIZED TO--
YEAH, I GET IT. I'VE SIGNED NON-DISCLOSURE AGREEMENTS BEFORE.
THIS IS NO ORDINARY NDA.
IF YOU VIOLATE THIS ONE, IT'S A FELONY. YOU'D BE CHARGED WITH TREASON UNDER THE ELLIS ACT.
TREASON?
THERE'S INTERNATIONAL IMPLICATIONS. WE CLAIMED EMINENT DOMAIN DUE TO THE PROXIMITY OF A US-WEATHER STATION, BUT THE RUSSIANS DEMANDED A JOINT RETRIEVAL.
WAIT, WHY IS NAVAL INTELLIGENCE INVOLVED IN A DIG SITE?

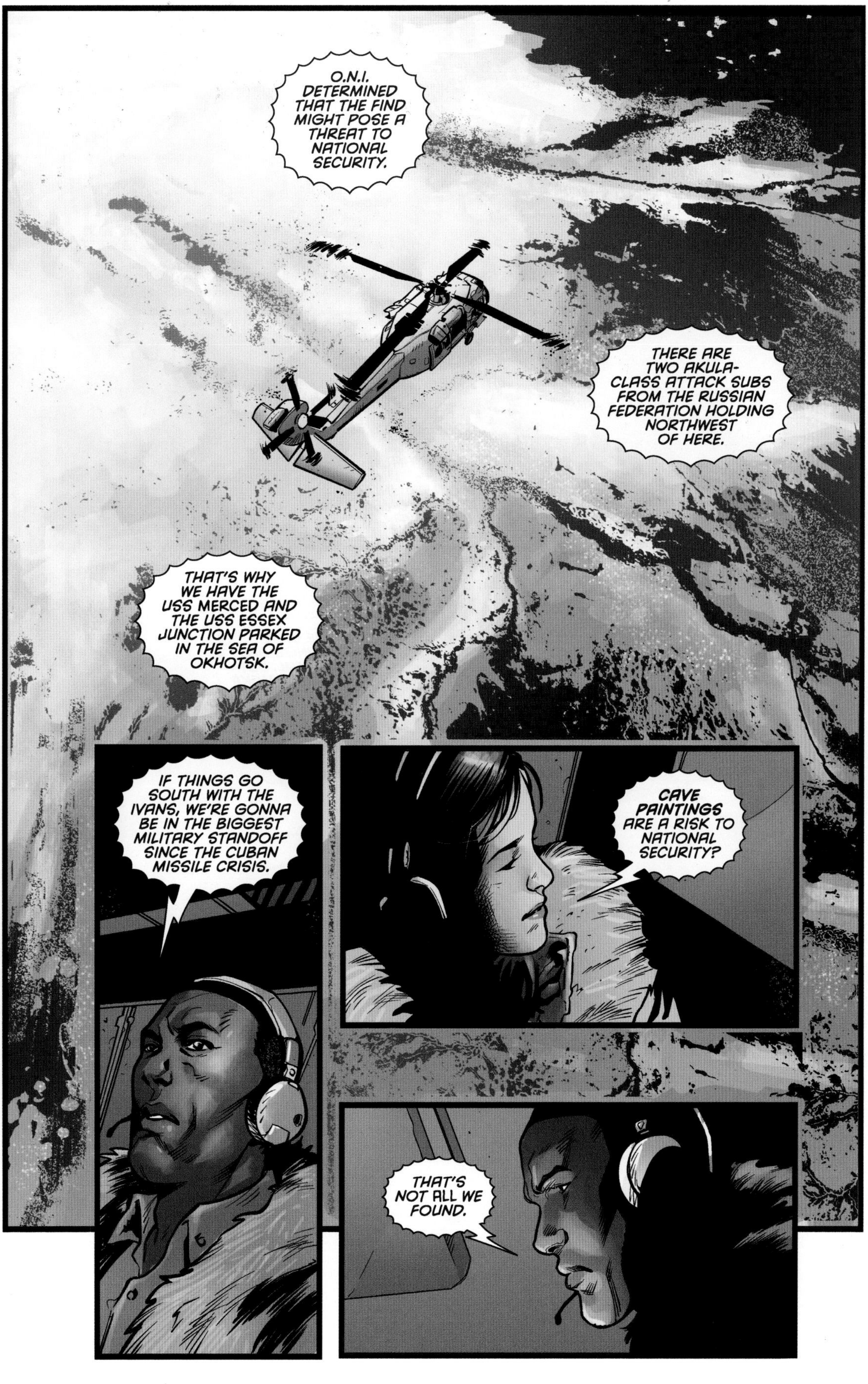
O.N.I. DETERMINED THAT THE FIND MIGHT POSE A THREAT TO NATIONAL SECURITY.
THERE ARE TWO AKULA-CLASS ATTACK SUBS FROM THE RUSSIAN FEDERATION HOLDING NORTHWEST OF HERE.
THAT'S WHY WE HAVE THE USS MERCED AND THE USS ESSEX JUNCTION PARKED IN THE SEA OF OKHOTSK.
IF THINGS GO SOUTH WITH THE IVANS, WE'RE GONNA BE IN THE BIGGEST MILITARY STANDOFF SINCE THE CUBAN MISSILE CRISIS.
CAVE PAINTINGS ARE A RISK TO NATIONAL SECURITY?
THAT'S NOT ALL WE FOUND.

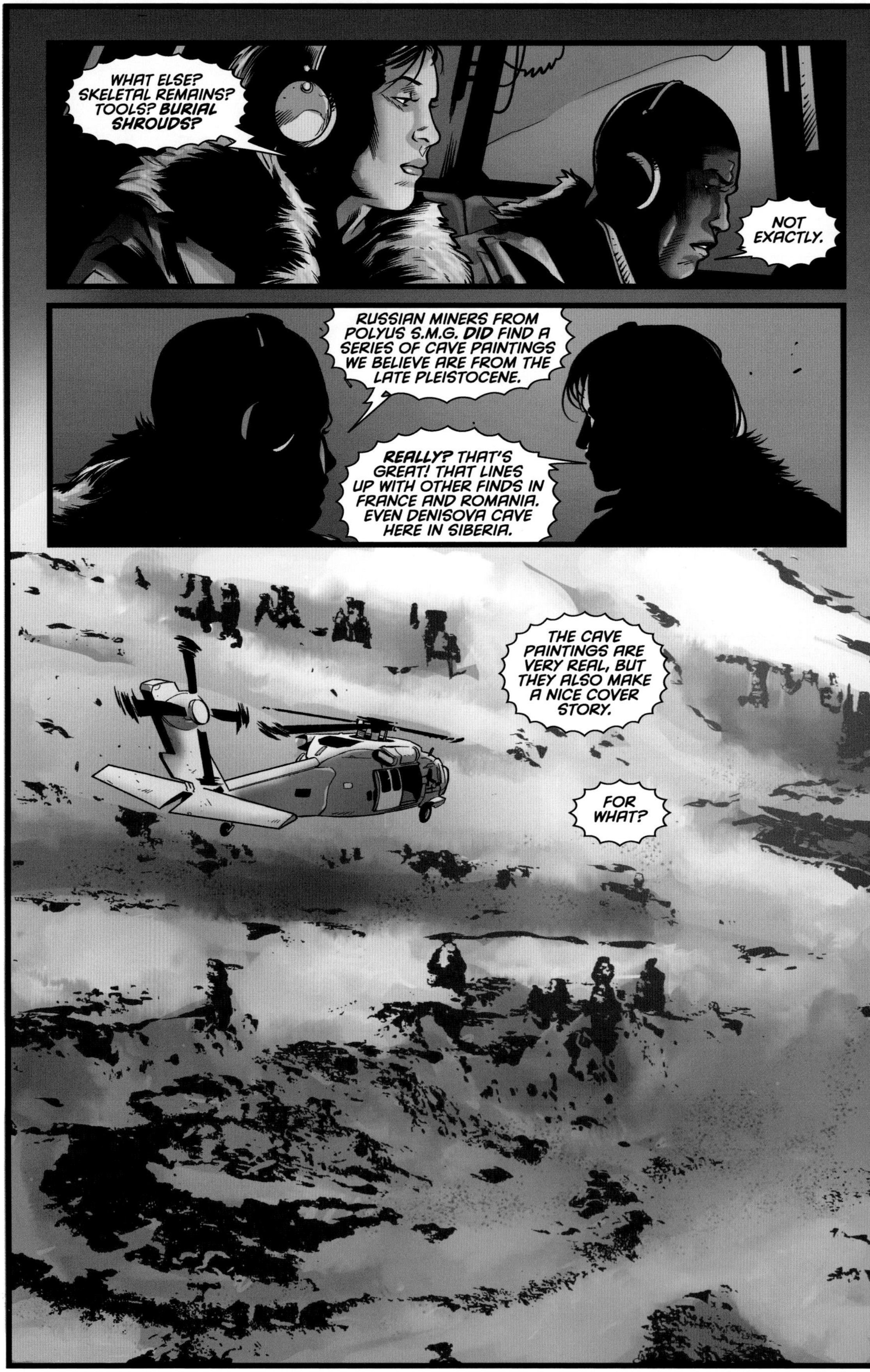
WHAT ELSE? SKELETAL REMAINS? TOOLS? BURIAL SHROUDS?
NOT EXACTLY.
RUSSIAN MINERS FROM POLYUS S.M.G. DID FIND A SERIES OF CAVE PAINTINGS WE BELIEVE ARE FROM THE LATE PLEISTOCENE.
REALLY? THAT'S GREAT! THAT LINES UP WITH OTHER FINDS IN FRANCE AND ROMANIA. EVEN DENISOVA CAVE HERE IN SIBERIA.
THE CAVE PAINTINGS ARE VERY REAL, BUT THEY ALSO MAKE A NICE COVER STORY.
FOR WHAT?

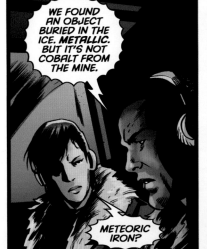

WE FOUND AN OBJECT BURIED IN THE ICE. METALLIC. BUT IT'S NOT COBALT FROM THE MINE.

METEORIC IRON?

GOOD GUESS, BUT NO. THE OBJECT IS OF UNKNOWN ORIGIN.

LOOK, I'M A CULTURAL ANTHROPOLOGIST, NOT A CONSPIRACY THEORIST.

THAT'S EXACTLY WHY YOU'RE HERE. THE SERIOUS NATURE OF YOUR PUBLISHED WORK.

WE NEED YOU TO MANAGE THE TEST PROTOCOLS, TRY TO AUTHENTICATE--

THUD

SORRY IT'S A LITTLE BUMPY! WE'RE CATCHING THERMALS ON THE DESCENT!

BAG! GIMME THE BAG!

HRRK!

SORRY.

PINCH THE BRIDGE OF YOUR NOSE. THERE'S A PRESSURE POINT HERE THAT'LL SETTLE YOUR STOMACH.

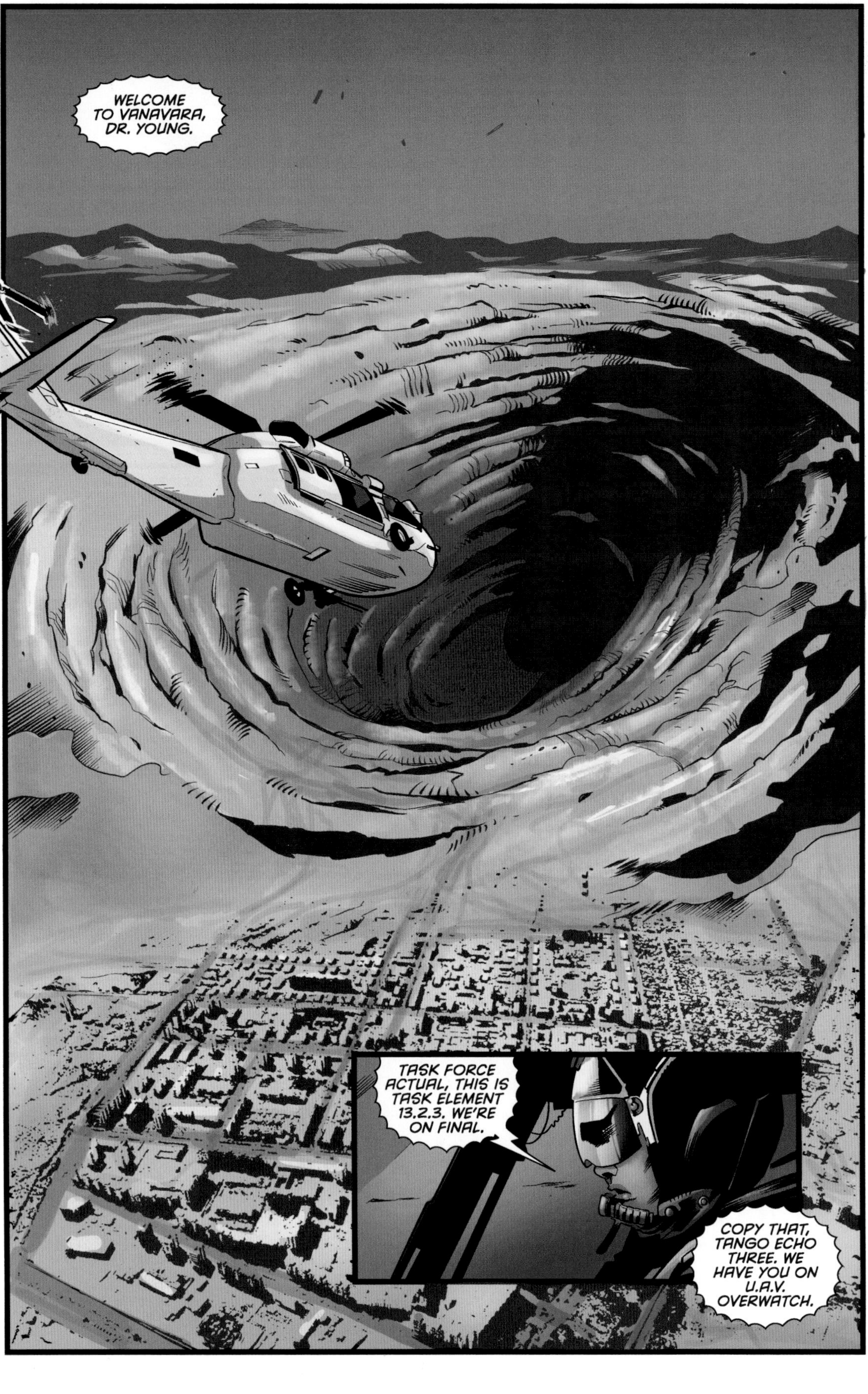
WELCOME TO VANAVARA, DR. YOUNG.
TASK FORCE ACTUAL, THIS IS TASK ELEMENT 13.2.3. WE'RE ON FINAL.
COPY THAT, TANGO ECHO THREE. WE HAVE YOU ON U.A.V. OVERWATCH.

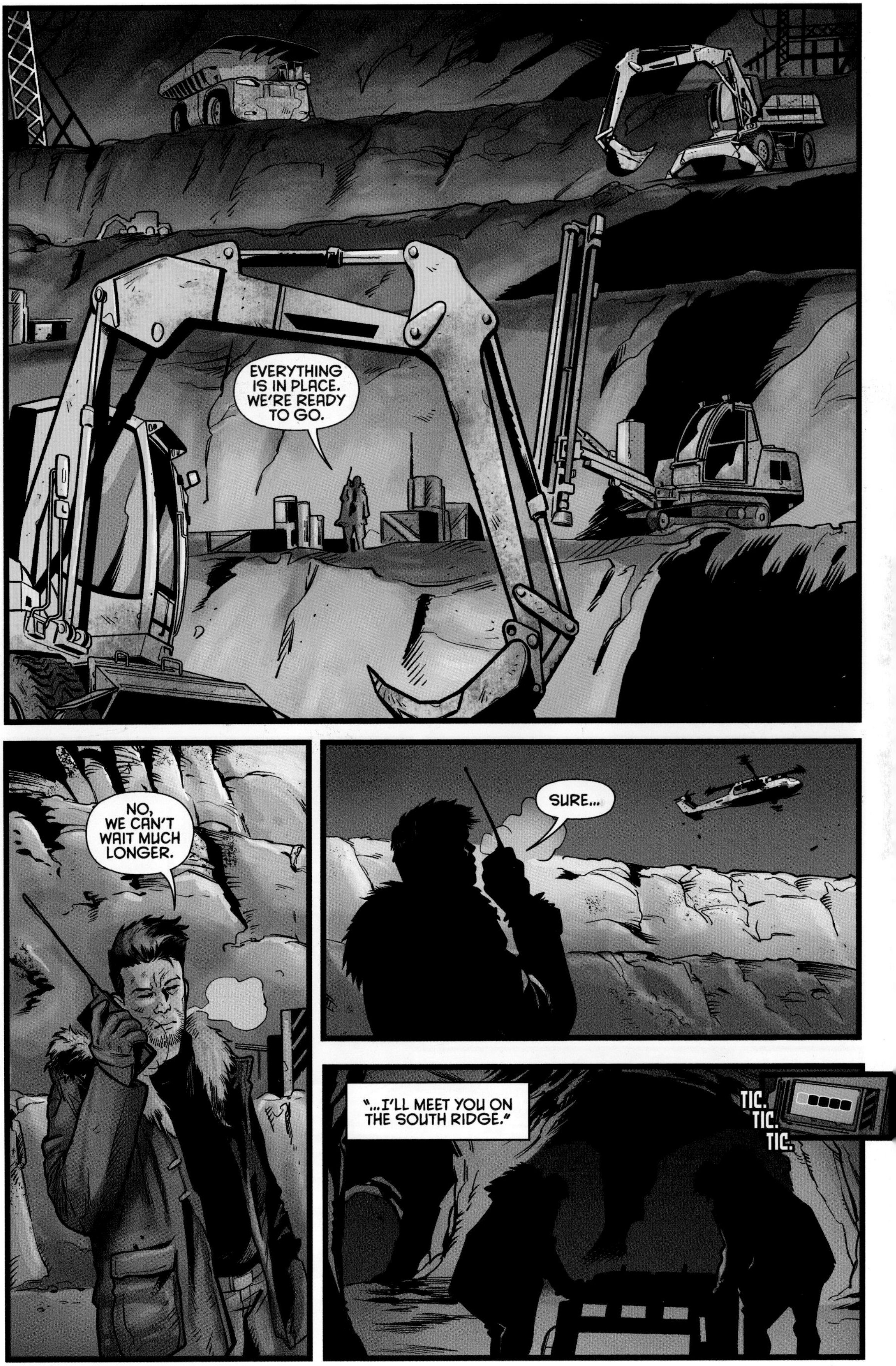
EVERYTHING IS IN PLACE. WE'RE READY TO GO.
NO, WE CAN'T WAIT MUCH LONGER.
SURE...
"...I'LL MEET YOU ON THE SOUTH RIDGE."
TIC. TIC. TIC.

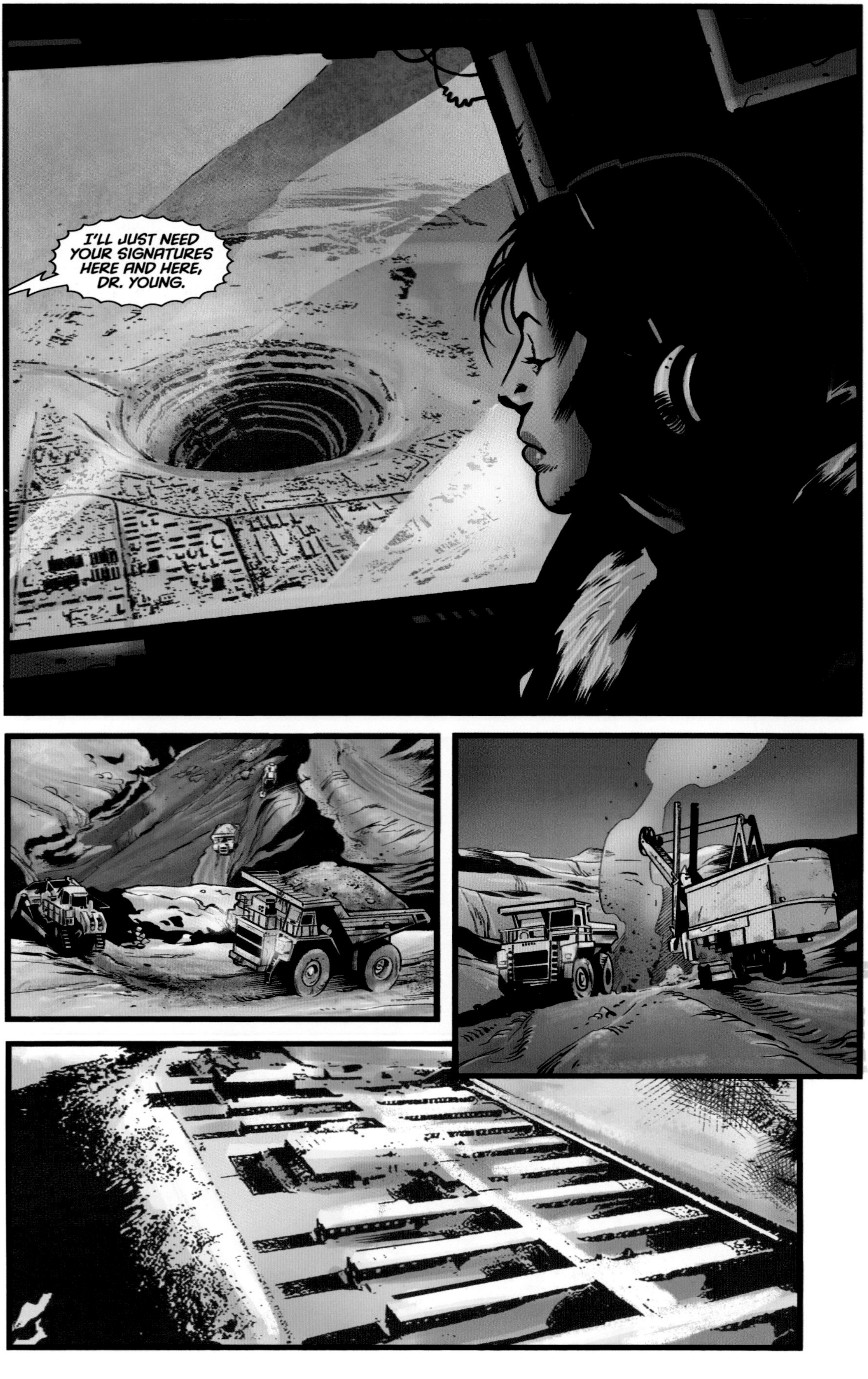
I'LL JUST NEED YOUR SIGNATURES HERE AND HERE, DR. YOUNG.

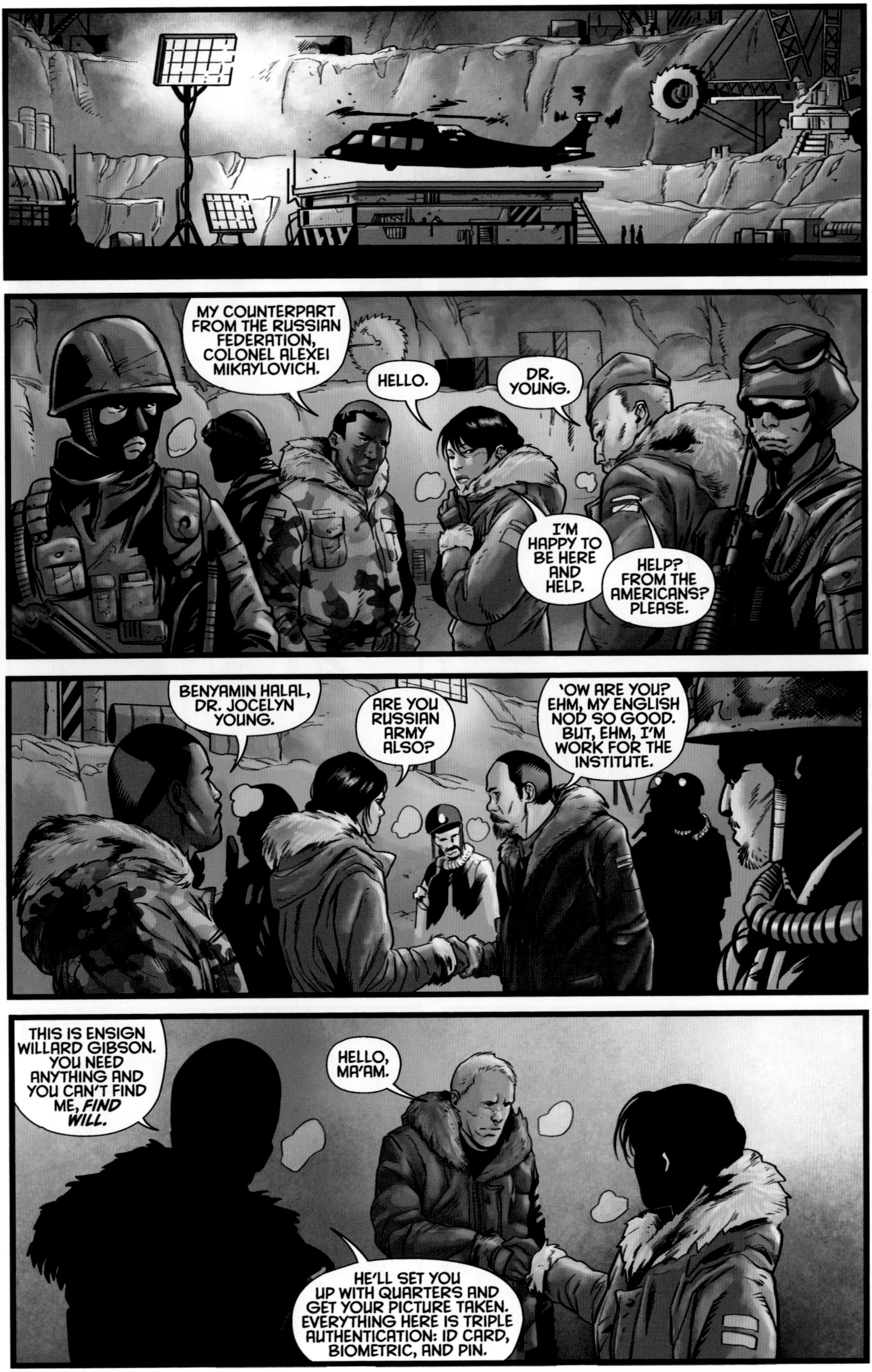
MY COUNTERPART FROM THE RUSSIAN FEDERATION, COLONEL ALEXEI MIKAYLOVICH.
HELLO.
DR. YOUNG.
I'M HAPPY TO BE HERE AND HELP.
HELP? FROM THE AMERICANS? PLEASE.
BENYAMIN HALAL, DR. JOCELYN YOUNG.
ARE YOU RUSSIAN ARMY ALSO?
'OW ARE YOU? EHM, MY ENGLISH NOD SO GOOD. BUT, EHM, I'M WORK FOR THE INSTITUTE.
THIS IS ENSIGN WILLARD GIBSON. YOU NEED ANYTHING AND YOU CAN'T FIND ME, *FIND WILL.*
HELLO, MA'AM.
HE'LL SET YOU UP WITH QUARTERS AND GET YOUR PICTURE TAKEN. EVERYTHING HERE IS TRIPLE AUTHENTICATION: ID CARD, BIOMETRIC, AND PIN.

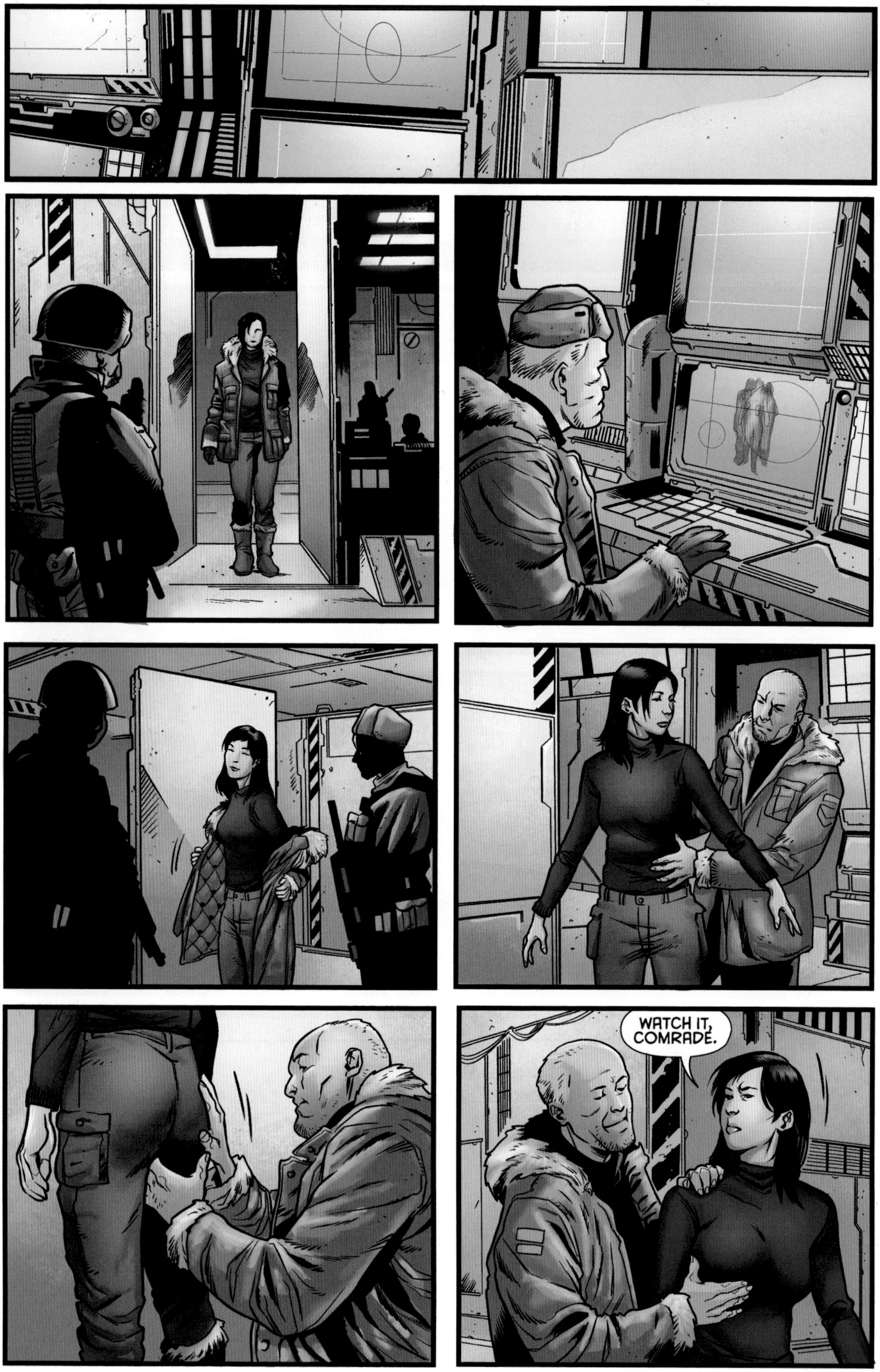
WATCH IT, COMRADE.

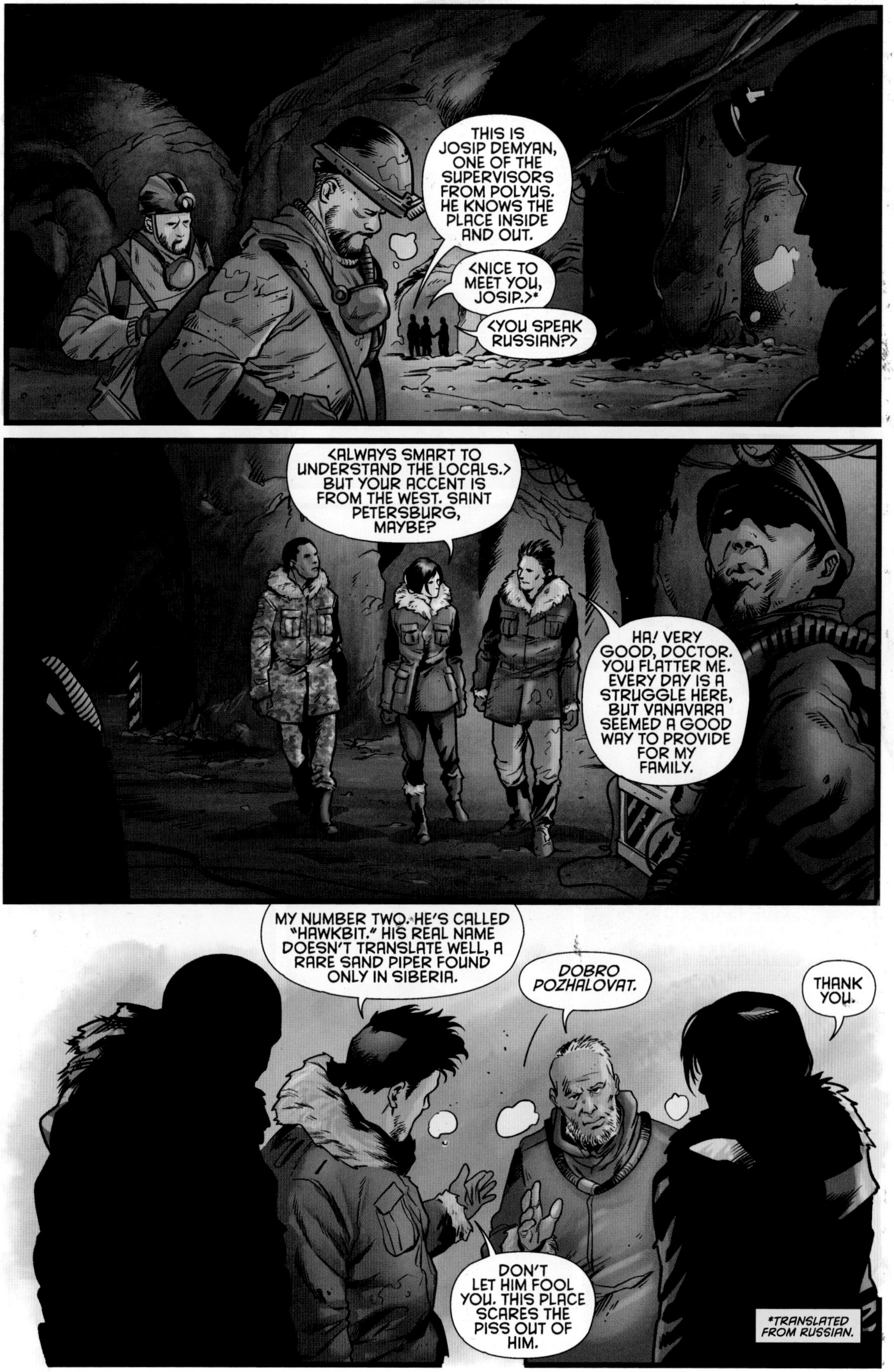
THIS IS JOSIP DEMYAN, ONE OF THE SUPERVISORS FROM POLYUS. HE KNOWS THE PLACE INSIDE AND OUT.
<NICE TO MEET YOU, JOSIP.>*
<YOU SPEAK RUSSIAN?>
<ALWAYS SMART TO UNDERSTAND THE LOCALS.> BUT YOUR ACCENT IS FROM THE WEST. SAINT PETERSBURG, MAYBE?
HA! VERY GOOD, DOCTOR. YOU FLATTER ME. EVERY DAY IS A STRUGGLE HERE, BUT VANAVARA SEEMED A GOOD WAY TO PROVIDE FOR MY FAMILY.
MY NUMBER TWO. HE'S CALLED "HAWKBIT." HIS REAL NAME DOESN'T TRANSLATE WELL, A RARE SAND PIPER FOUND ONLY IN SIBERIA.
DOBRO POZHALOVAT.
THANK YOU.
DON'T LET HIM FOOL YOU. THIS PLACE SCARES THE PISS OUT OF HIM.
*TRANSLATED FROM RUSSIAN.

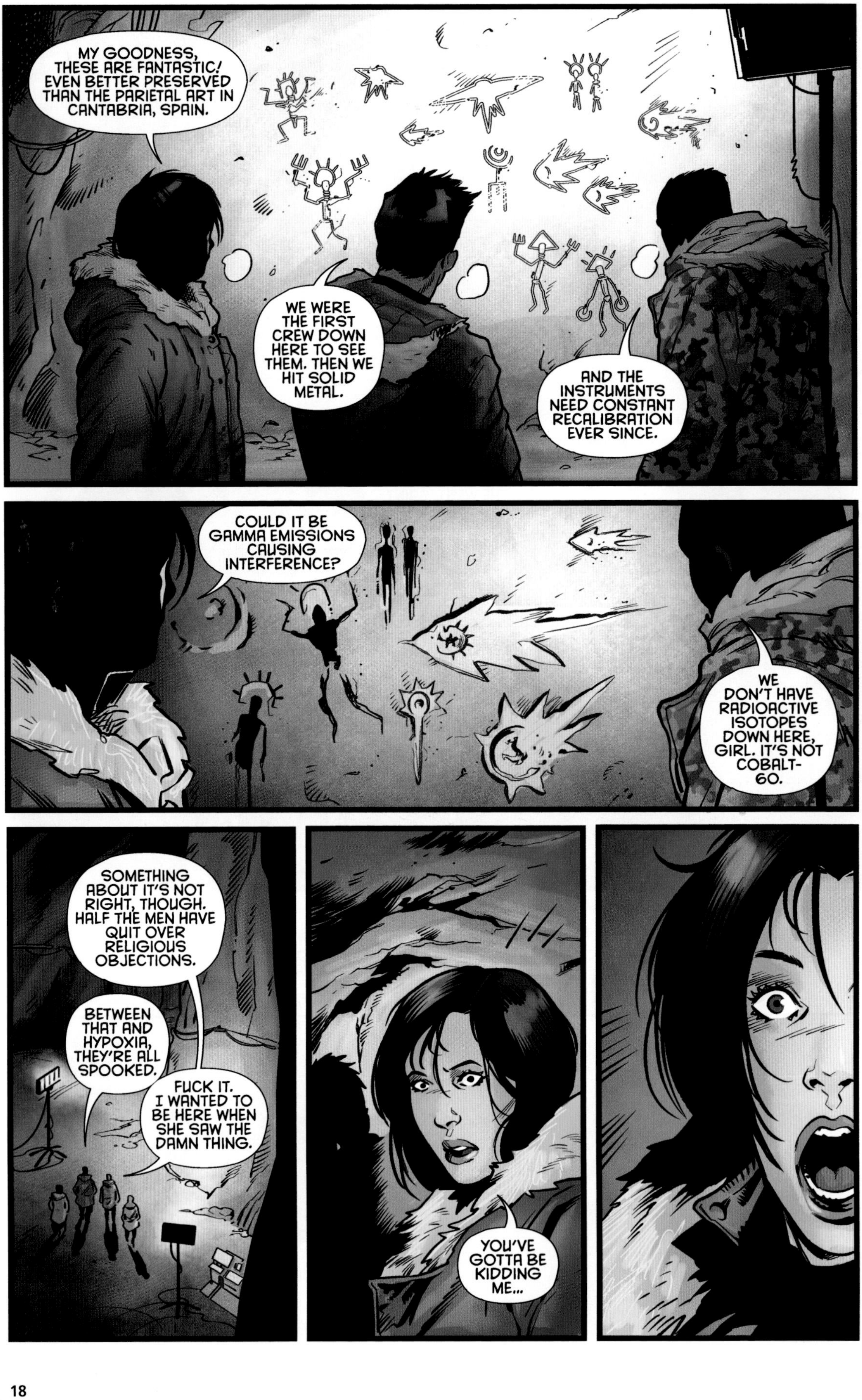
MY GOODNESS, THESE ARE FANTASTIC! EVEN BETTER PRESERVED THAN THE PARIETAL ART IN CANTABRIA, SPAIN.
WE WERE THE FIRST CREW DOWN HERE TO SEE THEM. THEN WE HIT SOLID METAL.
AND THE INSTRUMENTS NEED CONSTANT RECALIBRATION EVER SINCE.
COULD IT BE GAMMA EMISSIONS CAUSING INTERFERENCE?
WE DON'T HAVE RADIOACTIVE ISOTOPES DOWN HERE, GIRL. IT'S NOT COBALT-60.
SOMETHING ABOUT IT'S NOT RIGHT, THOUGH. HALF THE MEN HAVE QUIT OVER RELIGIOUS OBJECTIONS.
BETWEEN THAT AND HYPOXIA, THEY'RE ALL SPOOKED.
FUCK IT. I WANTED TO BE HERE WHEN SHE SAW THE DAMN THING.
YOU'VE GOTTA BE KIDDING ME...

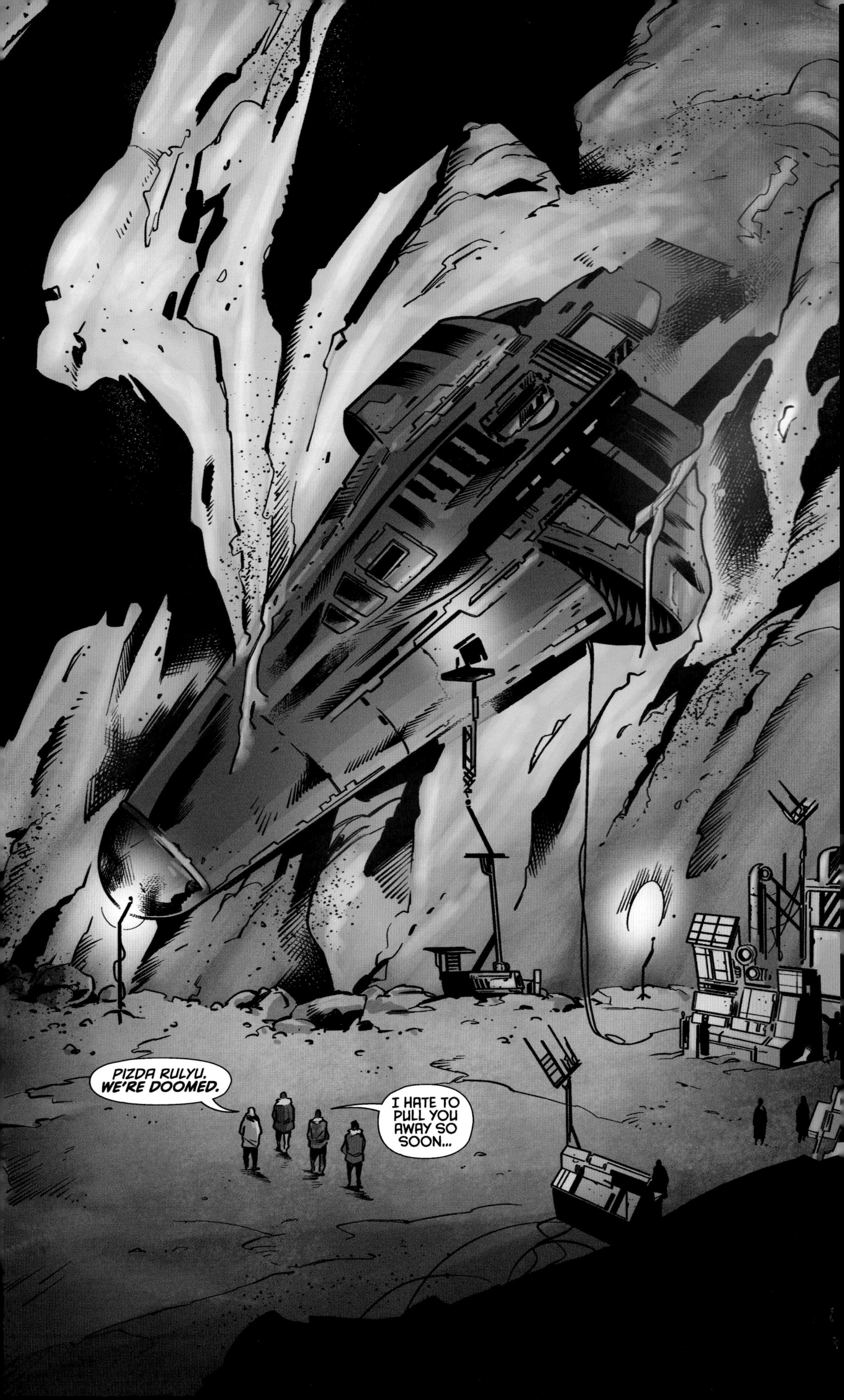
PIZDA RULYU. WE'RE DOOMED.
I HATE TO PULL YOU AWAY SO SOON...

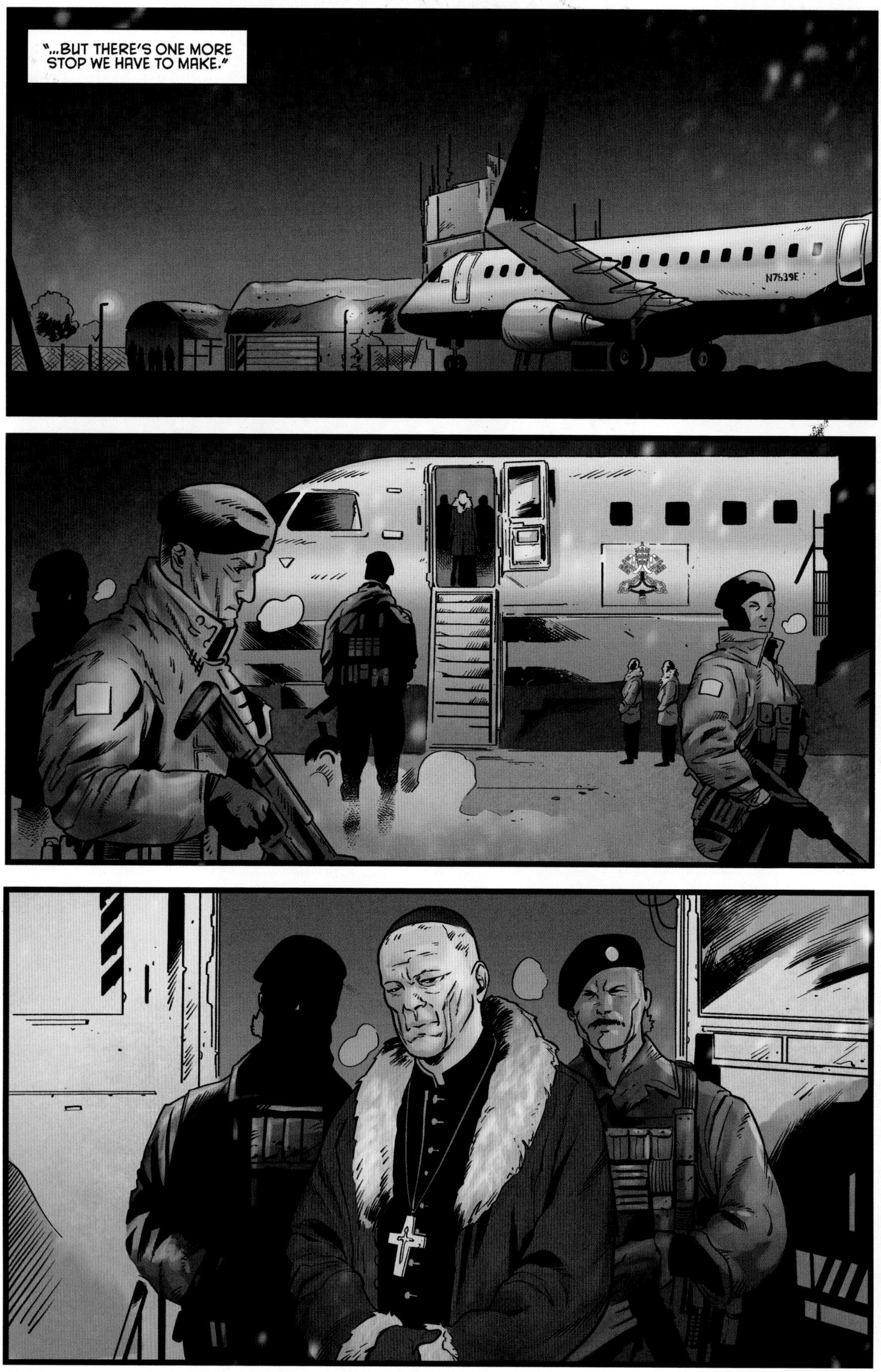
"...BUT THERE'S ONE MORE
STOP WE HAVE TO MAKE."

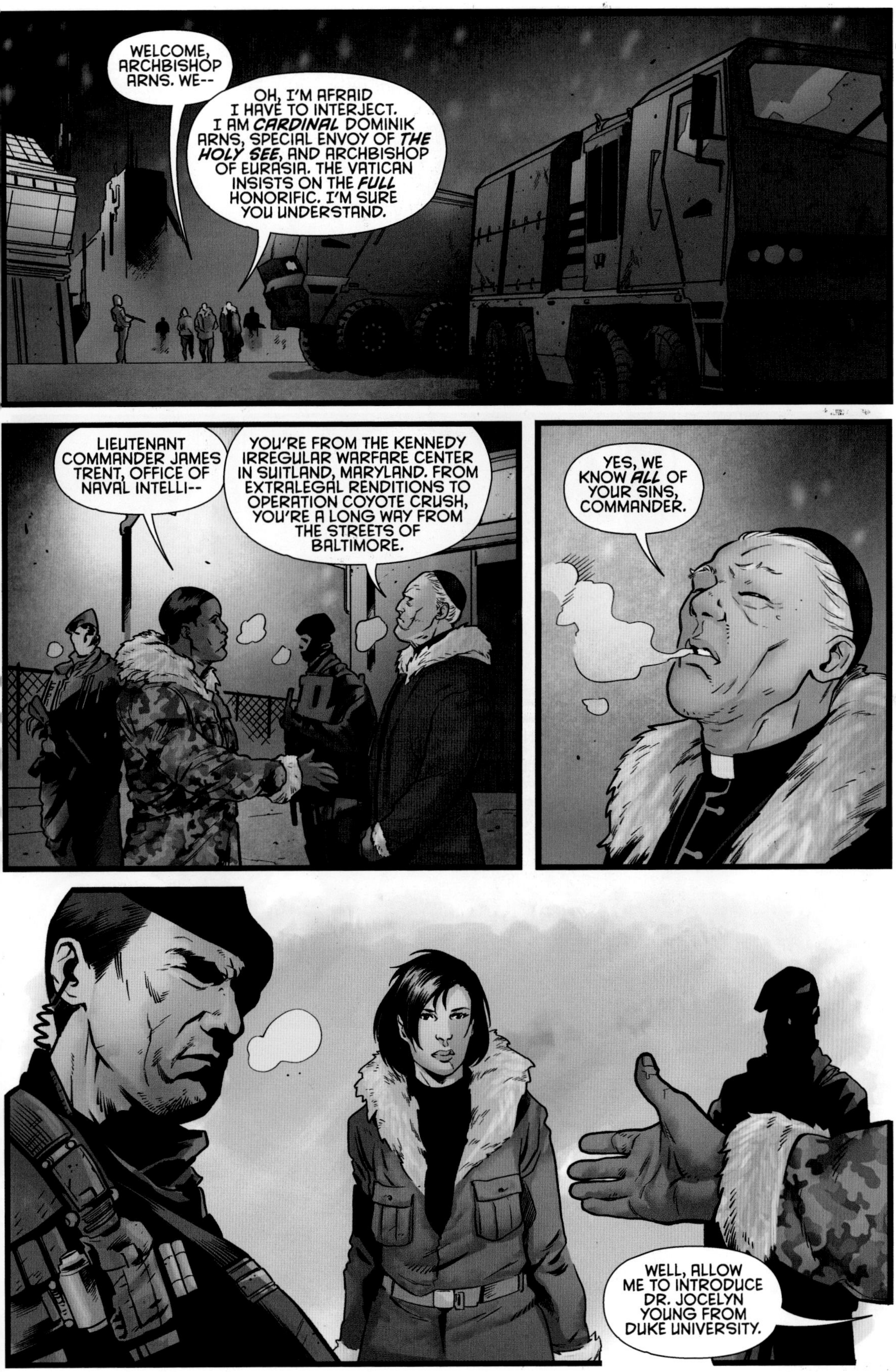
WELCOME, ARCHBISHOP ARNS. WE--
OH, I'M AFRAID I HAVE TO INTERJECT. I AM CARDINAL DOMINIK ARNS, SPECIAL ENVOY OF THE HOLY SEE, AND ARCHBISHOP OF EURASIA. THE VATICAN INSISTS ON THE FULL HONORIFIC. I'M SURE YOU UNDERSTAND.
LIEUTENANT COMMANDER JAMES TRENT, OFFICE OF NAVAL INTELLI--
YOU'RE FROM THE KENNEDY IRREGULAR WARFARE CENTER IN SUITLAND, MARYLAND. FROM EXTRALEGAL RENDITIONS TO OPERATION COYOTE CRUSH, YOU'RE A LONG WAY FROM THE STREETS OF BALTIMORE.
YES, WE KNOW ALL OF YOUR SINS, COMMANDER.
...
WELL, ALLOW ME TO INTRODUCE DR. JOCELYN YOUNG FROM DUKE UNIVERSITY.

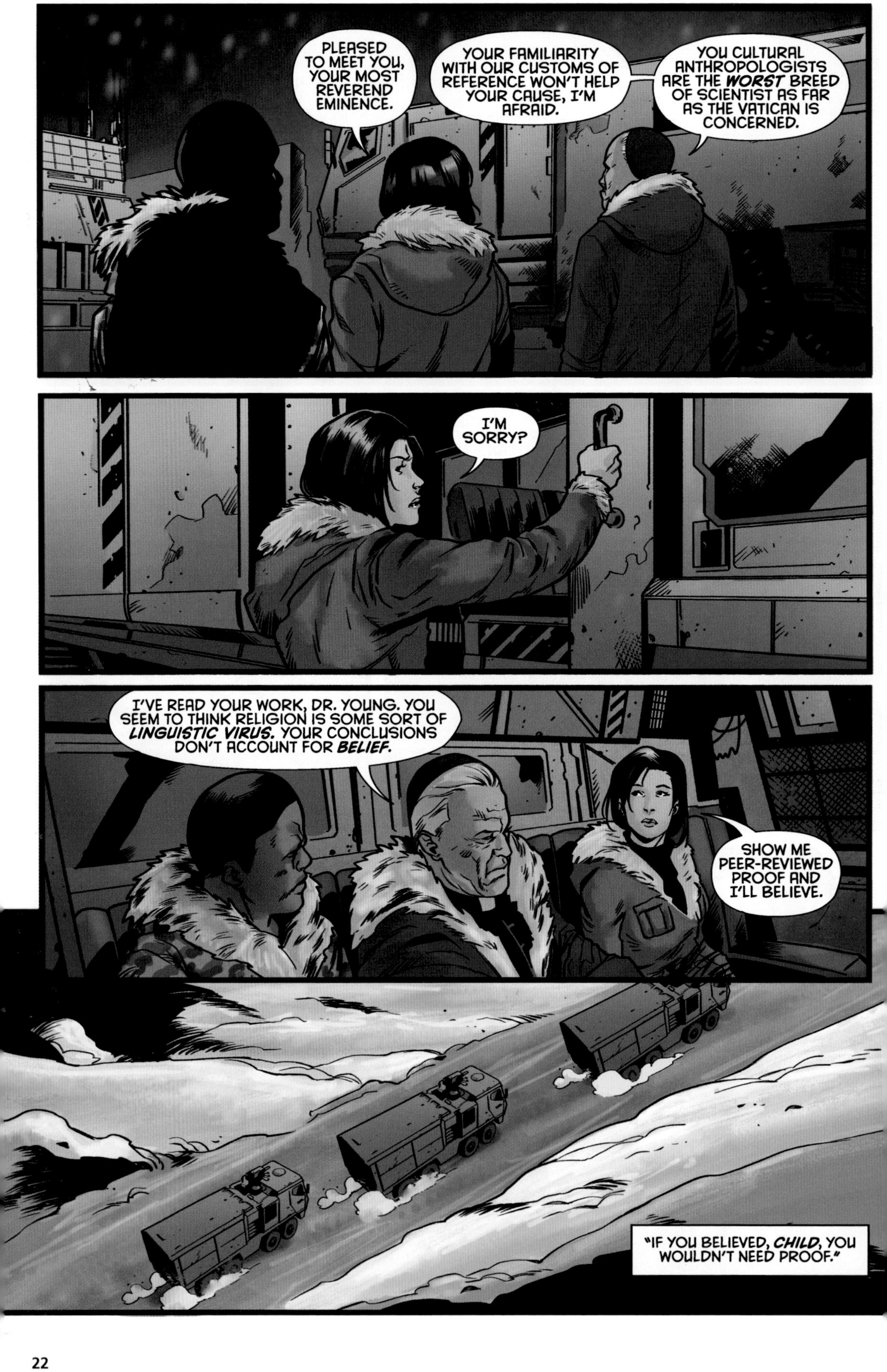
PLEASED TO MEET YOU, YOUR MOST REVEREND EMINENCE.
YOUR FAMILIARITY WITH OUR CUSTOMS OF REFERENCE WON'T HELP YOUR CAUSE, I'M AFRAID.
YOU CULTURAL ANTHROPOLOGISTS ARE THE *WORST* BREED OF SCIENTIST AS FAR AS THE VATICAN IS CONCERNED.
I'M SORRY?
I'VE READ YOUR WORK, DR. YOUNG. YOU SEEM TO THINK RELIGION IS SOME SORT OF *LINGUISTIC VIRUS.* YOUR CONCLUSIONS DON'T ACCOUNT FOR *BELIEF.*
SHOW ME PEER-REVIEWED PROOF AND I'LL BELIEVE.
"IF YOU BELIEVED, *CHILD,* YOU WOULDN'T NEED PROOF."

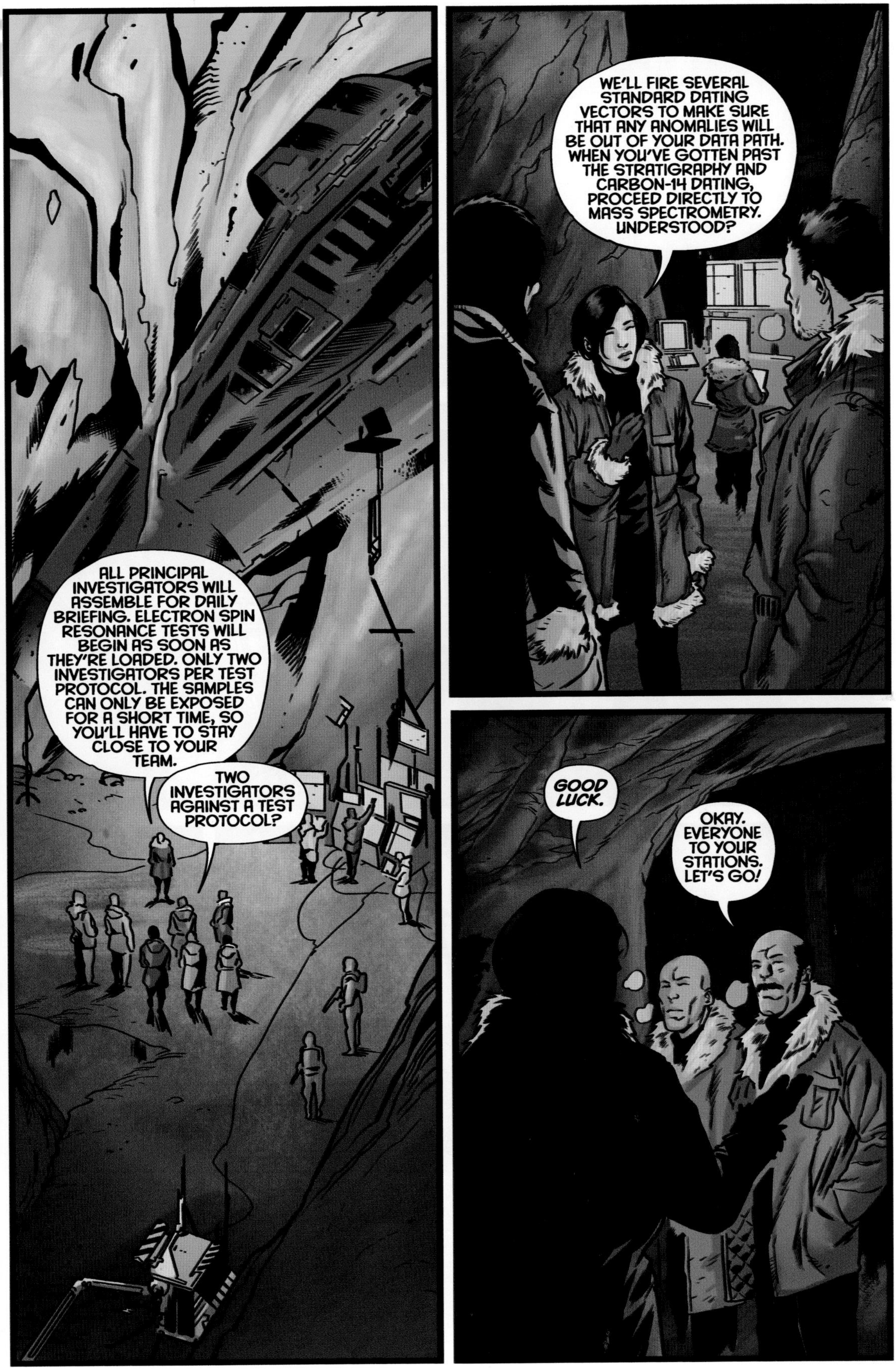
ALL PRINCIPAL INVESTIGATORS WILL ASSEMBLE FOR DAILY BRIEFING. ELECTRON SPIN RESONANCE TESTS WILL BEGIN AS SOON AS THEY'RE LOADED. ONLY TWO INVESTIGATORS PER TEST PROTOCOL. THE SAMPLES CAN ONLY BE EXPOSED FOR A SHORT TIME, SO YOU'LL HAVE TO STAY CLOSE TO YOUR TEAM.
TWO INVESTIGATORS AGAINST A TEST PROTOCOL?
WE'LL FIRE SEVERAL STANDARD DATING VECTORS TO MAKE SURE THAT ANY ANOMALIES WILL BE OUT OF YOUR DATA PATH. WHEN YOU'VE GOTTEN PAST THE STRATIGRAPHY AND CARBON-14 DATING, PROCEED DIRECTLY TO MASS SPECTROMETRY. UNDERSTOOD?
GOOD LUCK.
OKAY. EVERYONE TO YOUR STATIONS. LET'S GO!

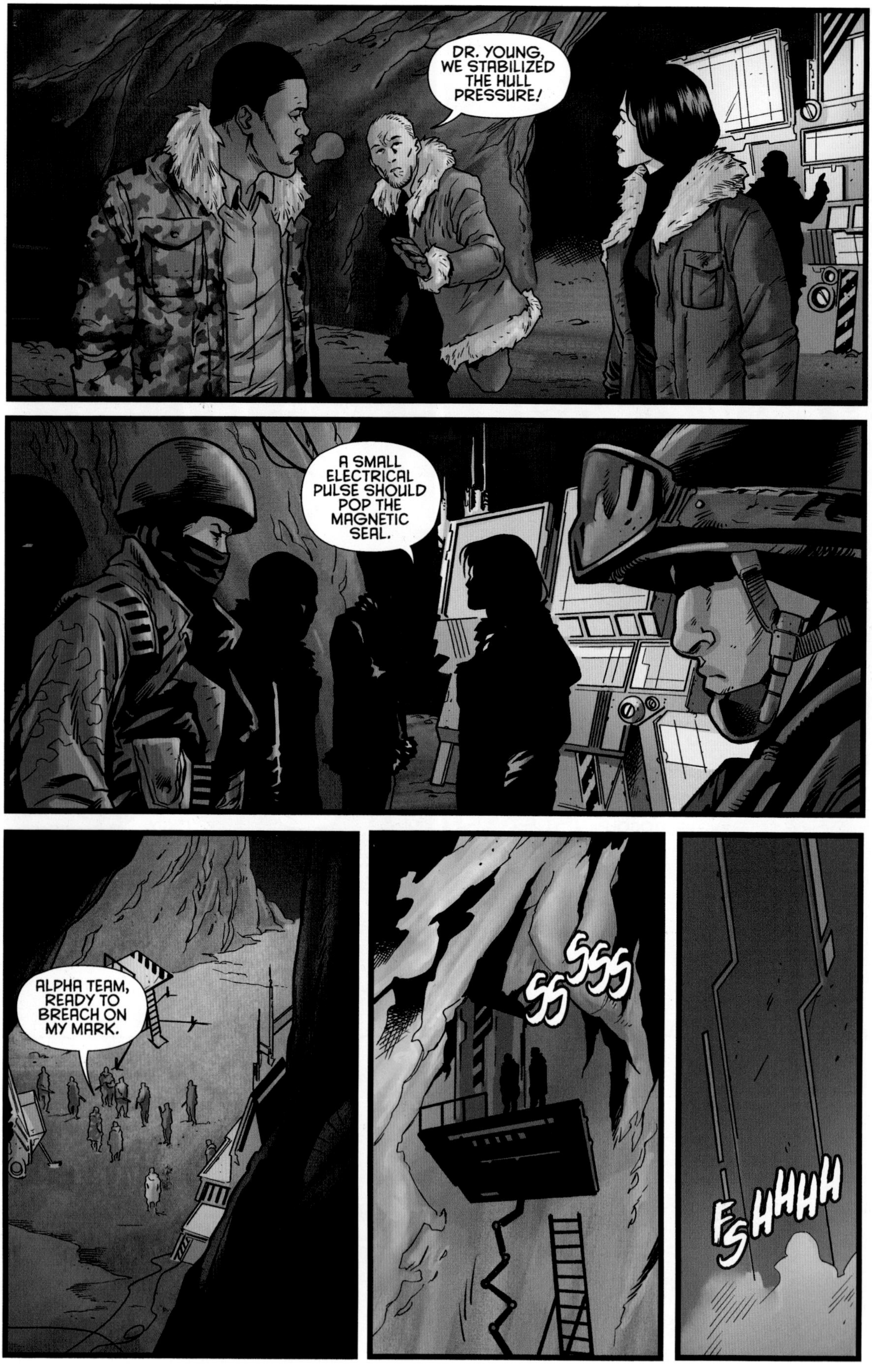
DR. YOUNG, WE STABILIZED THE HULL PRESSURE!
A SMALL ELECTRICAL PULSE SHOULD POP THE MAGNETIC SEAL.
ALPHA TEAM, READY TO BREACH ON MY MARK.
SSSSS
FSHHHH

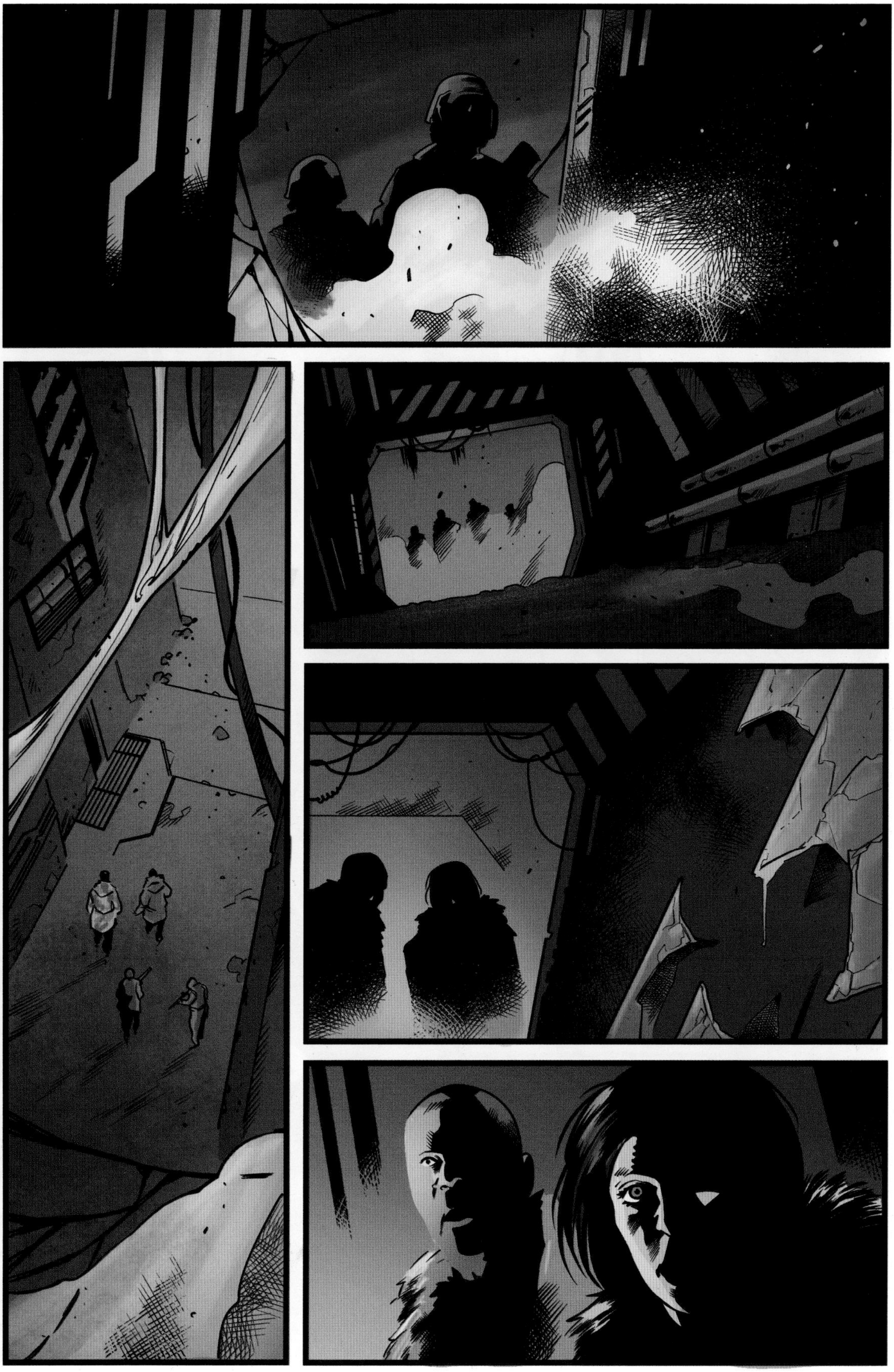

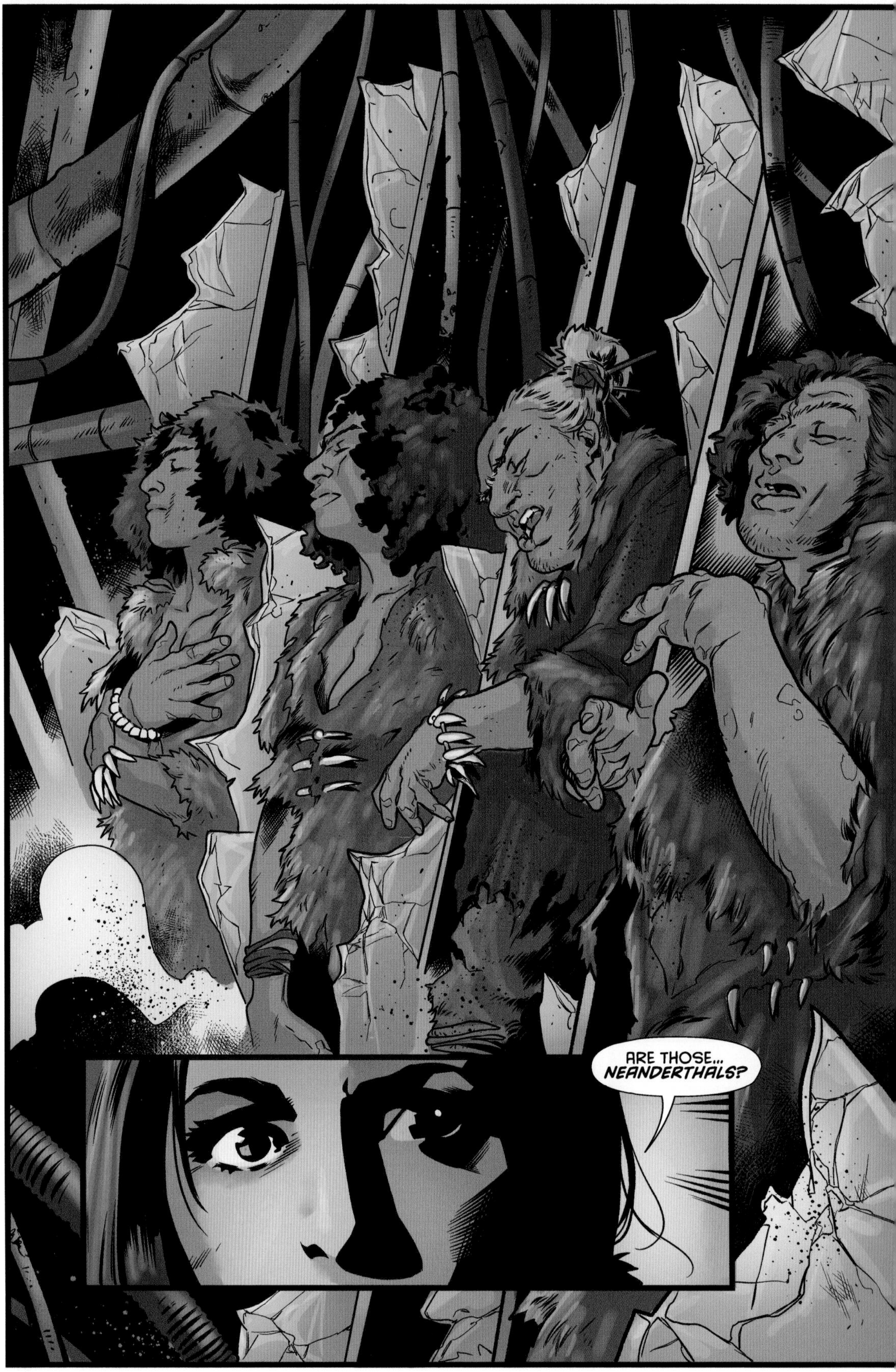
ARE THOSE... NEANDERTHALS?

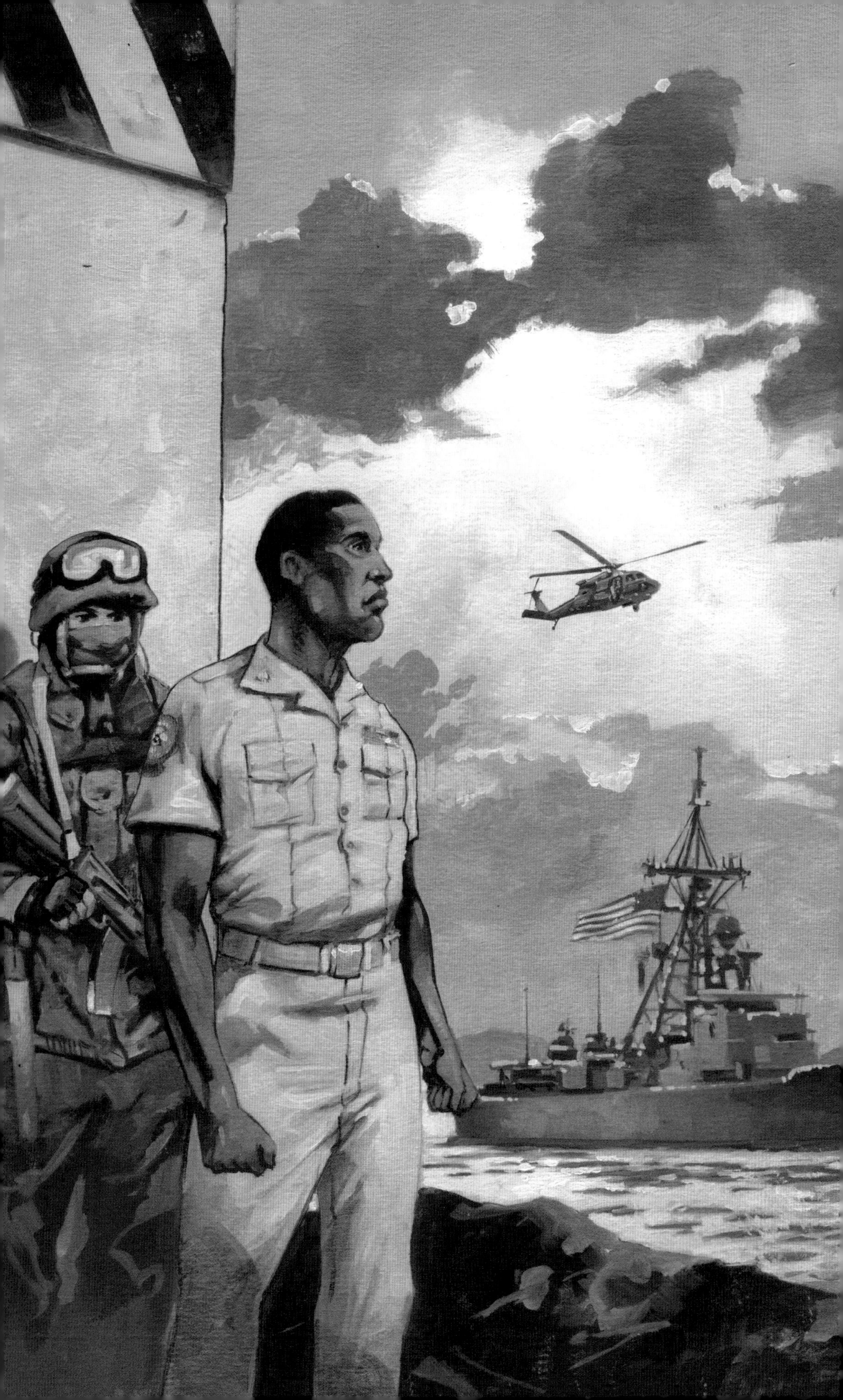

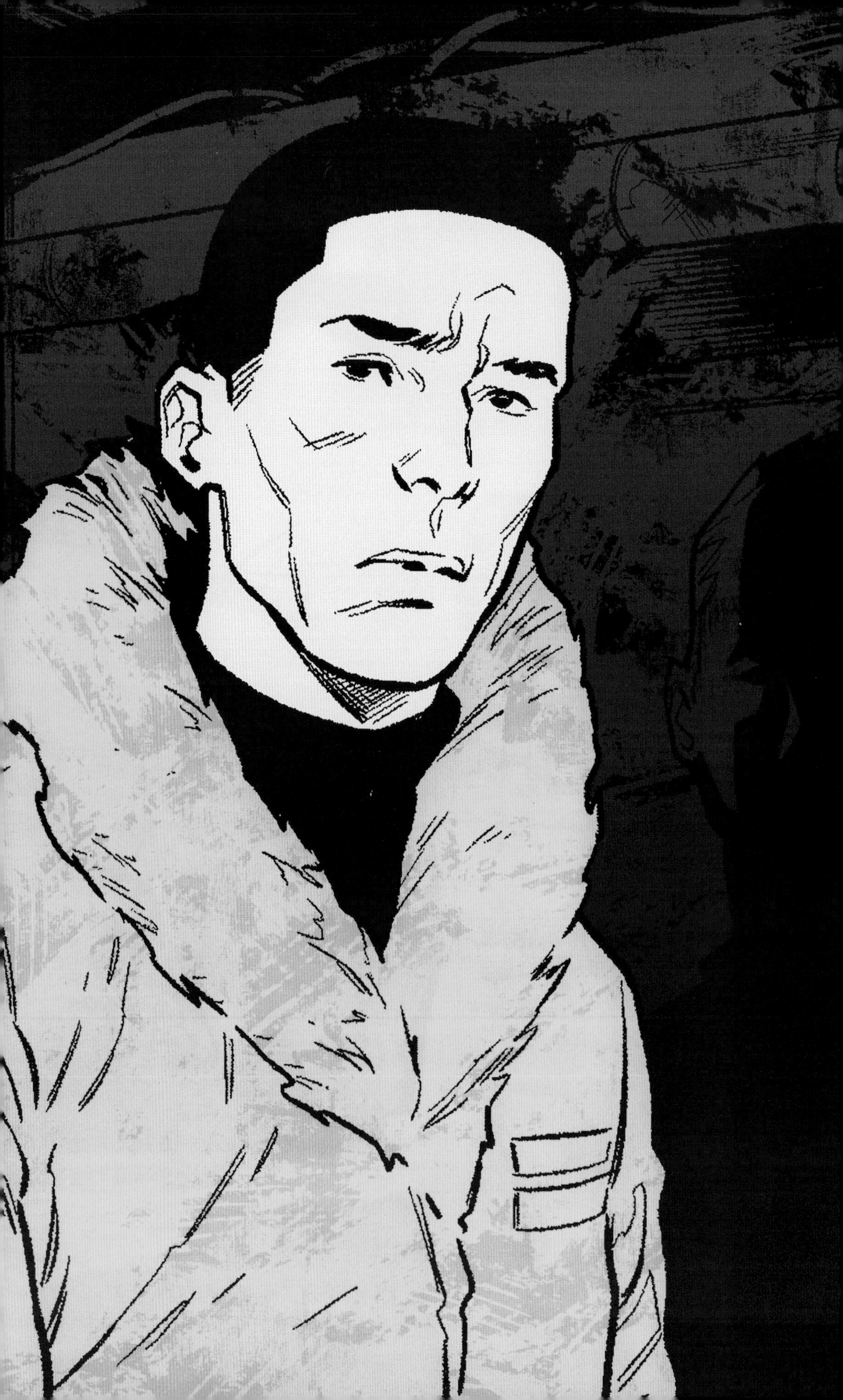

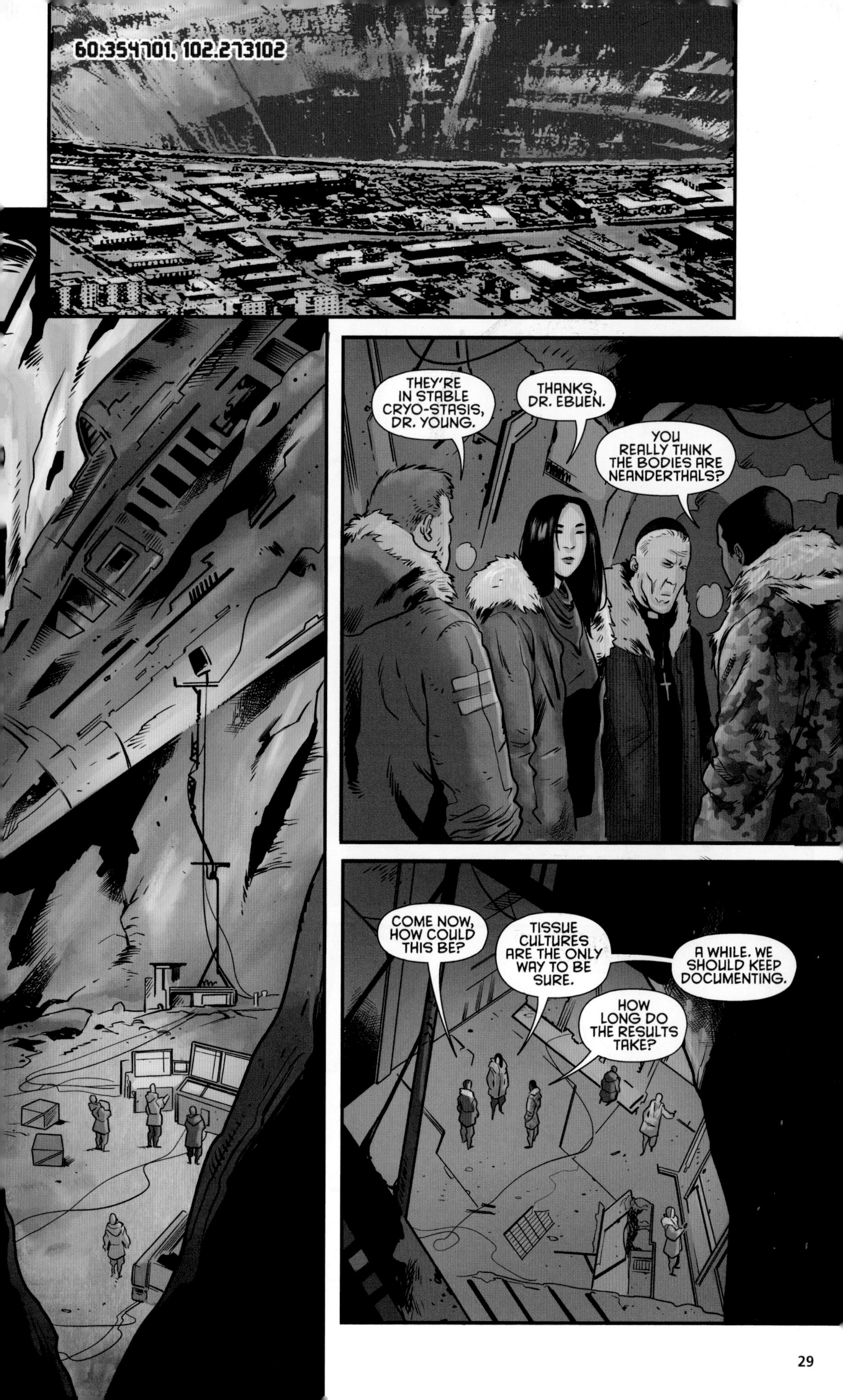
60.354701, 102.273102
THEY'RE IN STABLE CRYO-STASIS, DR. YOUNG.
THANKS, DR. EBUEN.
YOU REALLY THINK THE BODIES ARE NEANDERTHALS?
COME NOW, HOW COULD THIS BE?
TISSUE CULTURES ARE THE ONLY WAY TO BE SURE.
HOW LONG DO THE RESULTS TAKE?
A WHILE. WE SHOULD KEEP DOCUMENTING.

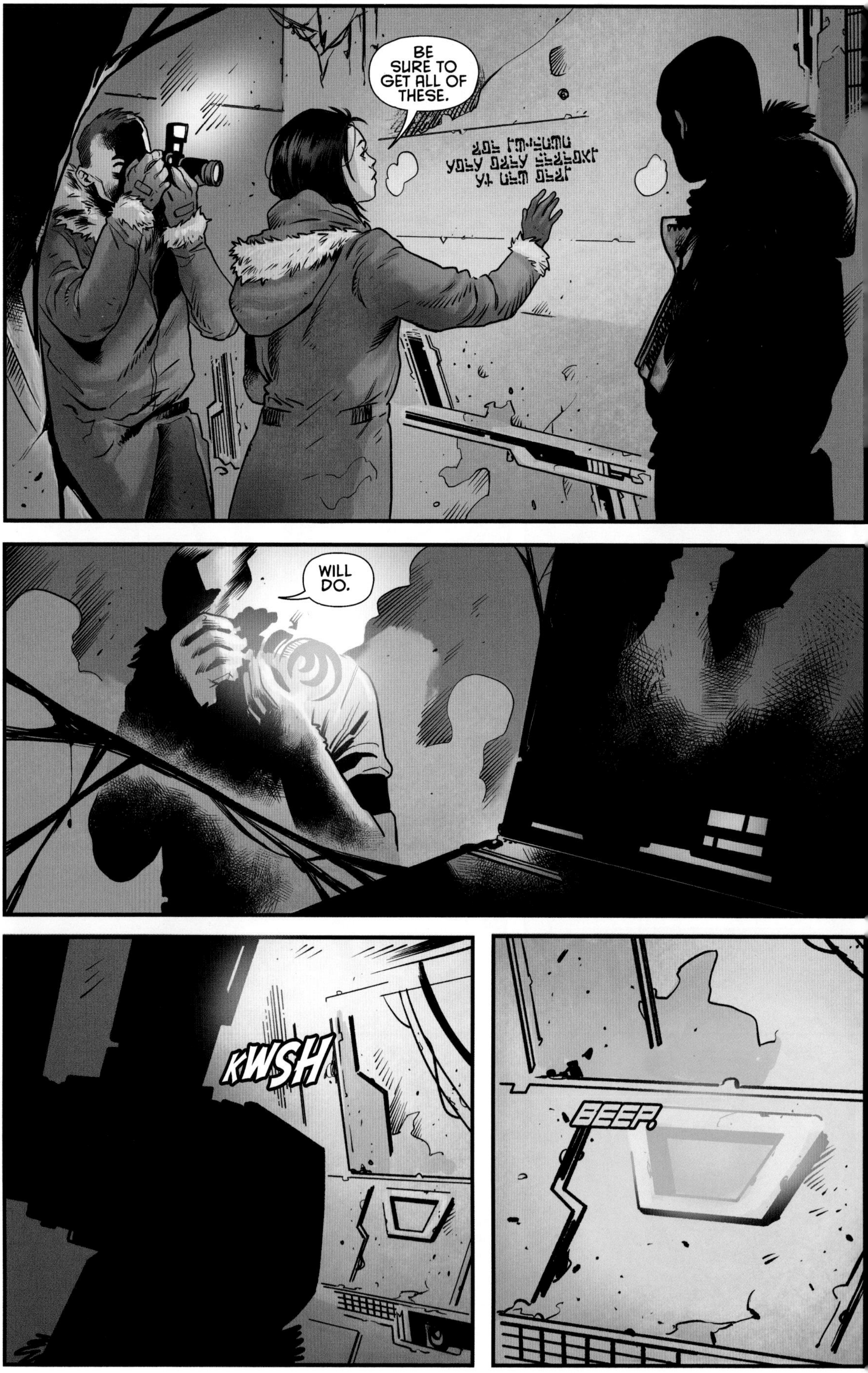
BE SURE TO GET ALL OF THESE.
WILL DO.
KWSH
BEEP.

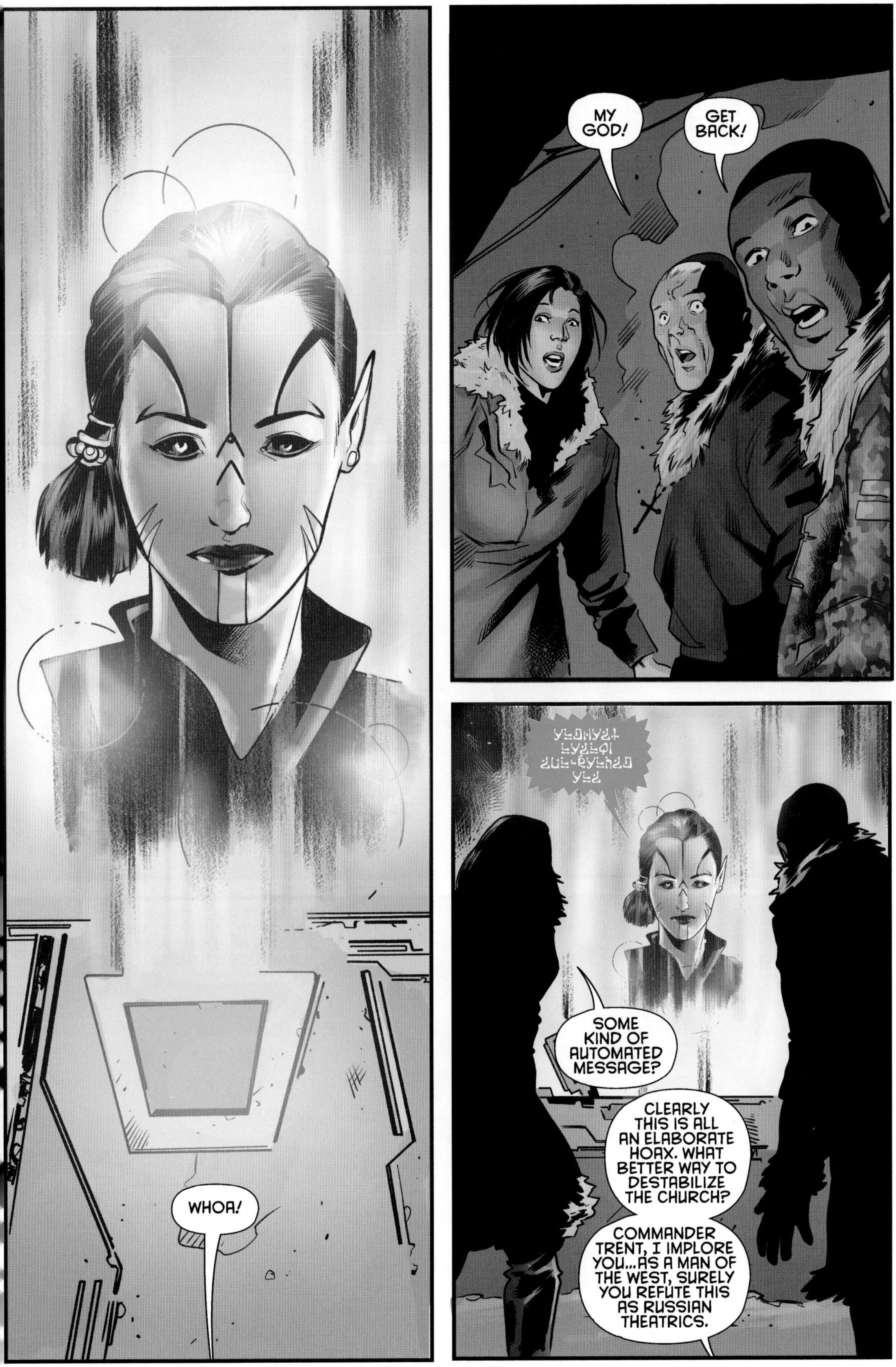
WHOA!
MY GOD!
GET BACK!
SOME KIND OF AUTOMATED MESSAGE?
CLEARLY THIS IS ALL AN ELABORATE HOAX. WHAT BETTER WAY TO DESTABILIZE THE CHURCH?
COMMANDER TRENT, I IMPLORE YOU...AS A MAN OF THE WEST, SURELY YOU REFUTE THIS AS RUSSIAN THEATRICS.

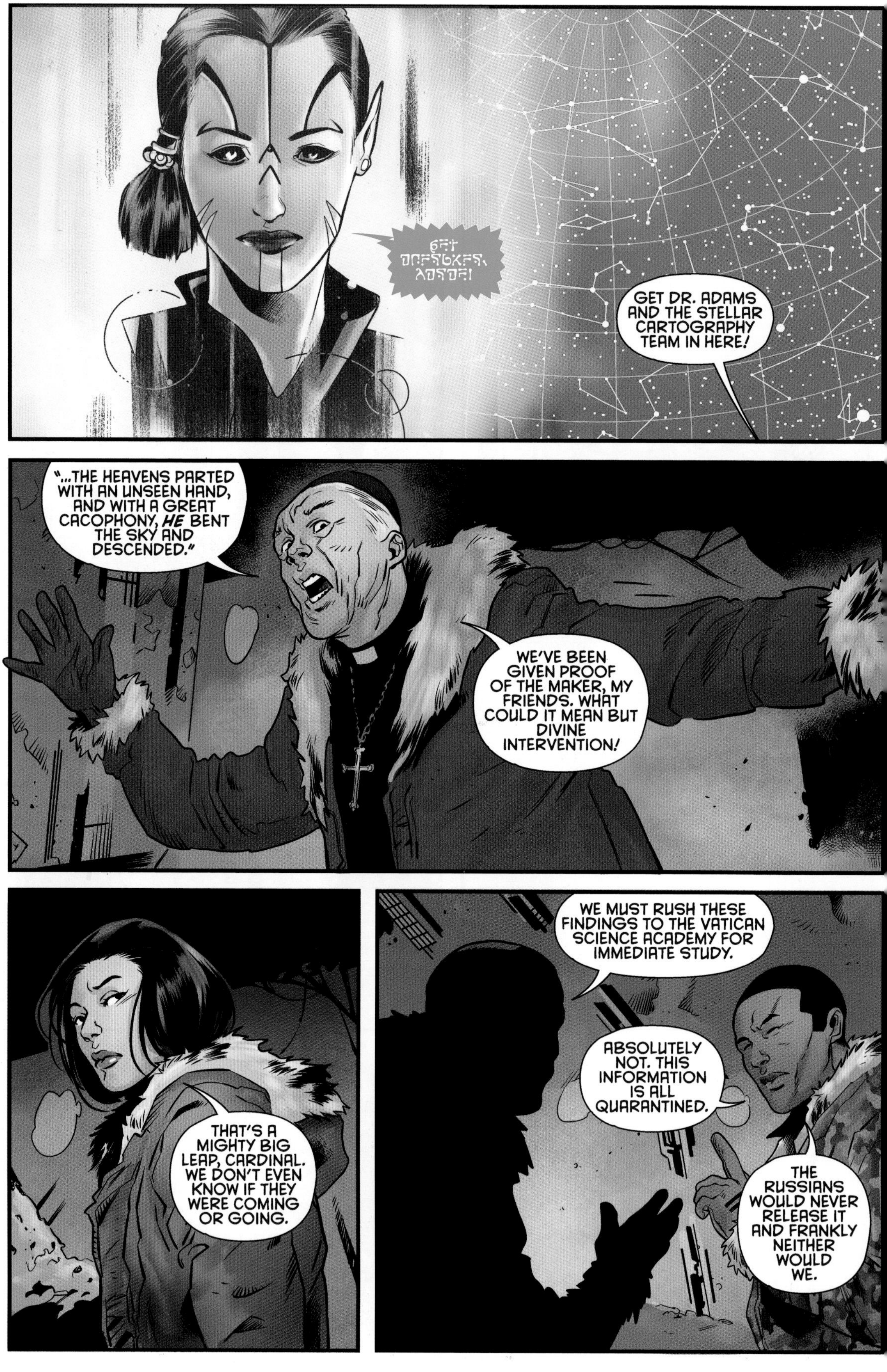
GET DR. ADAMS AND THE STELLAR CARTOGRAPHY TEAM IN HERE!
"...THE HEAVENS PARTED WITH AN UNSEEN HAND, AND WITH A GREAT CACOPHONY, HE BENT THE SKY AND DESCENDED."
WE'VE BEEN GIVEN PROOF OF THE MAKER, MY FRIENDS. WHAT COULD IT MEAN BUT DIVINE INTERVENTION!
THAT'S A MIGHTY BIG LEAP, CARDINAL. WE DON'T EVEN KNOW IF THEY WERE COMING OR GOING.
WE MUST RUSH THESE FINDINGS TO THE VATICAN SCIENCE ACADEMY FOR IMMEDIATE STUDY.
ABSOLUTELY NOT. THIS INFORMATION IS ALL QUARANTINED.
THE RUSSIANS WOULD NEVER RELEASE IT AND FRANKLY NEITHER WOULD WE.

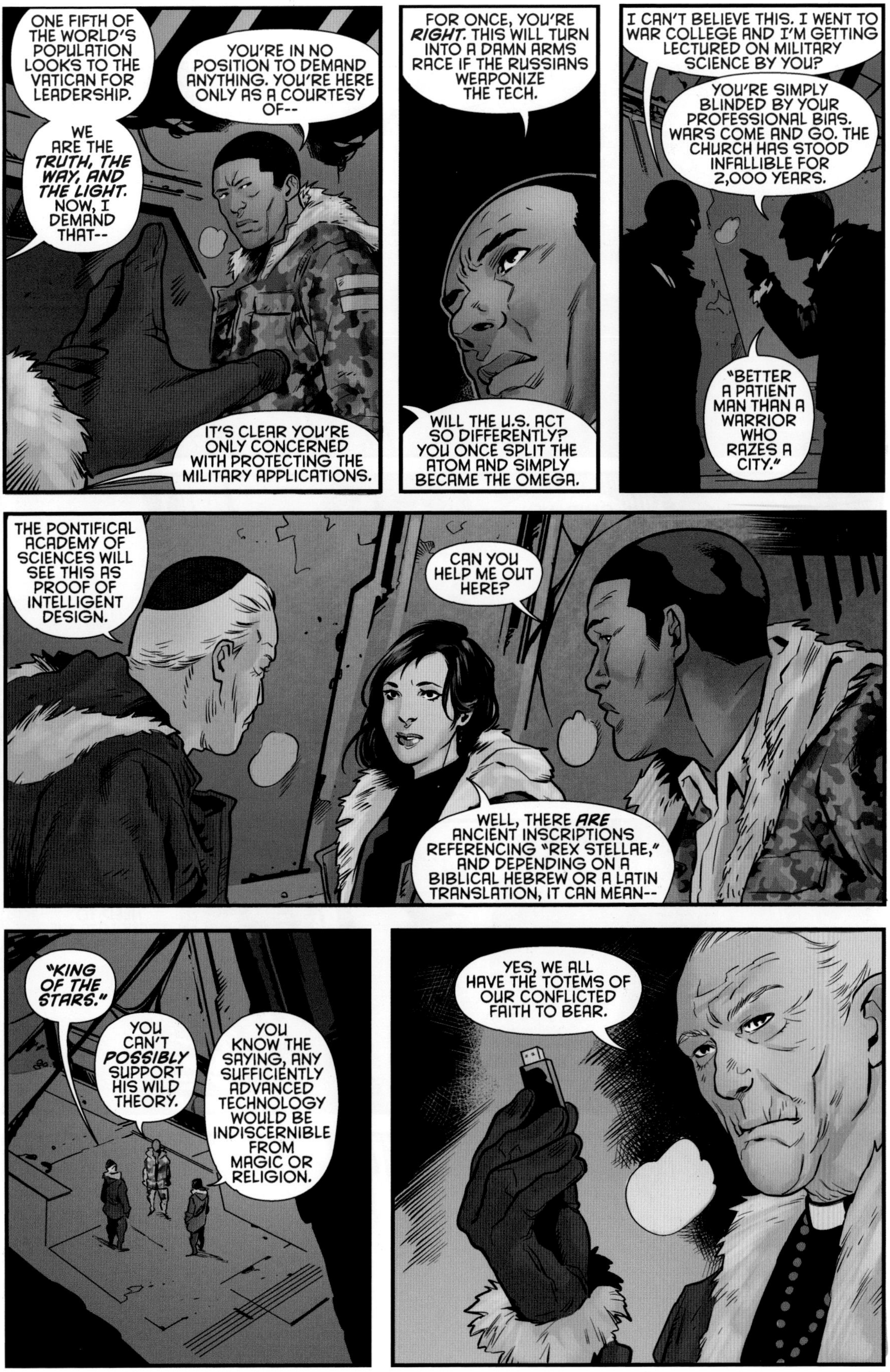

ONE FIFTH OF THE WORLD'S POPULATION LOOKS TO THE VATICAN FOR LEADERSHIP.
YOU'RE IN NO POSITION TO DEMAND ANYTHING. YOU'RE HERE ONLY AS A COURTESY OF--
WE ARE THE *TRUTH, THE WAY, AND THE LIGHT*. NOW, I DEMAND THAT--
IT'S CLEAR YOU'RE ONLY CONCERNED WITH PROTECTING THE MILITARY APPLICATIONS.
FOR ONCE, YOU'RE *RIGHT*. THIS WILL TURN INTO A DAMN ARMS RACE IF THE RUSSIANS WEAPONIZE THE TECH.
WILL THE U.S. ACT SO DIFFERENTLY? YOU ONCE SPLIT THE ATOM AND SIMPLY BECAME THE OMEGA.
I CAN'T BELIEVE THIS. I WENT TO WAR COLLEGE AND I'M GETTING LECTURED ON MILITARY SCIENCE BY YOU?
YOU'RE SIMPLY BLINDED BY YOUR PROFESSIONAL BIAS. WARS COME AND GO. THE CHURCH HAS STOOD INFALLIBLE FOR 2,000 YEARS.
"BETTER A PATIENT MAN THAN A WARRIOR WHO RAZES A CITY."
THE PONTIFICAL ACADEMY OF SCIENCES WILL SEE THIS AS PROOF OF INTELLIGENT DESIGN.
CAN YOU HELP ME OUT HERE?
WELL, THERE *ARE* ANCIENT INSCRIPTIONS REFERENCING "REX STELLAE," AND DEPENDING ON A BIBLICAL HEBREW OR A LATIN TRANSLATION, IT CAN MEAN--
"KING OF THE STARS."
YOU CAN'T *POSSIBLY* SUPPORT HIS WILD THEORY.
YOU KNOW THE SAYING, ANY SUFFICIENTLY ADVANCED TECHNOLOGY WOULD BE INDISCERNIBLE FROM MAGIC OR RELIGION.
YES, WE ALL HAVE THE TOTEMS OF OUR CONFLICTED FAITH TO BEAR.

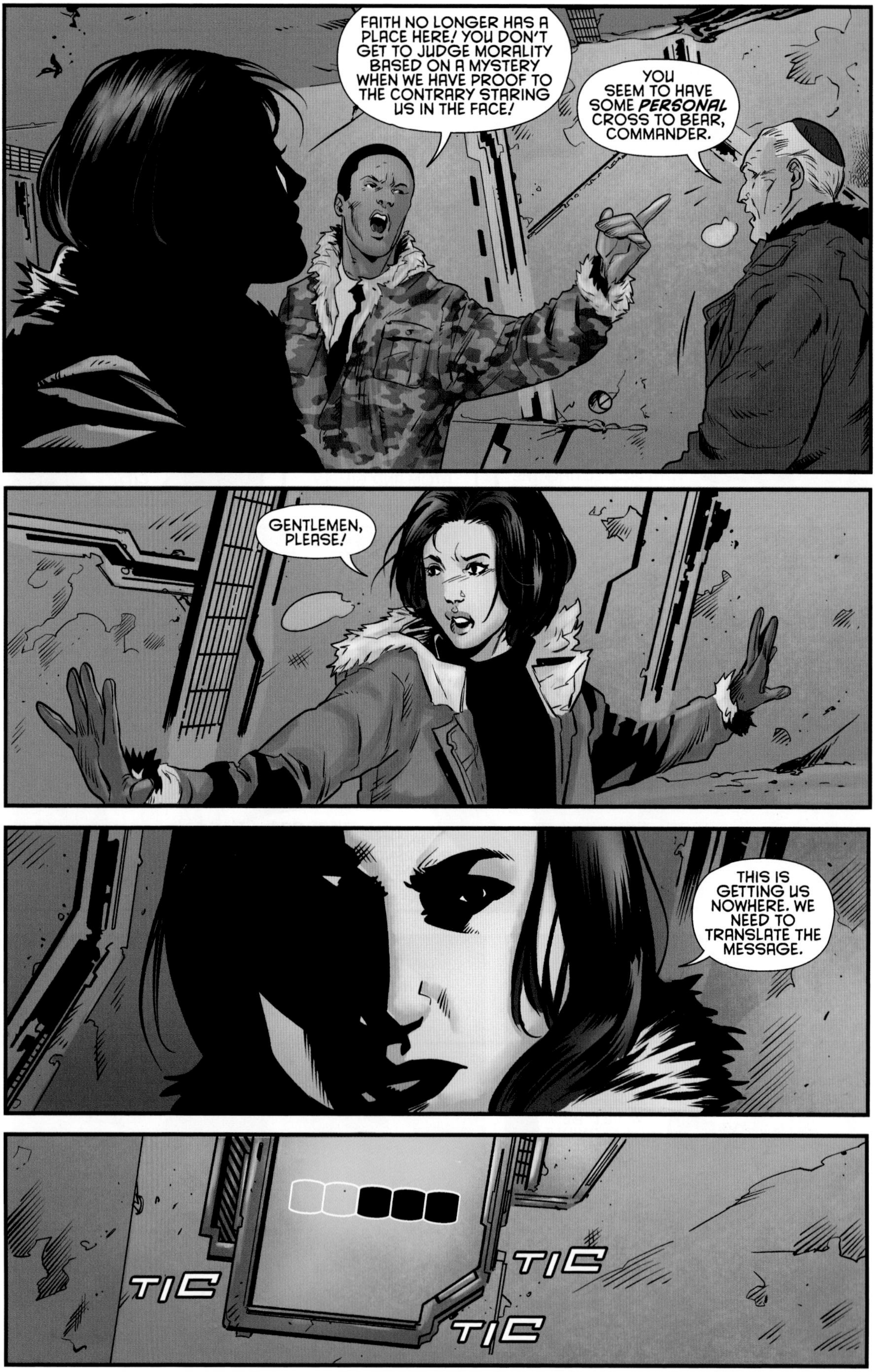
FAITH NO LONGER HAS A PLACE HERE! YOU DON'T GET TO JUDGE MORALITY BASED ON A MYSTERY WHEN WE HAVE PROOF TO THE CONTRARY STARING US IN THE FACE!
YOU SEEM TO HAVE SOME *PERSONAL* CROSS TO BEAR, COMMANDER.
GENTLEMEN, PLEASE!
THIS IS GETTING US NOWHERE. WE NEED TO TRANSLATE THE MESSAGE.
TIC
TIC
TIC

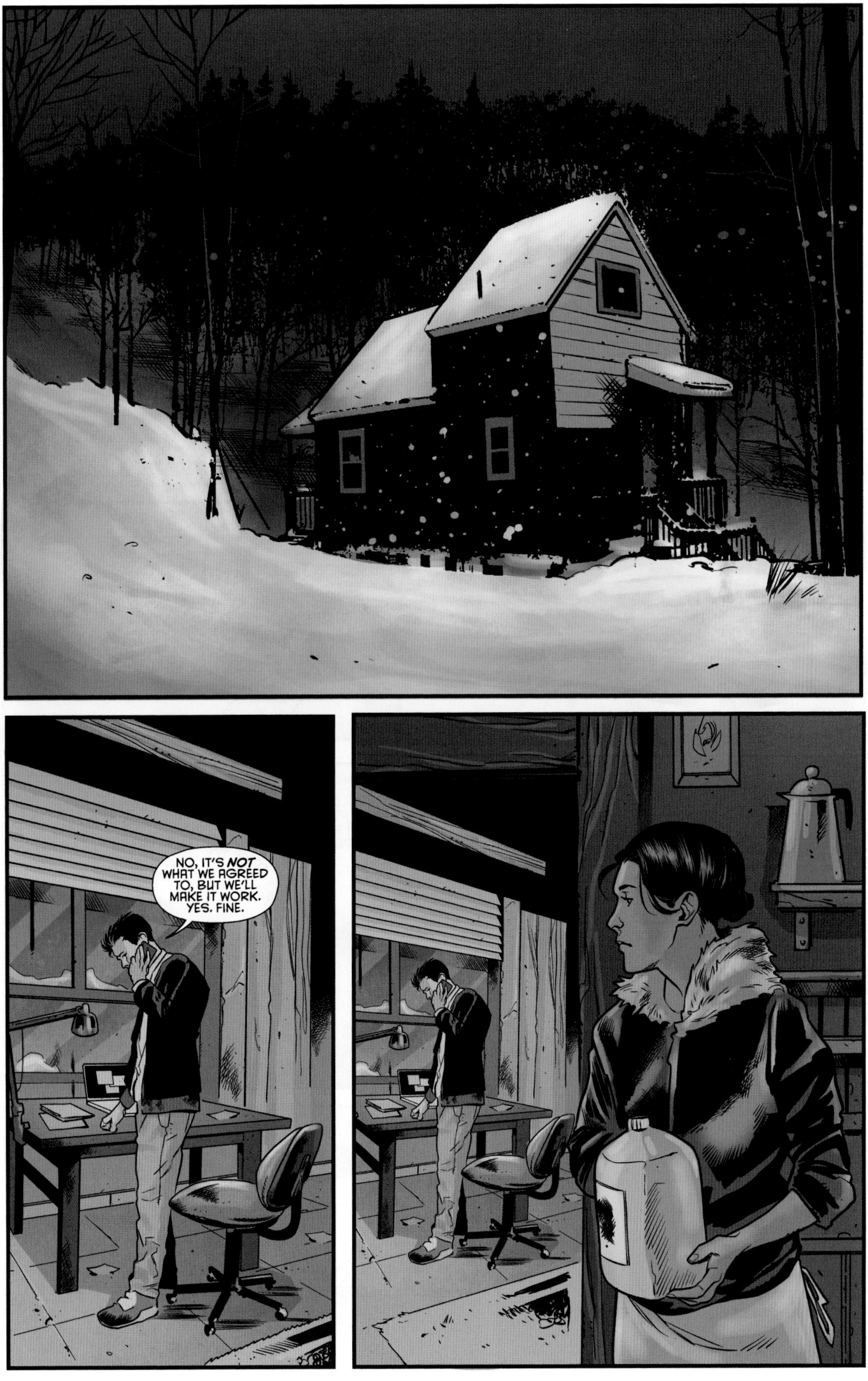
NO, IT'S NOT WHAT WE AGREED TO, BUT WE'LL MAKE IT WORK. YES. FINE.

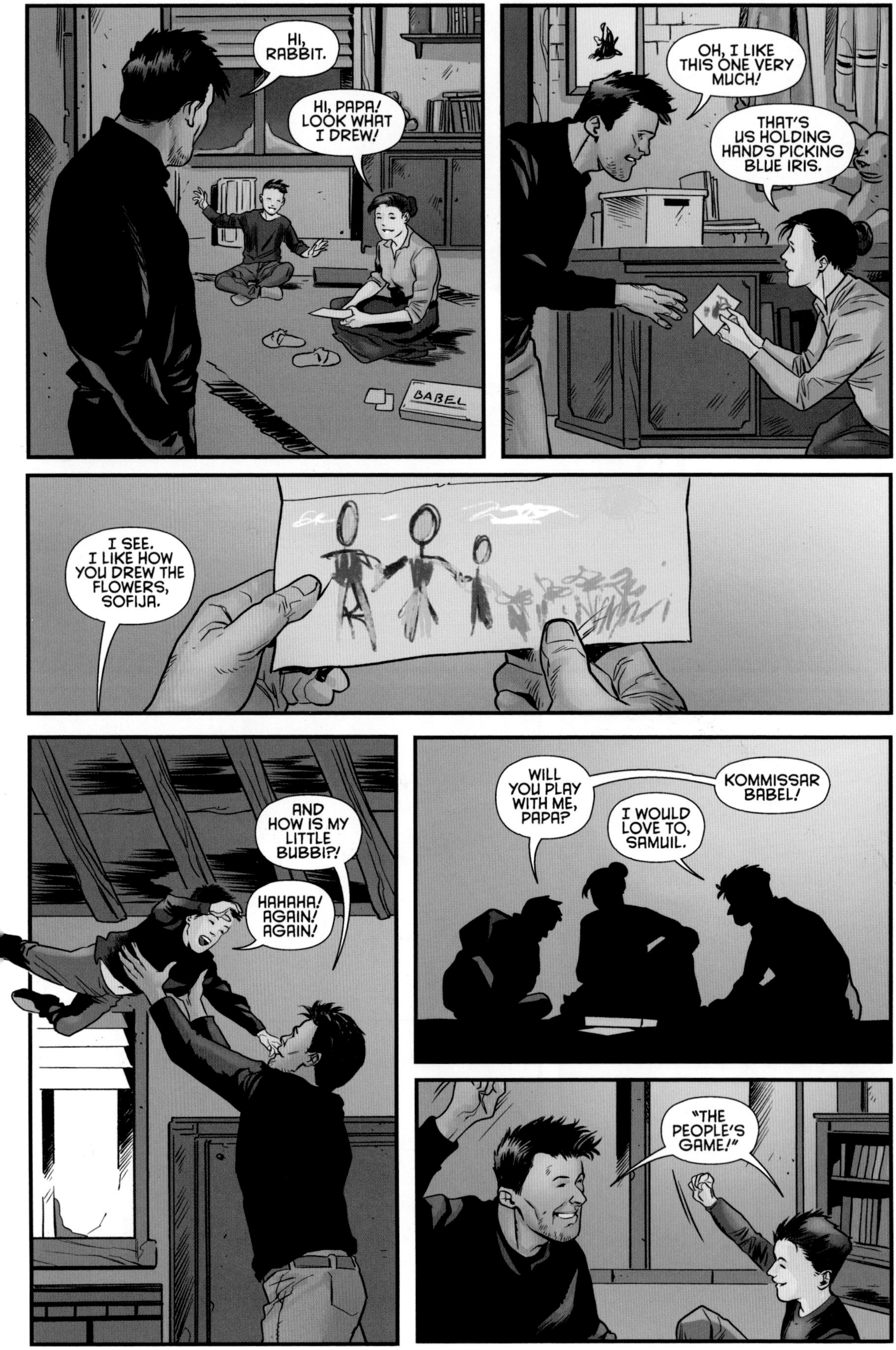
HI, RABBIT.
HI, PAPA! LOOK WHAT I DREW!
BABEL
OH, I LIKE THIS ONE VERY MUCH!
THAT'S US HOLDING HANDS PICKING BLUE IRIS.
I SEE. I LIKE HOW YOU DREW THE FLOWERS, SOFIJA.
AND HOW IS MY LITTLE BUBBI?!
HAHAHA! AGAIN! AGAIN!
WILL YOU PLAY WITH ME, PAPA?
KOMMISSAR BABEL!
I WOULD LOVE TO, SAMUIL.
"THE PEOPLE'S GAME!"

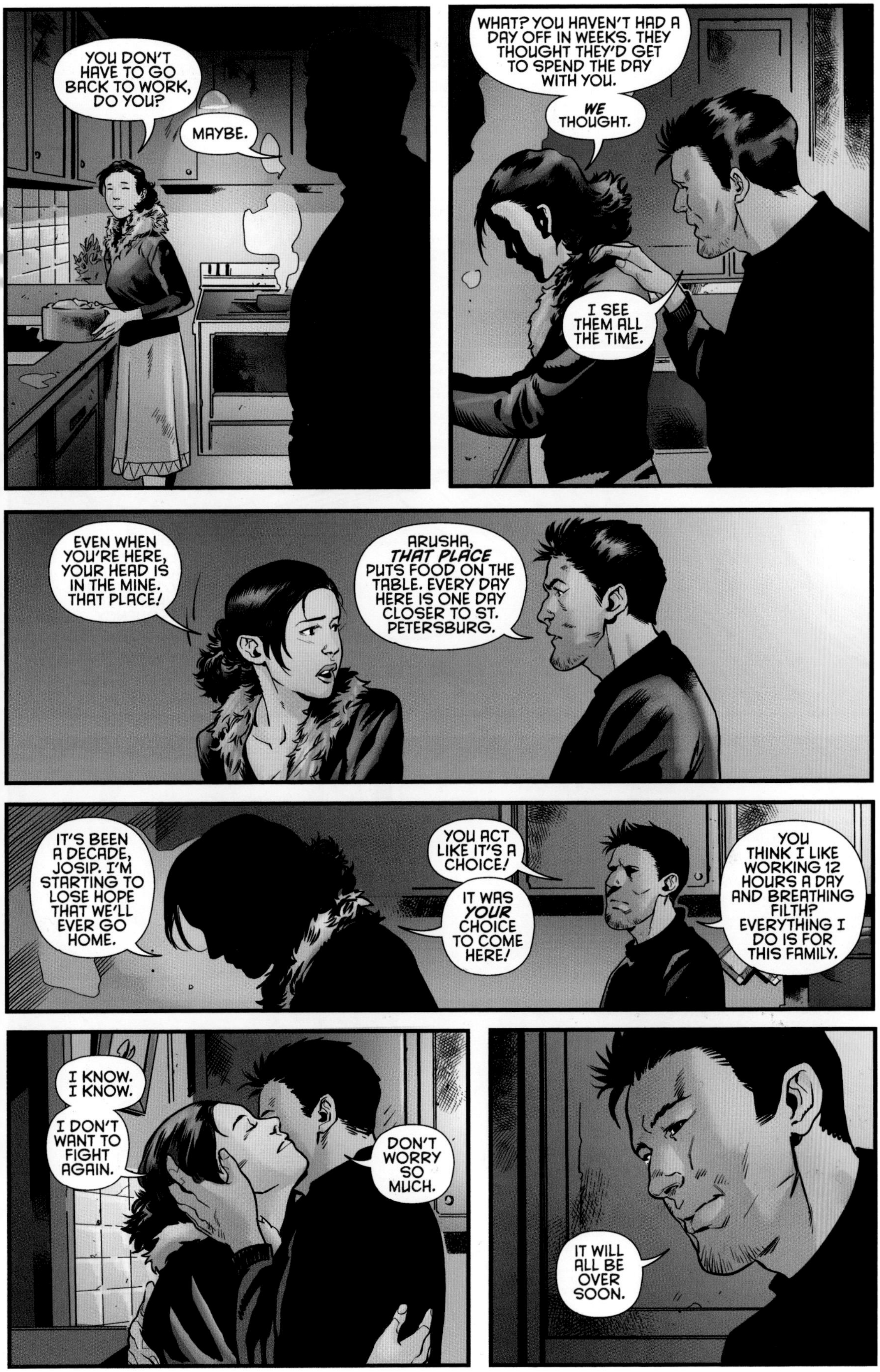

YOU DON'T HAVE TO GO BACK TO WORK, DO YOU?
MAYBE.
WHAT? YOU HAVEN'T HAD A DAY OFF IN WEEKS. THEY THOUGHT THEY'D GET TO SPEND THE DAY WITH YOU.
WE THOUGHT.
I SEE THEM ALL THE TIME.
EVEN WHEN YOU'RE HERE, YOUR HEAD IS IN THE MINE. THAT PLACE!
ARUSHA, THAT PLACE PUTS FOOD ON THE TABLE. EVERY DAY HERE IS ONE DAY CLOSER TO ST. PETERSBURG.
IT'S BEEN A DECADE, JOSIP. I'M STARTING TO LOSE HOPE THAT WE'LL EVER GO HOME.
YOU ACT LIKE IT'S A CHOICE!
IT WAS YOUR CHOICE TO COME HERE!
YOU THINK I LIKE WORKING 12 HOURS A DAY AND BREATHING FILTH? EVERYTHING I DO IS FOR THIS FAMILY.
I KNOW. I KNOW.
I DON'T WANT TO FIGHT AGAIN.
DON'T WORRY SO MUCH.
IT WILL ALL BE OVER SOON.

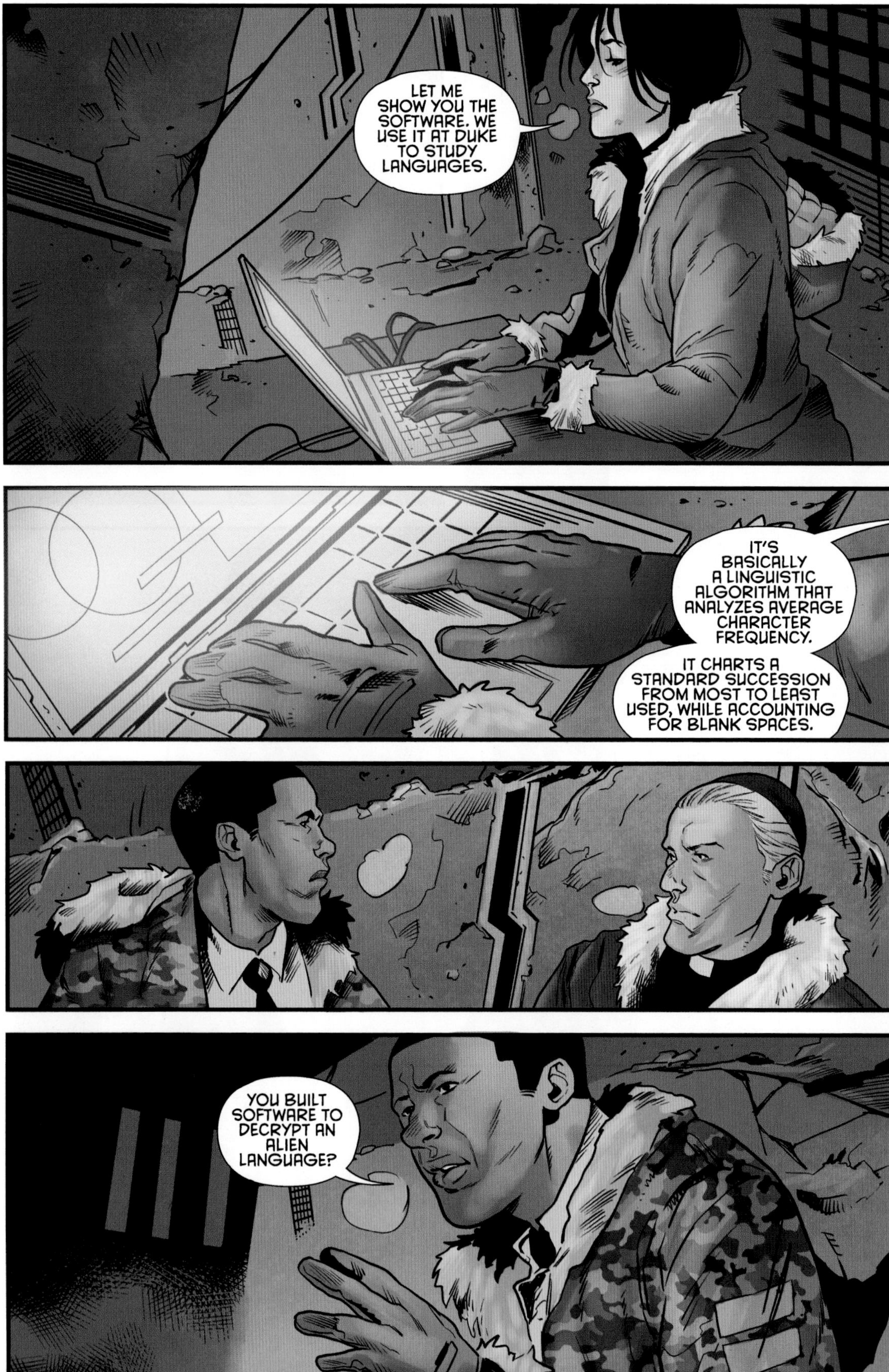
LET ME SHOW YOU THE SOFTWARE. WE USE IT AT DUKE TO STUDY LANGUAGES.
IT'S BASICALLY A LINGUISTIC ALGORITHM THAT ANALYZES AVERAGE CHARACTER FREQUENCY.
IT CHARTS A STANDARD SUCCESSION FROM MOST TO LEAST USED, WHILE ACCOUNTING FOR BLANK SPACES.
YOU BUILT SOFTWARE TO DECRYPT AN ALIEN LANGUAGE?

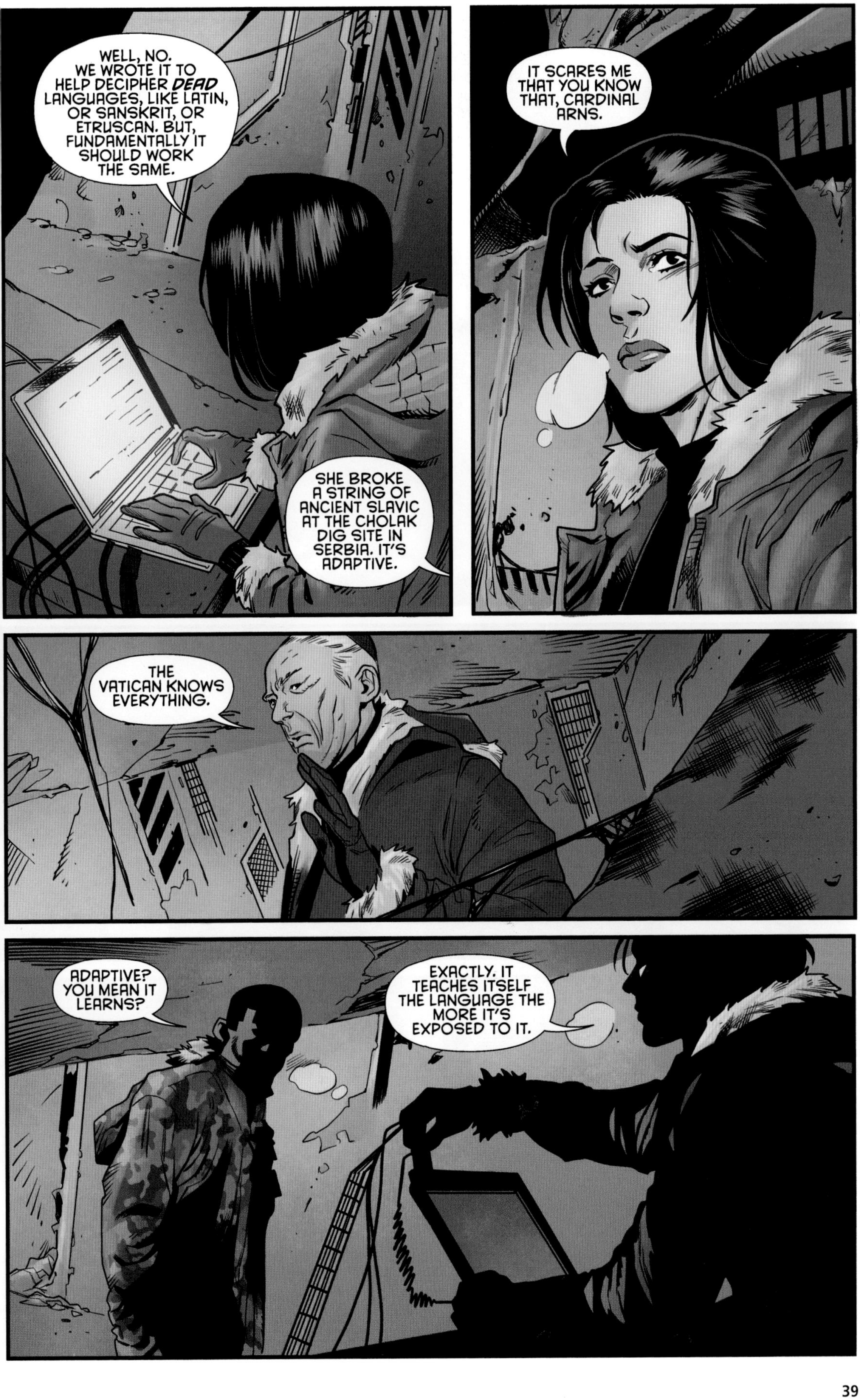
WELL, NO. WE WROTE IT TO HELP DECIPHER *DEAD* LANGUAGES, LIKE LATIN, OR SANSKRIT, OR ETRUSCAN. BUT, FUNDAMENTALLY IT SHOULD WORK THE SAME.
IT SCARES ME THAT YOU KNOW THAT, CARDINAL ARNS.
SHE BROKE A STRING OF ANCIENT SLAVIC AT THE CHOLAK DIG SITE IN SERBIA. IT'S ADAPTIVE.
THE VATICAN KNOWS EVERYTHING.
ADAPTIVE? YOU MEAN IT LEARNS?
EXACTLY. IT TEACHES ITSELF THE LANGUAGE THE MORE IT'S EXPOSED TO IT.

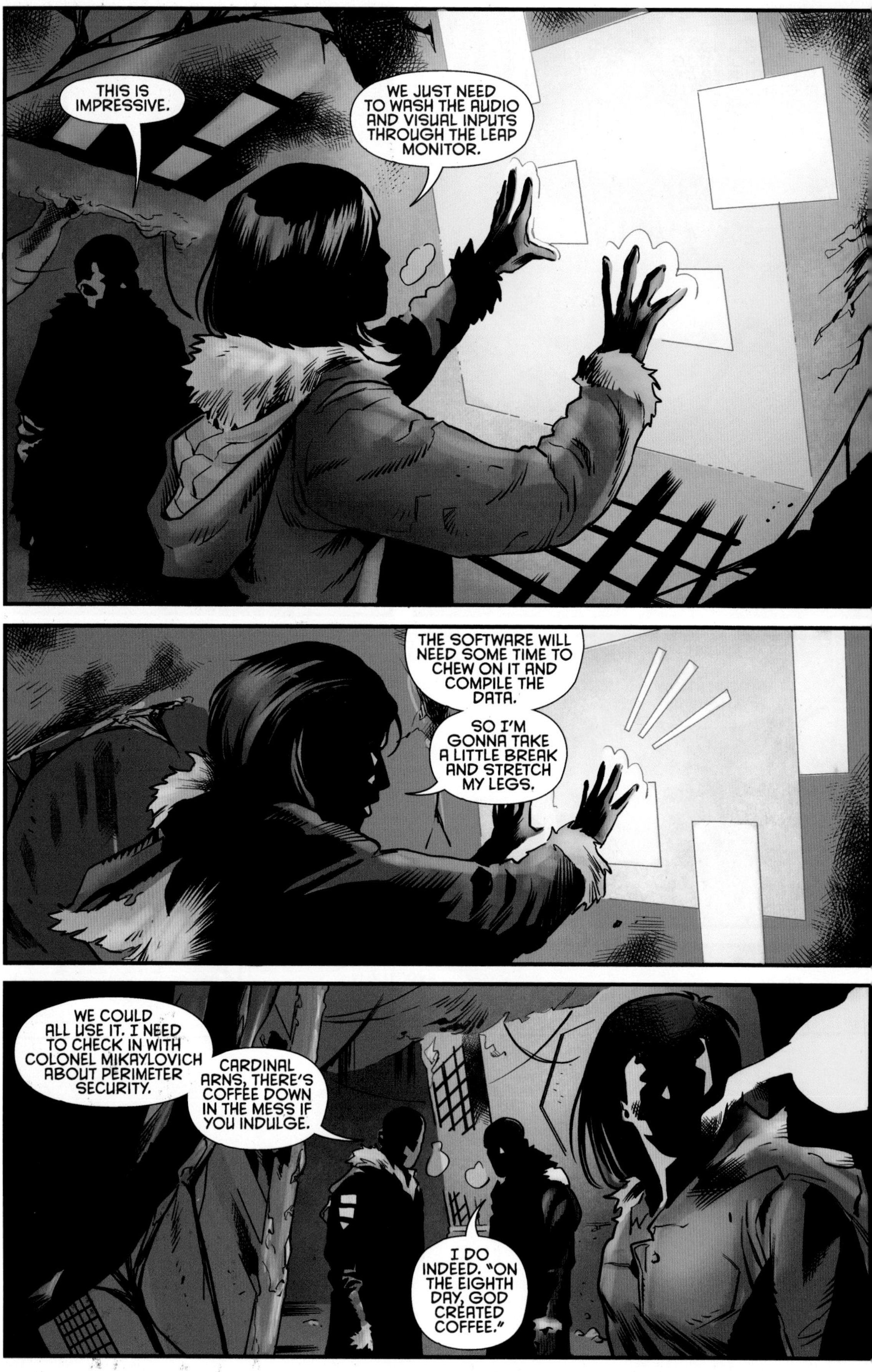
THIS IS IMPRESSIVE.
WE JUST NEED TO WASH THE AUDIO AND VISUAL INPUTS THROUGH THE LEAP MONITOR.
THE SOFTWARE WILL NEED SOME TIME TO CHEW ON IT AND COMPILE THE DATA.
SO I'M GONNA TAKE A LITTLE BREAK AND STRETCH MY LEGS.
WE COULD ALL USE IT. I NEED TO CHECK IN WITH COLONEL MIKAYLOVICH ABOUT PERIMETER SECURITY.
CARDINAL ARNS, THERE'S COFFEE DOWN IN THE MESS IF YOU INDULGE.
I DO INDEED. "ON THE EIGHTH DAY, GOD CREATED COFFEE."

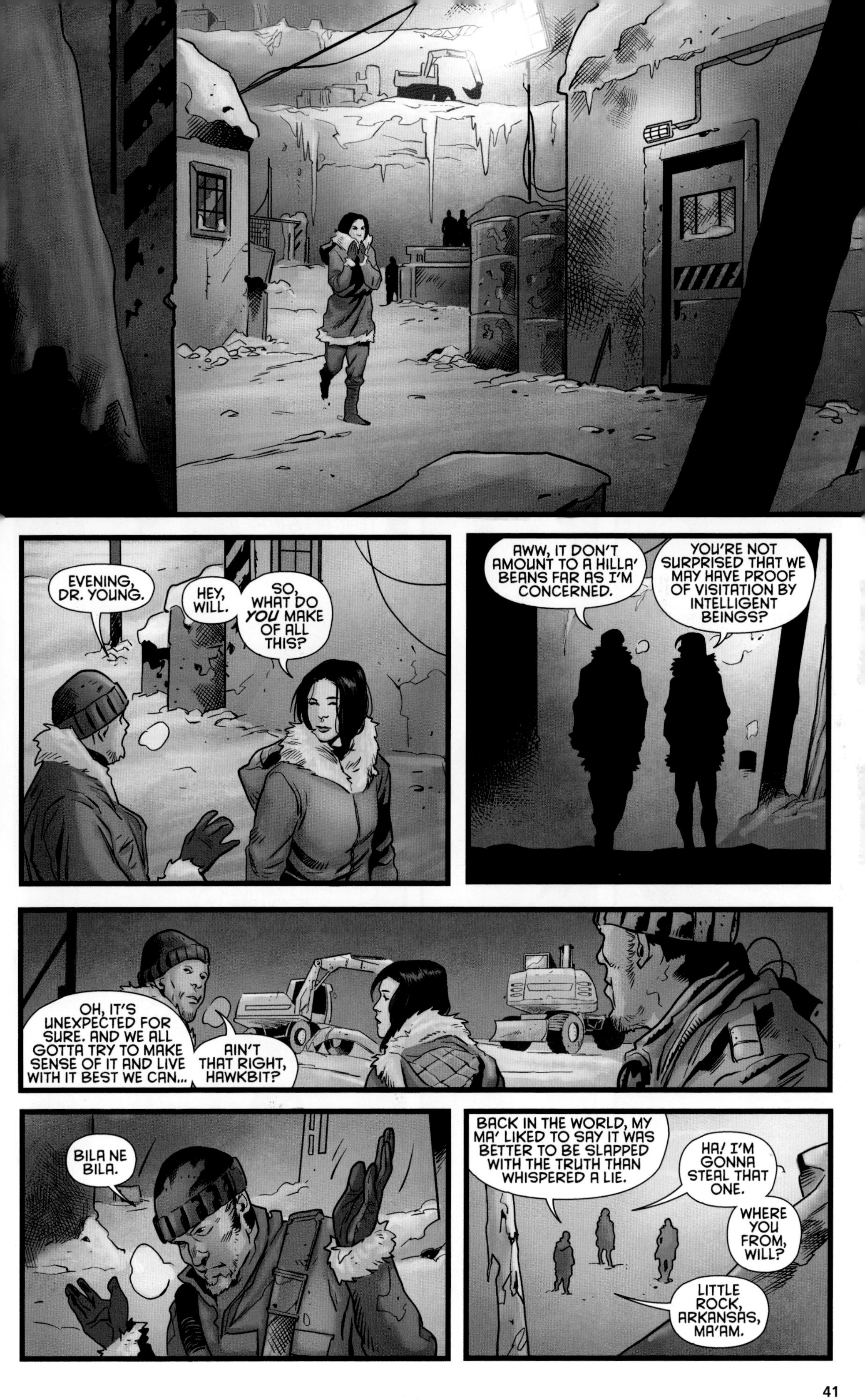

EVENING, DR. YOUNG.
HEY, WILL.
SO, WHAT DO *YOU* MAKE OF ALL THIS?
AWW, IT DON'T AMOUNT TO A HILLA' BEANS FAR AS I'M CONCERNED.
YOU'RE NOT SURPRISED THAT WE MAY HAVE PROOF OF VISITATION BY INTELLIGENT BEINGS?
OH, IT'S UNEXPECTED FOR SURE. AND WE ALL GOTTA TRY TO MAKE SENSE OF IT AND LIVE WITH IT BEST WE CAN...
AIN'T THAT RIGHT, HAWKBIT?
BILA NE BILA.
BACK IN THE WORLD, MY MA' LIKED TO SAY IT WAS BETTER TO BE SLAPPED WITH THE TRUTH THAN WHISPERED A LIE.
HA! I'M GONNA STEAL THAT ONE.
WHERE YOU FROM, WILL?
LITTLE ROCK, ARKANSAS, MA'AM.

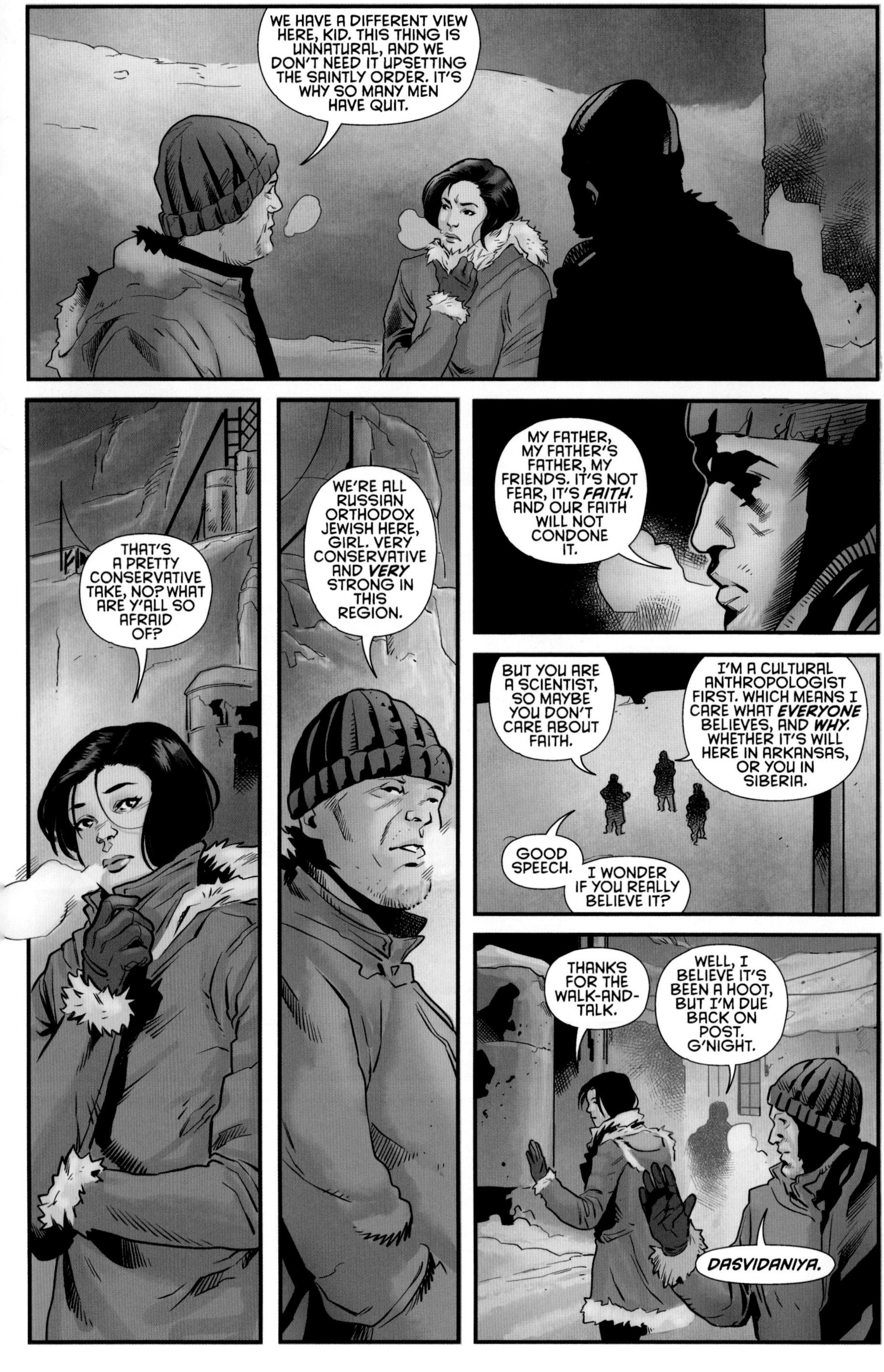
WE HAVE A DIFFERENT VIEW HERE, KID. THIS THING IS UNNATURAL, AND WE DON'T NEED IT UPSETTING THE SAINTLY ORDER. IT'S WHY SO MANY MEN HAVE QUIT.
THAT'S A PRETTY CONSERVATIVE TAKE, NO? WHAT ARE Y'ALL SO AFRAID OF?
WE'RE ALL RUSSIAN ORTHODOX JEWISH HERE, GIRL. VERY CONSERVATIVE AND VERY STRONG IN THIS REGION.
MY FATHER, MY FATHER'S FATHER, MY FRIENDS. IT'S NOT FEAR, IT'S FAITH. AND OUR FAITH WILL NOT CONDONE IT.
BUT YOU ARE A SCIENTIST, SO MAYBE YOU DON'T CARE ABOUT FAITH.
I'M A CULTURAL ANTHROPOLOGIST FIRST. WHICH MEANS I CARE WHAT EVERYONE BELIEVES, AND WHY. WHETHER IT'S WILL HERE IN ARKANSAS, OR YOU IN SIBERIA.
GOOD SPEECH.
I WONDER IF YOU REALLY BELIEVE IT?
THANKS FOR THE WALK-AND-TALK.
WELL, I BELIEVE IT'S BEEN A HOOT, BUT I'M DUE BACK ON POST. G'NIGHT.
DASVIDANIYA.

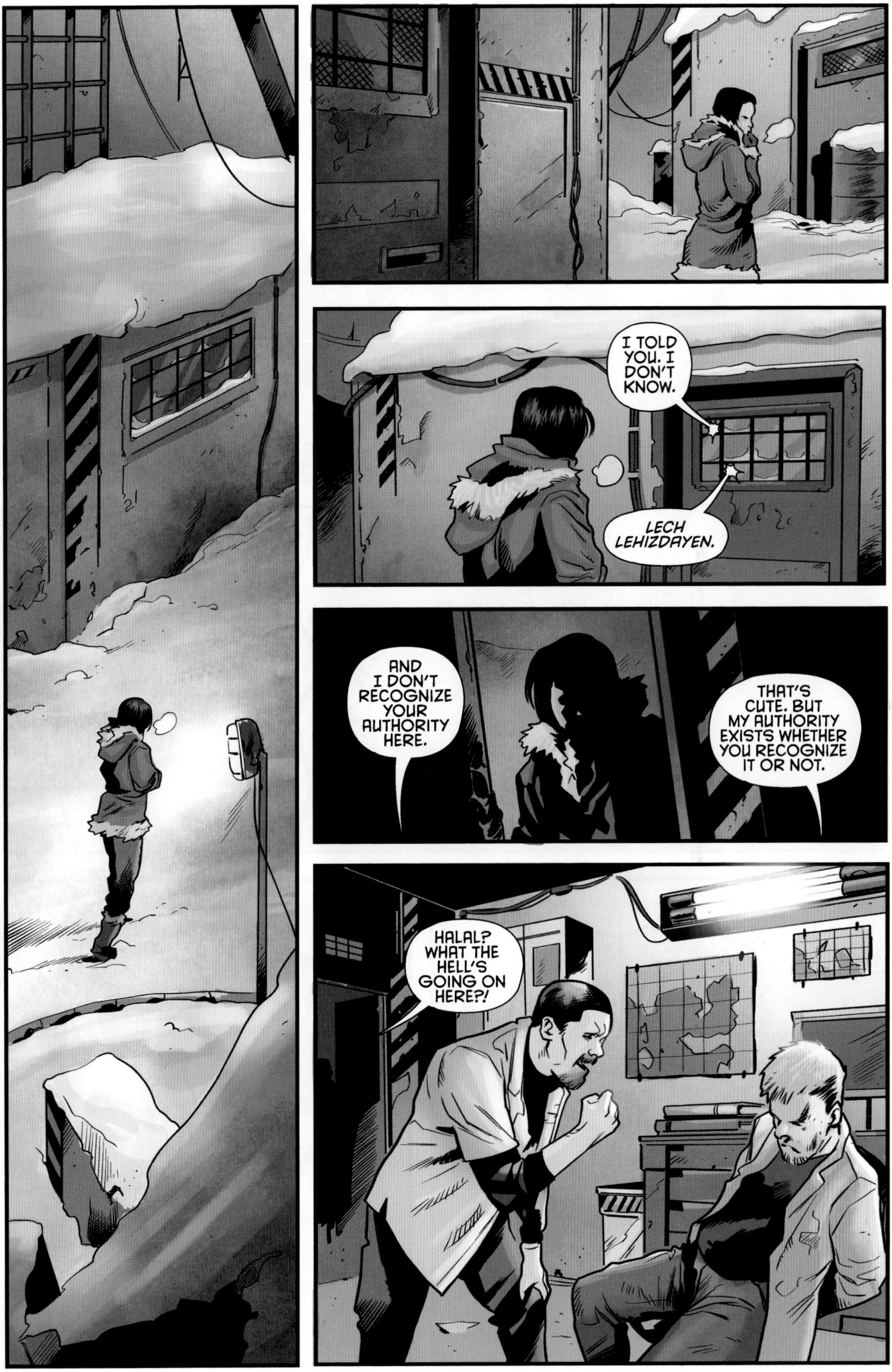
I TOLD YOU. I DON'T KNOW.
LECH LEHIZDAYEN.
AND I DON'T RECOGNIZE YOUR AUTHORITY HERE.
THAT'S CUTE. BUT MY AUTHORITY EXISTS WHETHER YOU RECOGNIZE IT OR NOT.
HALAL? WHAT THE HELL'S GOING ON HERE?!

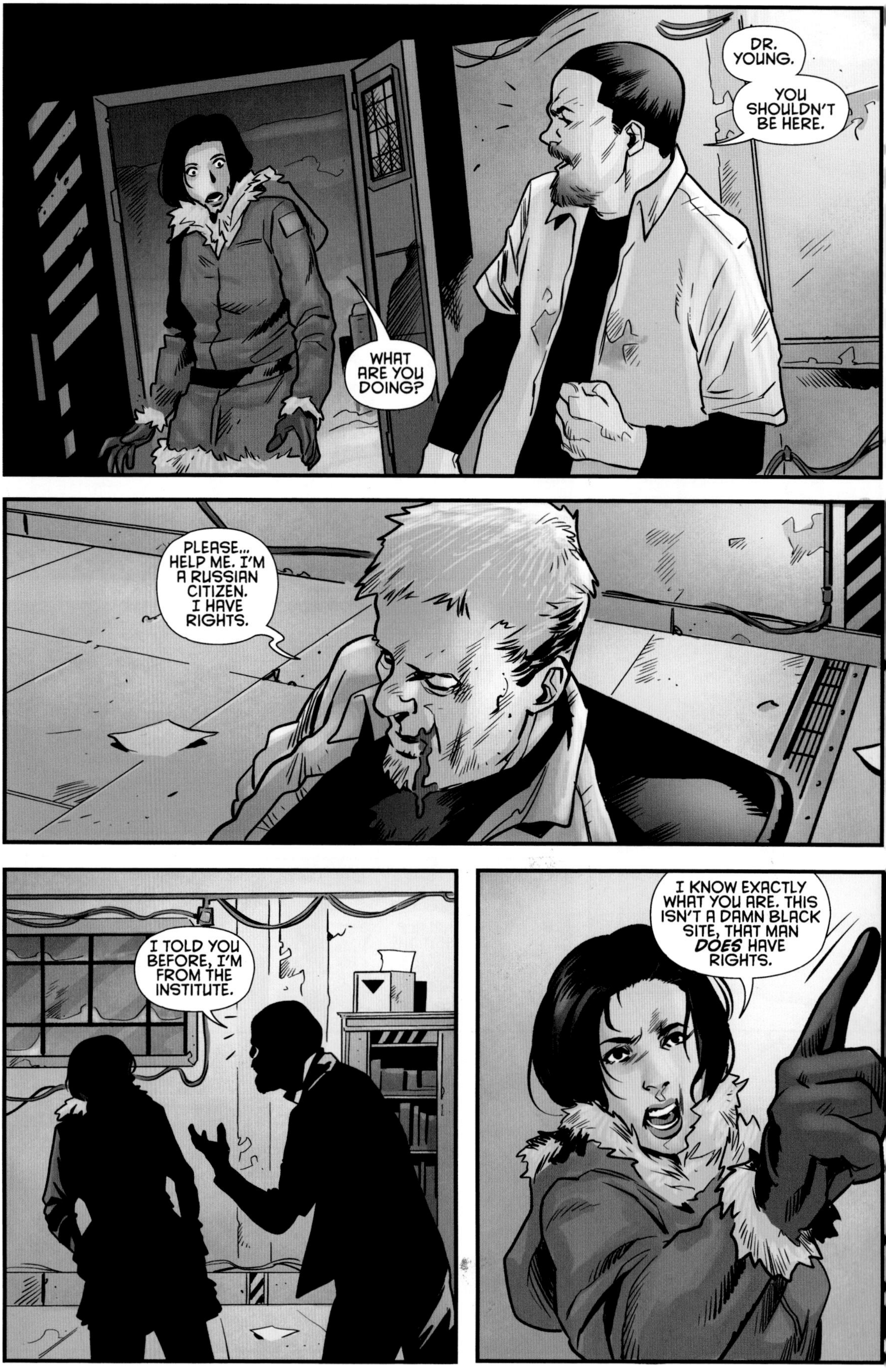
DR. YOUNG.
YOU SHOULDN'T BE HERE.
WHAT ARE YOU DOING?
PLEASE... HELP ME. I'M A RUSSIAN CITIZEN. I HAVE RIGHTS.
I TOLD YOU BEFORE, I'M FROM THE INSTITUTE.
I KNOW EXACTLY WHAT YOU ARE. THIS ISN'T A DAMN BLACK SITE, THAT MAN *DOES* HAVE RIGHTS.

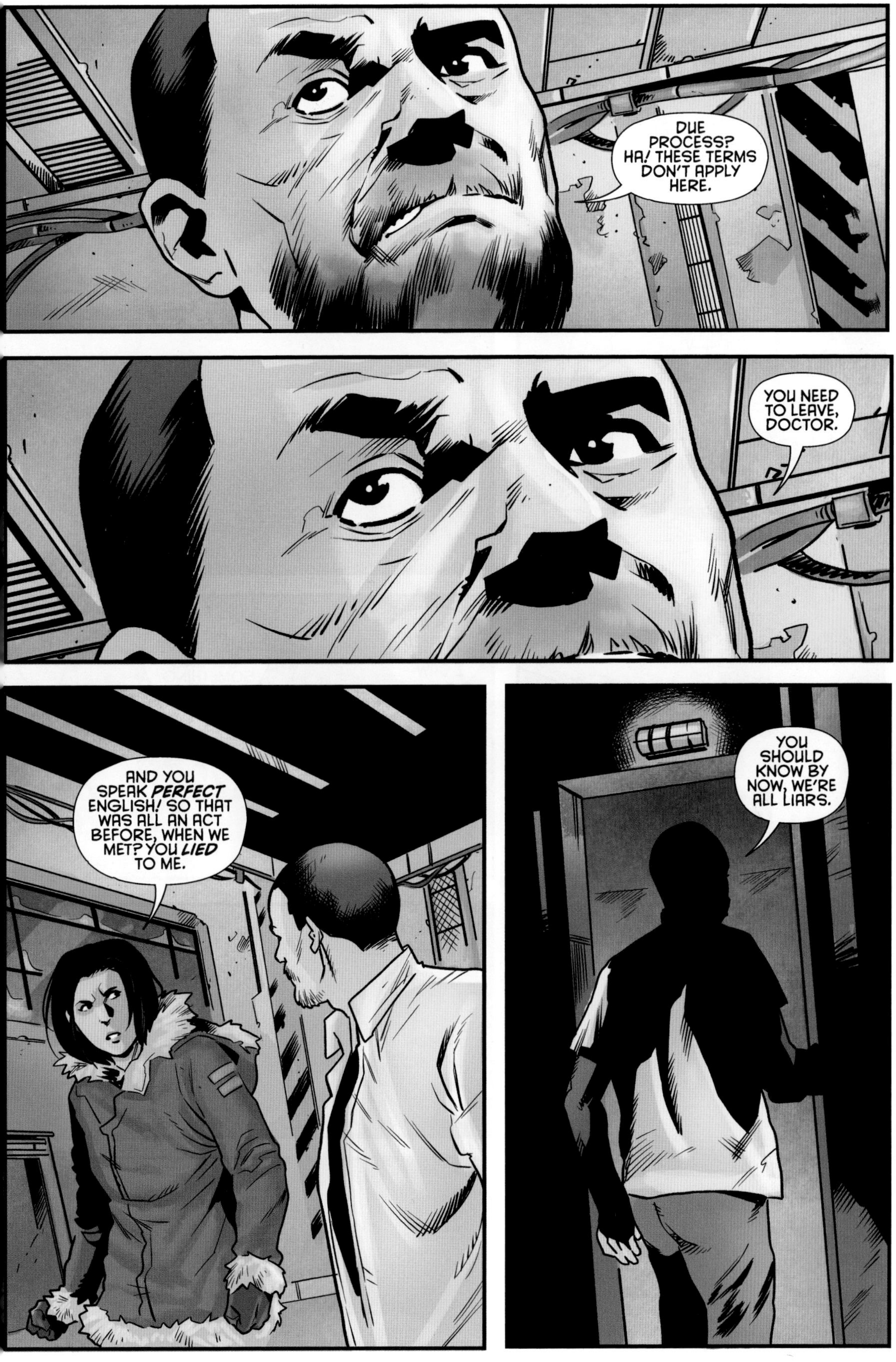
DUE PROCESS? HA! THESE TERMS DON'T APPLY HERE.
YOU NEED TO LEAVE, DOCTOR.
AND YOU SPEAK *PERFECT* ENGLISH! SO THAT WAS ALL AN ACT BEFORE, WHEN WE MET? YOU *LIED* TO ME.
YOU SHOULD KNOW BY NOW, WE'RE ALL LIARS.

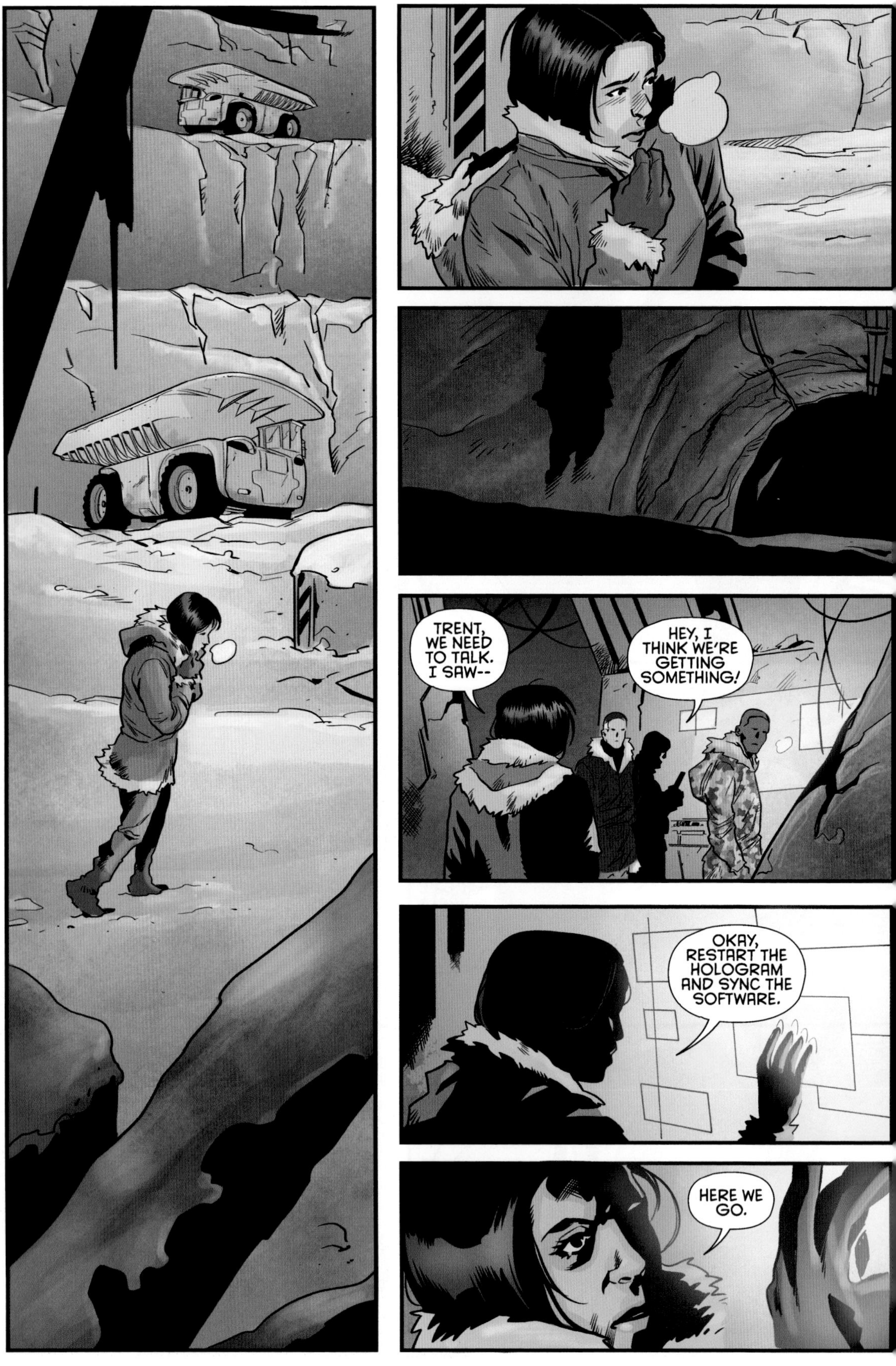
TRENT, WE NEED TO TALK. I SAW--
HEY, I THINK WE'RE GETTING SOMETHING!
OKAY, RESTART THE HOLOGRAM AND SYNC THE SOFTWARE.
HERE WE GO.

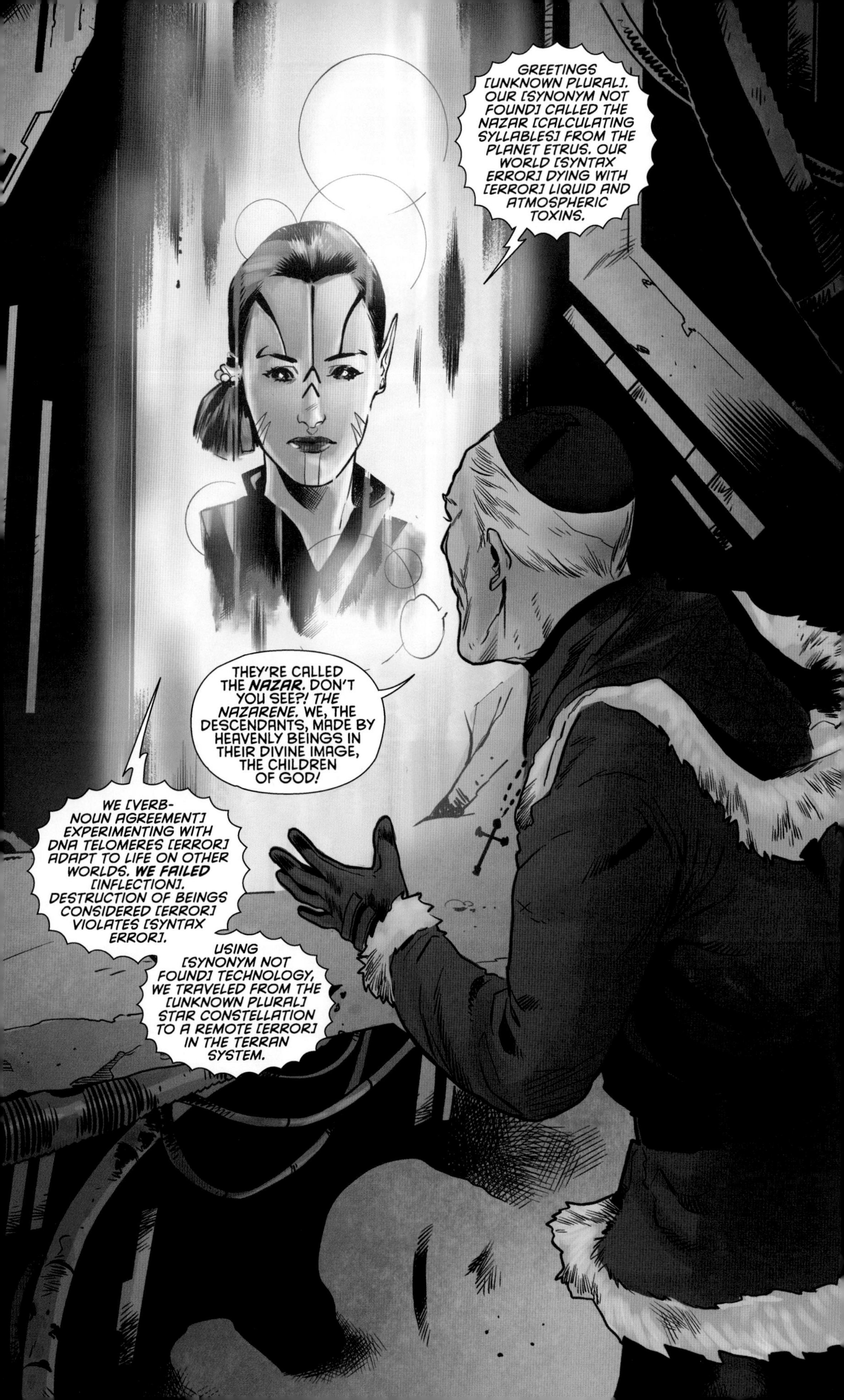
GREETINGS [UNKNOWN PLURAL]. OUR [SYNONYM NOT FOUND] CALLED THE NAZAR [CALCULATING SYLLABLES] FROM THE PLANET ETRUS. OUR WORLD [SYNTAX ERROR] DYING WITH [ERROR] LIQUID AND ATMOSPHERIC TOXINS.
THEY'RE CALLED THE ***NAZAR***. DON'T YOU SEE?! *THE NAZARENE*. WE, THE DESCENDANTS, MADE BY HEAVENLY BEINGS IN THEIR DIVINE IMAGE, THE CHILDREN OF GOD!
WE [VERB-NOUN AGREEMENT] EXPERIMENTING WITH DNA TELOMERES [ERROR] ADAPT TO LIFE ON OTHER WORLDS. **WE FAILED** [INFLECTION]. DESTRUCTION OF BEINGS CONSIDERED [ERROR] VIOLATES [SYNTAX ERROR].
USING [SYNONYM NOT FOUND] TECHNOLOGY, WE TRAVELED FROM THE [UNKNOWN PLURAL] STAR CONSTELLATION TO A REMOTE [ERROR] IN THE TERRAN SYSTEM.

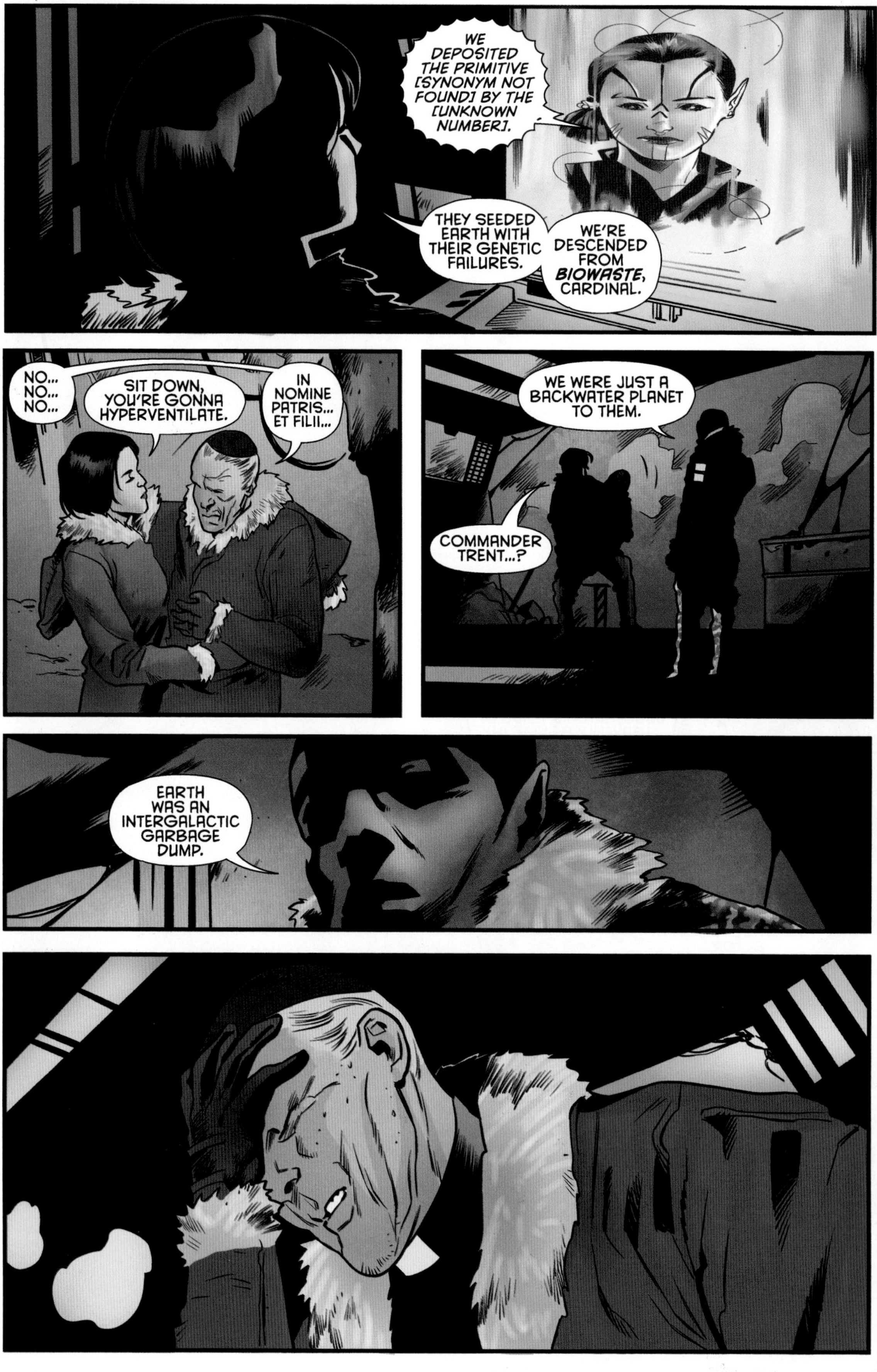
WE DEPOSITED THE PRIMITIVE [SYNONYM NOT FOUND] BY THE [UNKNOWN NUMBER].
THEY SEEDED EARTH WITH THEIR GENETIC FAILURES.
WE'RE DESCENDED FROM BIOWASTE, CARDINAL.
NO... NO... NO...
SIT DOWN, YOU'RE GONNA HYPERVENTILATE.
IN NOMINE PATRIS... ET FILII...
WE WERE JUST A BACKWATER PLANET TO THEM.
COMMANDER TRENT...?
EARTH WAS AN INTERGALACTIC GARBAGE DUMP.

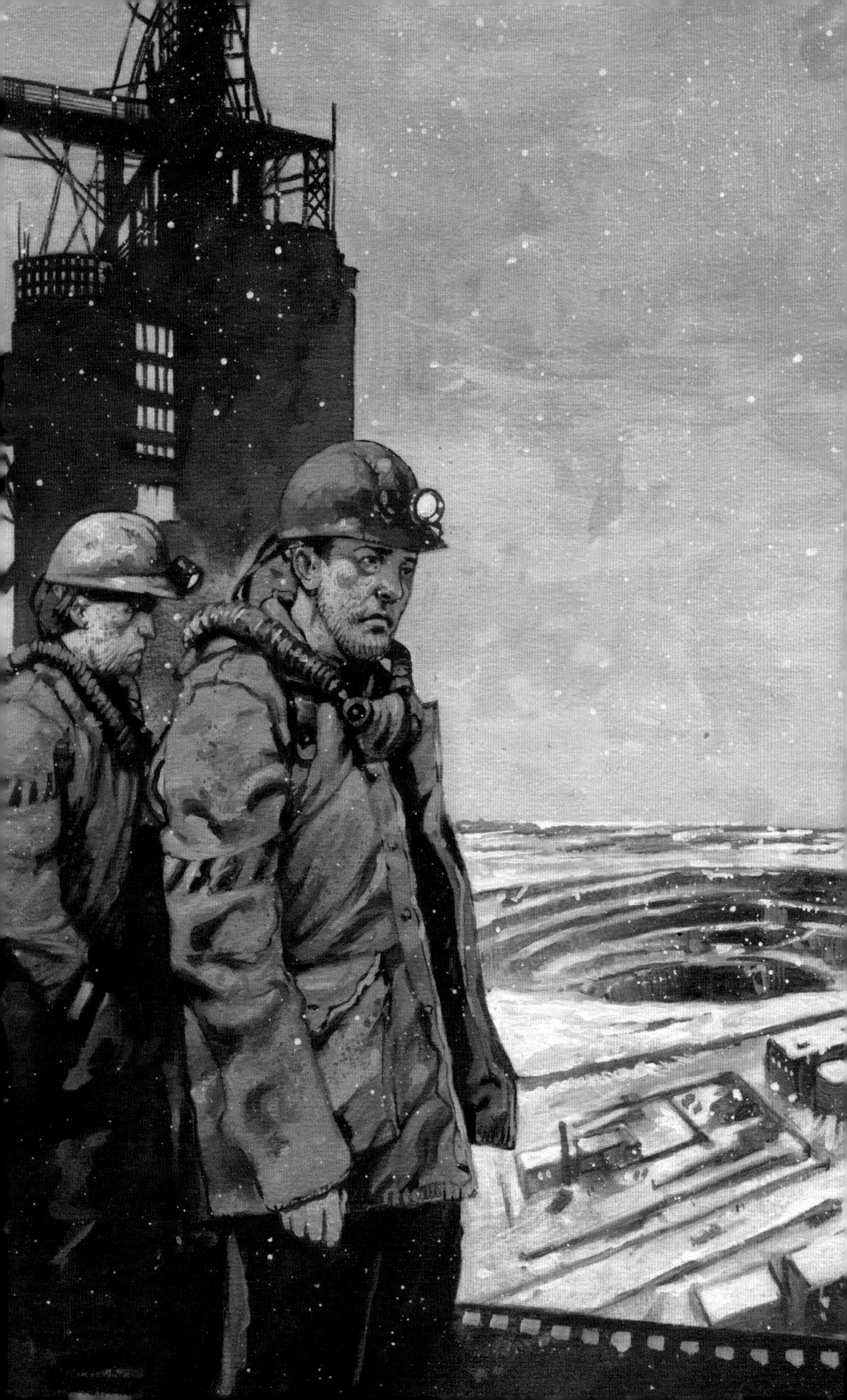

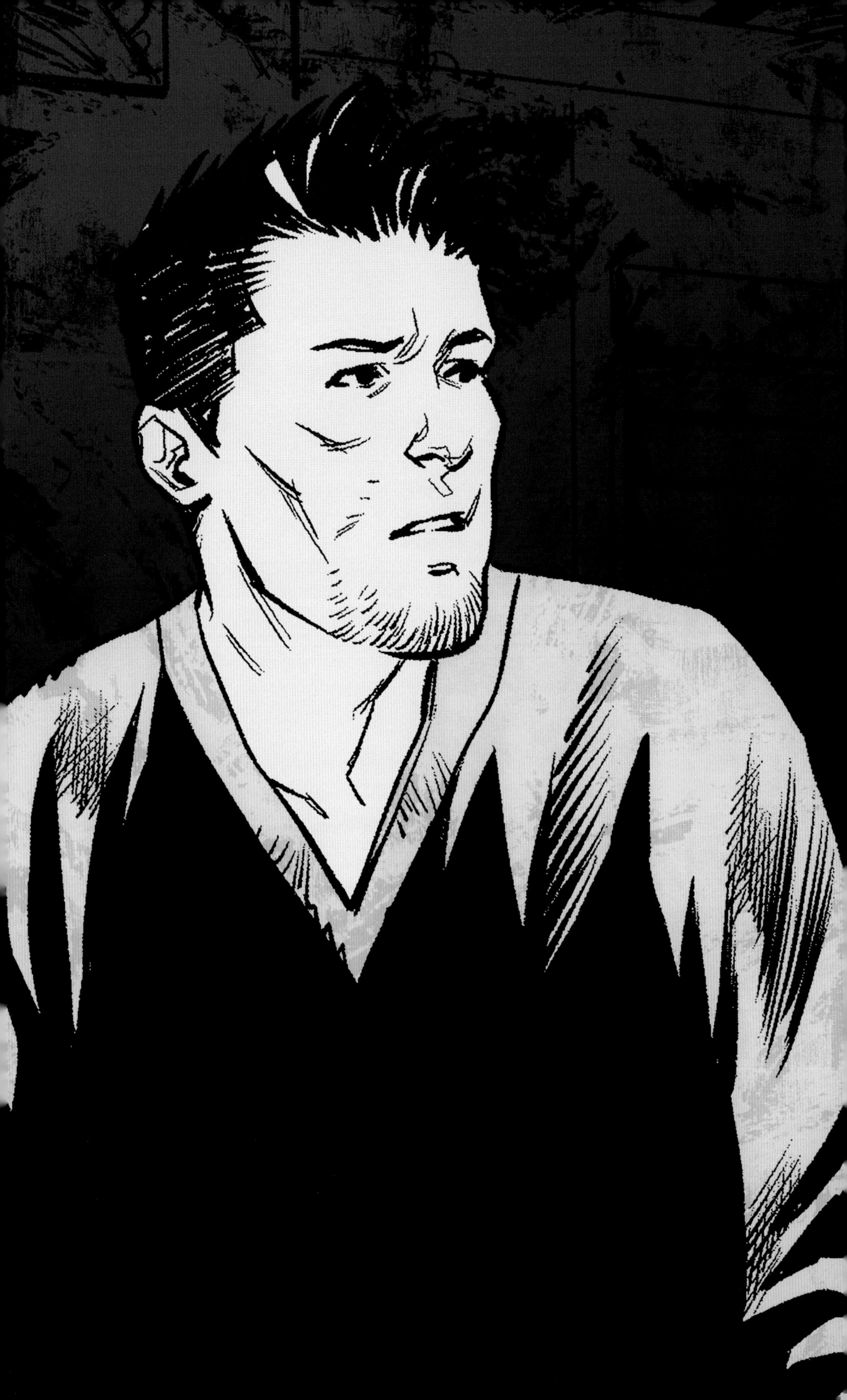

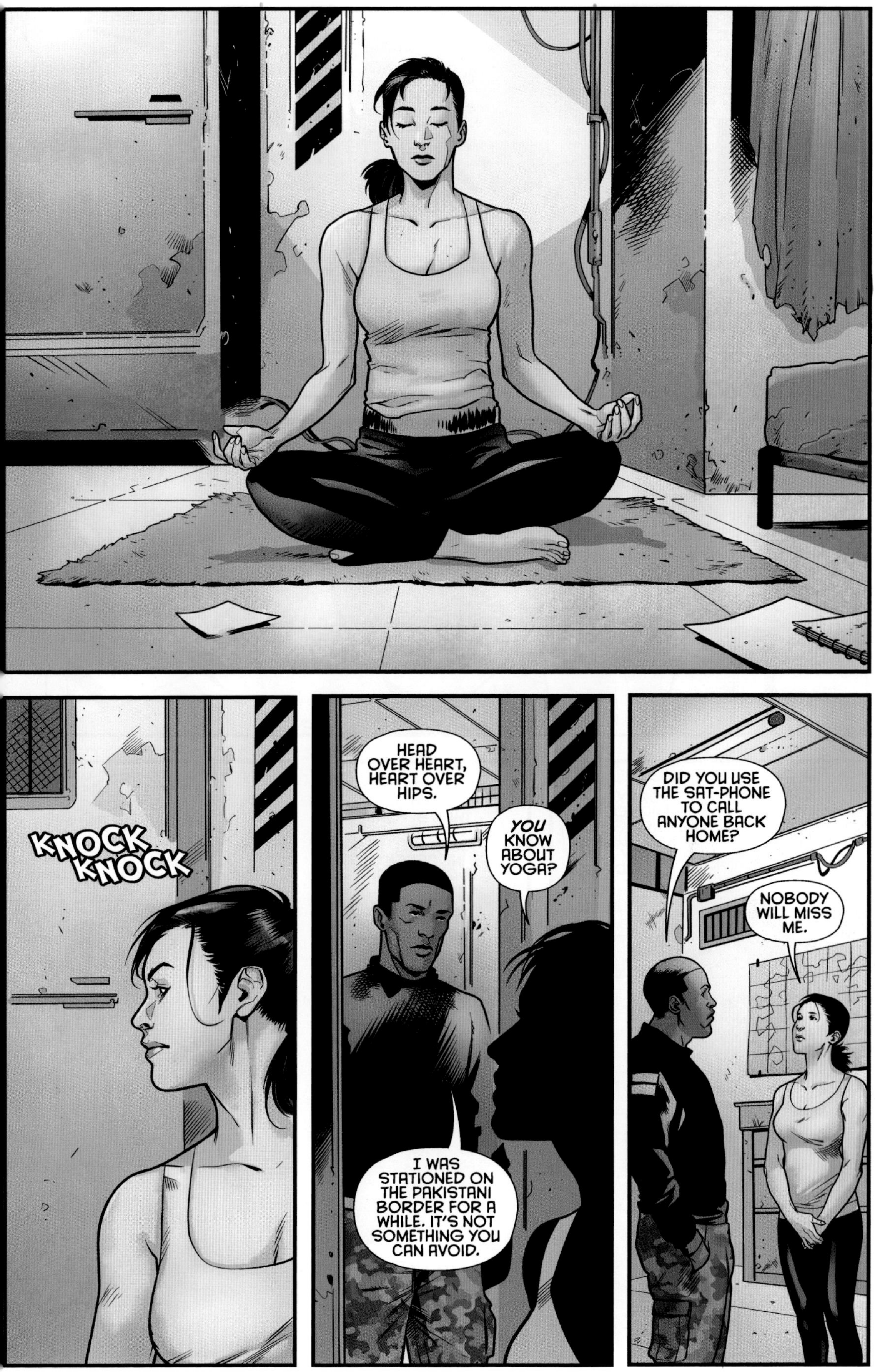
KNOCK KNOCK
HEAD OVER HEART, HEART OVER HIPS.
YOU KNOW ABOUT YOGA?
I WAS STATIONED ON THE PAKISTANI BORDER FOR A WHILE. IT'S NOT SOMETHING YOU CAN AVOID.
DID YOU USE THE SAT-PHONE TO CALL ANYONE BACK HOME?
NOBODY WILL MISS ME.

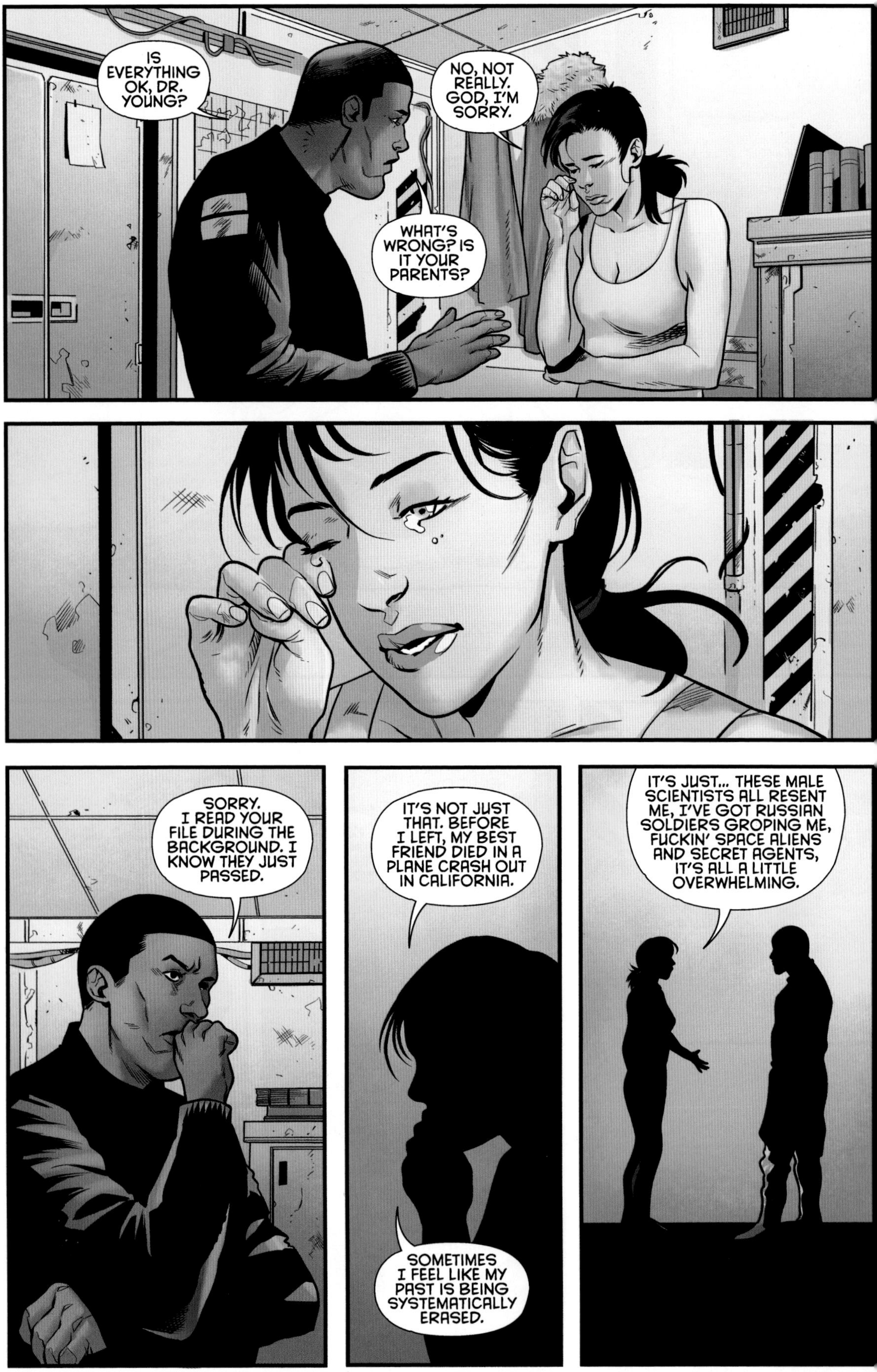
IS EVERYTHING OK, DR. YOUNG?
NO, NOT REALLY. GOD, I'M SORRY.
WHAT'S WRONG? IS IT YOUR PARENTS?
SORRY. I READ YOUR FILE DURING THE BACKGROUND. I KNOW THEY JUST PASSED.
IT'S NOT JUST THAT. BEFORE I LEFT, MY BEST FRIEND DIED IN A PLANE CRASH OUT IN CALIFORNIA.
SOMETIMES I FEEL LIKE MY PAST IS BEING SYSTEMATICALLY ERASED.
IT'S JUST... THESE MALE SCIENTISTS ALL RESENT ME, I'VE GOT RUSSIAN SOLDIERS GROPING ME, FUCKIN' SPACE ALIENS AND SECRET AGENTS, IT'S ALL A LITTLE OVERWHELMING.

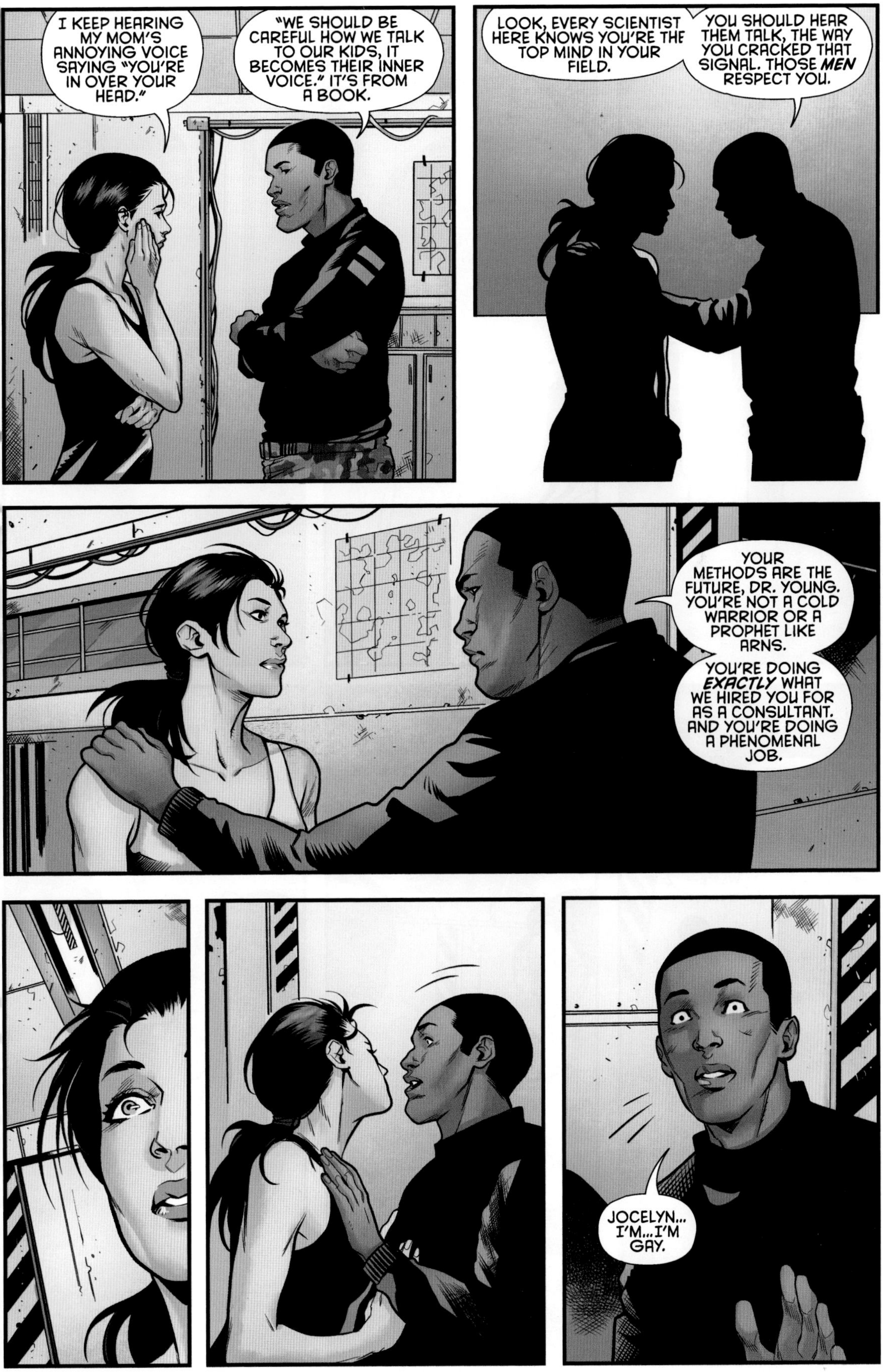
I KEEP HEARING MY MOM'S ANNOYING VOICE SAYING "YOU'RE IN OVER YOUR HEAD."
"WE SHOULD BE CAREFUL HOW WE TALK TO OUR KIDS, IT BECOMES THEIR INNER VOICE." IT'S FROM A BOOK.
LOOK, EVERY SCIENTIST HERE KNOWS YOU'RE THE TOP MIND IN YOUR FIELD.
YOU SHOULD HEAR THEM TALK, THE WAY YOU CRACKED THAT SIGNAL. THOSE *MEN* RESPECT YOU.
YOUR METHODS ARE THE FUTURE, DR. YOUNG. YOU'RE NOT A COLD WARRIOR OR A PROPHET LIKE ARNS.
YOU'RE DOING *EXACTLY* WHAT WE HIRED YOU FOR AS A CONSULTANT. AND YOU'RE DOING A PHENOMENAL JOB.
JOCELYN... I'M...I'M GAY.

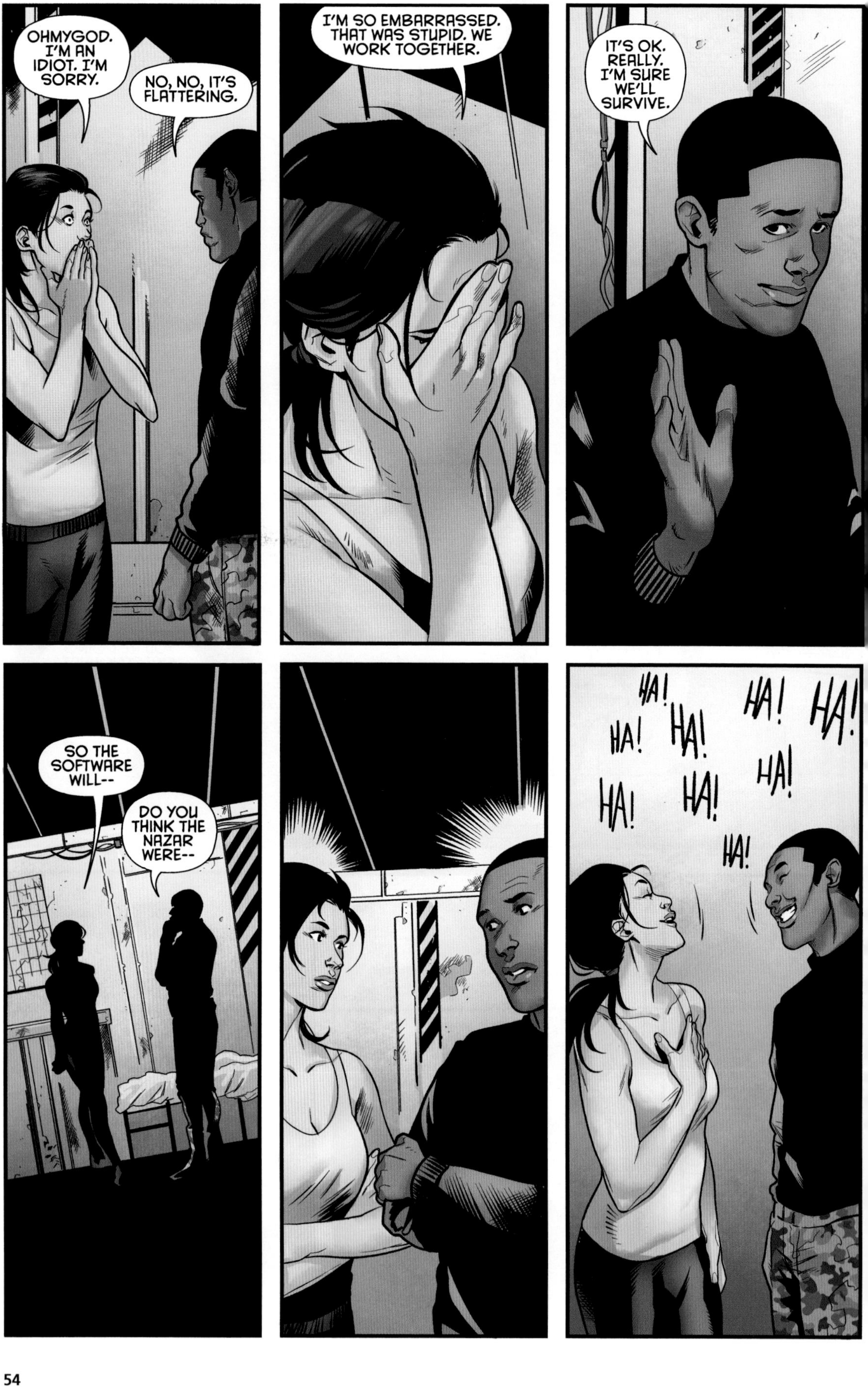
OHMYGOD. I'M AN IDIOT. I'M SORRY.
NO, NO, IT'S FLATTERING.
I'M SO EMBARRASSED. THAT WAS STUPID. WE WORK TOGETHER.
IT'S OK. REALLY. I'M SURE WE'LL SURVIVE.
SO THE SOFTWARE WILL--
DO YOU THINK THE NAZAR WERE--
HA! HA! HA! HA! HA! HA! HA! HA! HA!

...THEN WHO WERE YOU TALKING TO, JOSIP?!

I TOLD YOU IT'S JUST WORK.

ARE YOU GETTING INVOLVED IN HAWKBIT'S WEIRD CULT?

WHAT? NO! HOW CAN YOU ASK ME THAT, ARUSHA? I'VE BEEN TALKING TO THE PRESS, NOT THOSE RELIGIOUS NUTS.

THE PRESS? SINCE WHEN? YOU SIGNED AN NDA!

I'M TIRED OF WORKING SO HARD FOR OUR SURVIVAL. THEY OFFERED A LOT OF MONEY, OK?

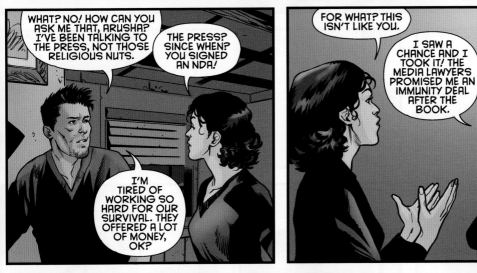

FOR WHAT? THIS ISN'T LIKE YOU.

I SAW A CHANCE AND I TOOK IT! THE MEDIA LAWYERS PROMISED ME AN IMMUNITY DEAL AFTER THE BOOK.

AND YOU *BELIEVED* THEM?!

THEY *NEED* ME.

THEY'RE *USING* YOU!

I DID THIS FOR *YOU!* FOR SAMUIL AND SOFIJA!

WHAT GOOD WILL IT DO US IF YOU'RE IN JAIL? YOU'RE JEOPARDIZING EVERYTHING WE'VE WORKED FOR!

WHAT HAVE WE WORKED FOR?! THIS 900 SQUARE FOOT HOVEL? CLOTHES AND FOOD WE CAN BARELY AFFORD?

I MEANT *US*. OUR MARRIAGE. OUR FAMILY.

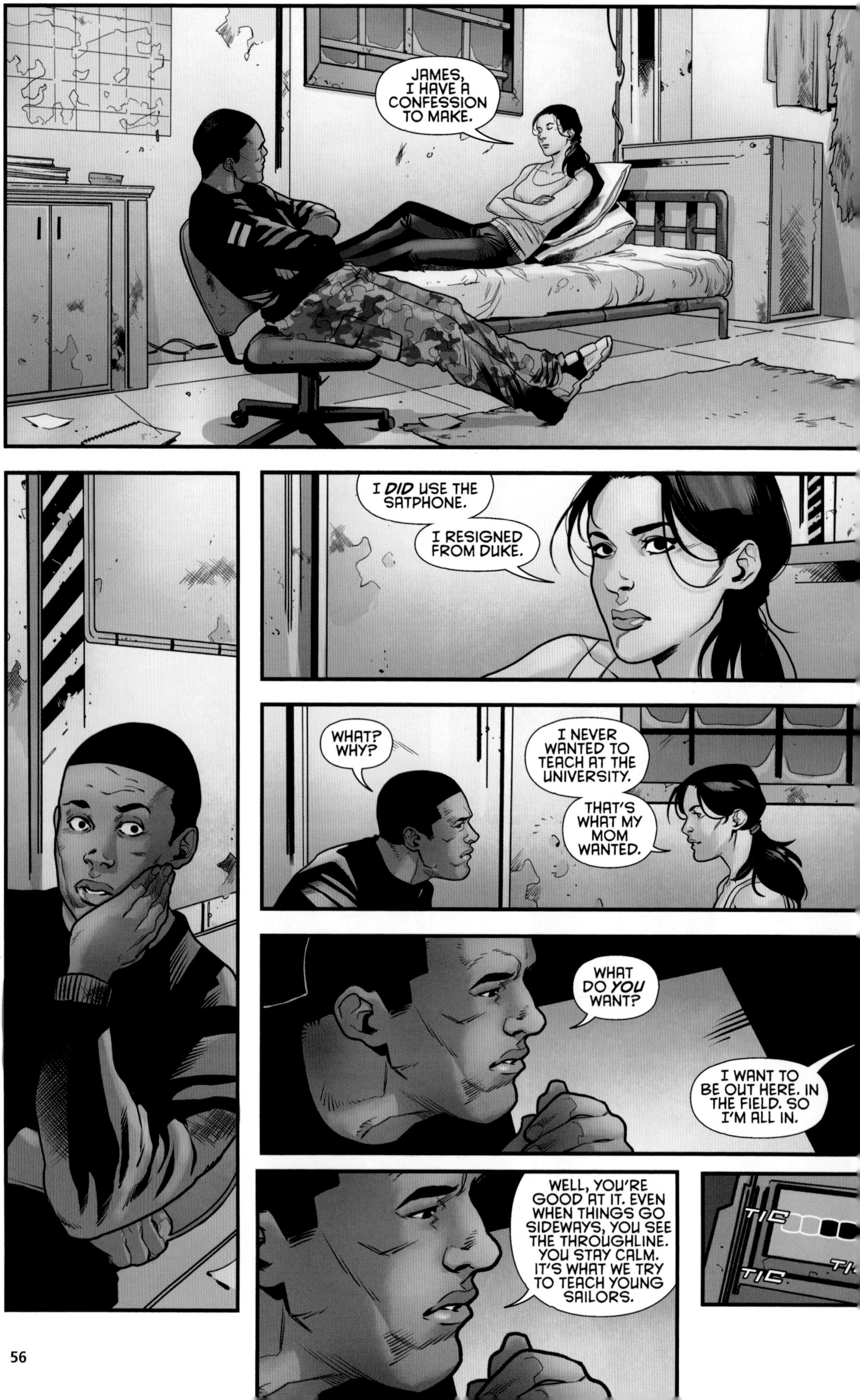
JAMES, I HAVE A CONFESSION TO MAKE.
I DID USE THE SATPHONE.
I RESIGNED FROM DUKE.
WHAT? WHY?
I NEVER WANTED TO TEACH AT THE UNIVERSITY.
THAT'S WHAT MY MOM WANTED.
WHAT DO YOU WANT?
I WANT TO BE OUT HERE. IN THE FIELD. SO I'M ALL IN.
WELL, YOU'RE GOOD AT IT. EVEN WHEN THINGS GO SIDEWAYS, YOU SEE THE THROUGHLINE. YOU STAY CALM. IT'S WHAT WE TRY TO TEACH YOUNG SAILORS.
TIC
TIC
TIC

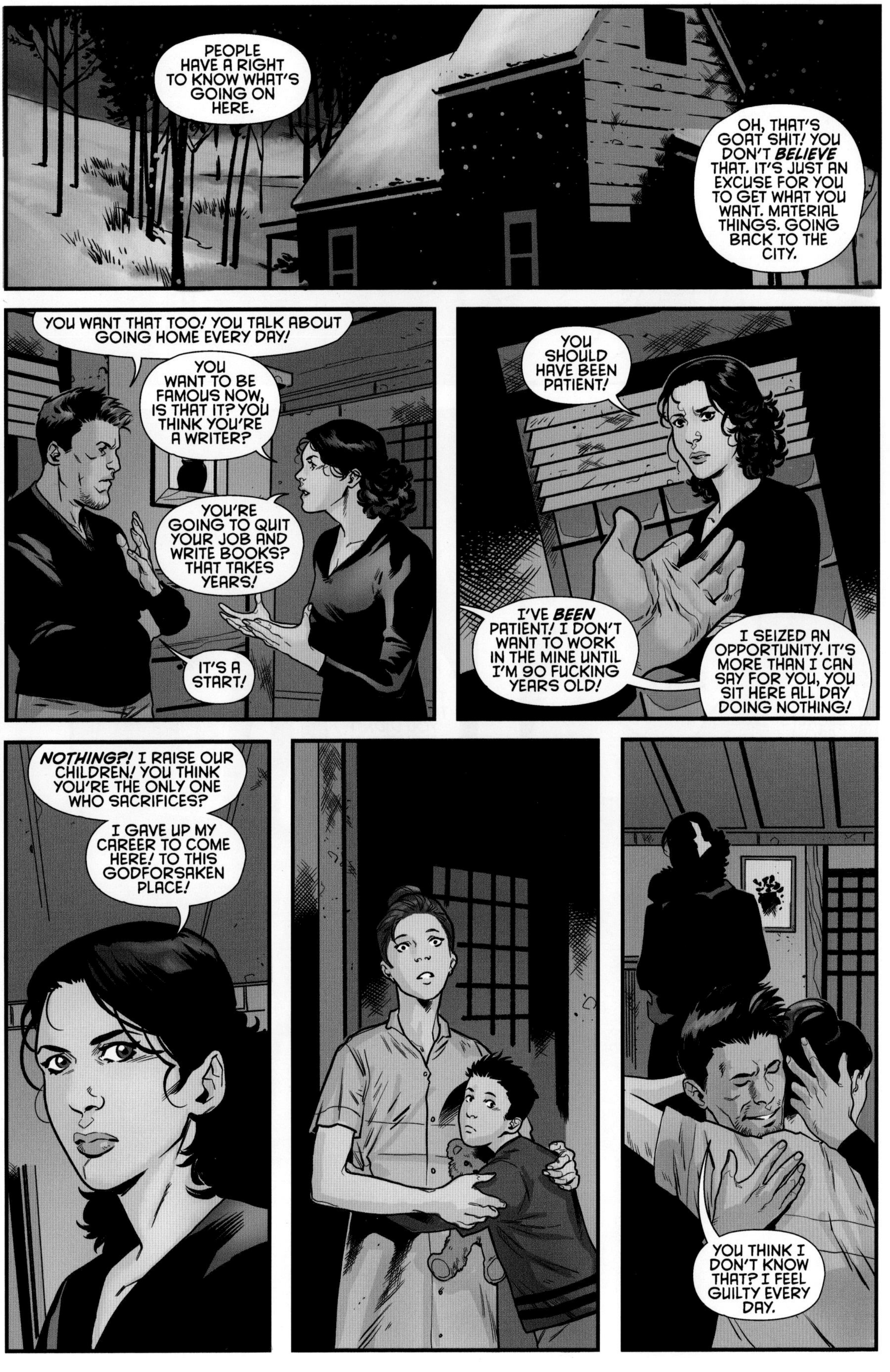
PEOPLE HAVE A RIGHT TO KNOW WHAT'S GOING ON HERE.
OH, THAT'S GOAT SHIT! YOU DON'T *BELIEVE* THAT. IT'S JUST AN EXCUSE FOR YOU TO GET WHAT YOU WANT. MATERIAL THINGS. GOING BACK TO THE CITY.
YOU WANT THAT TOO! YOU TALK ABOUT GOING HOME EVERY DAY!
YOU WANT TO BE FAMOUS NOW, IS THAT IT? YOU THINK YOU'RE A WRITER?
YOU'RE GOING TO QUIT YOUR JOB AND WRITE BOOKS? THAT TAKES YEARS!
IT'S A START!
YOU SHOULD HAVE BEEN PATIENT!
I'VE *BEEN* PATIENT! I DON'T WANT TO WORK IN THE MINE UNTIL I'M 90 FUCKING YEARS OLD!
I SEIZED AN OPPORTUNITY. IT'S MORE THAN I CAN SAY FOR YOU, YOU SIT HERE ALL DAY DOING NOTHING!
NOTHING?! I RAISE OUR CHILDREN! YOU THINK YOU'RE THE ONLY ONE WHO SACRIFICES?
I GAVE UP MY CAREER TO COME HERE! TO THIS GODFORSAKEN PLACE!
YOU THINK I DON'T KNOW THAT? I FEEL GUILTY EVERY DAY.

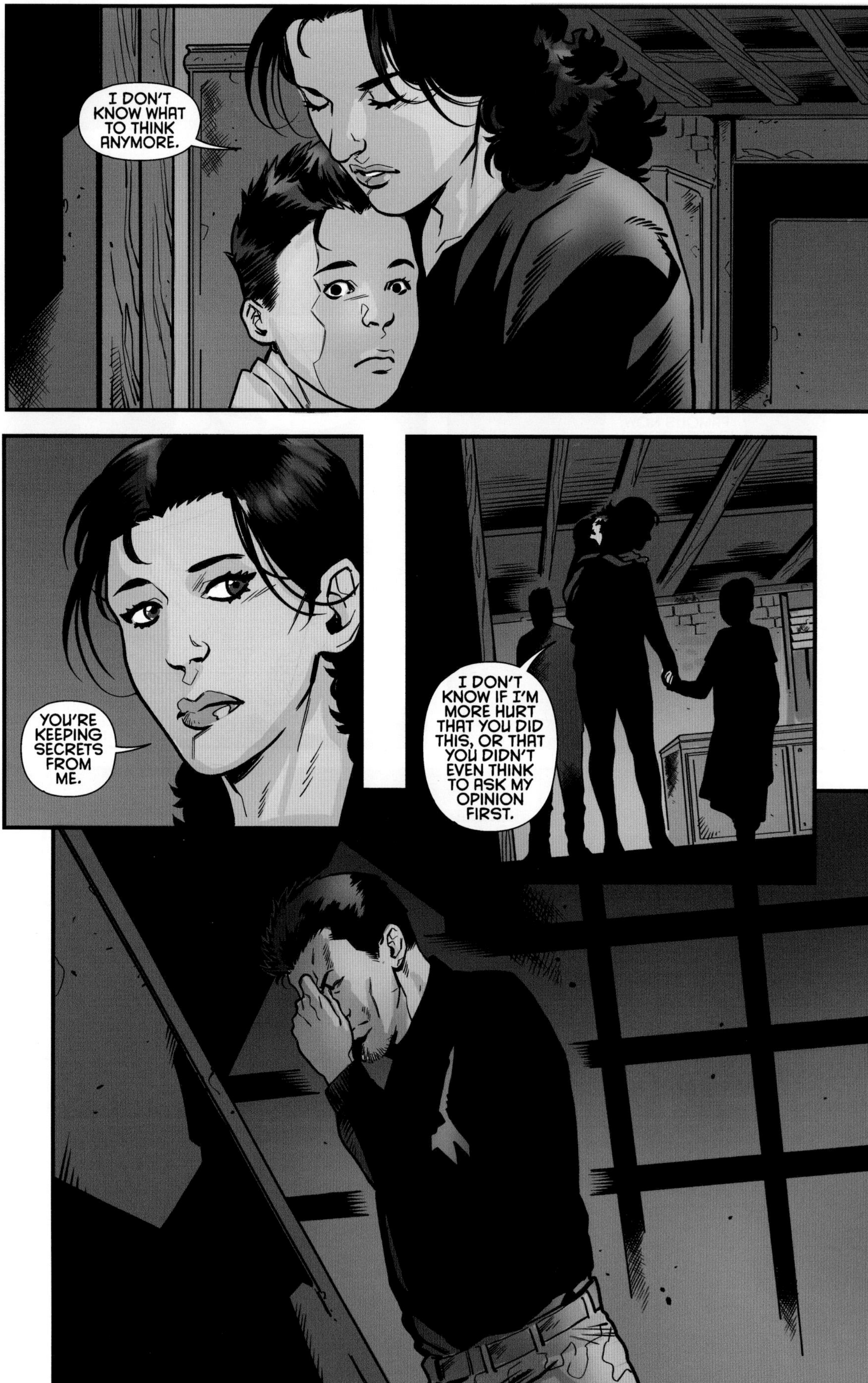
I DON'T KNOW WHAT TO THINK ANYMORE.
YOU'RE KEEPING SECRETS FROM ME.
I DON'T KNOW IF I'M MORE HURT THAT YOU DID THIS, OR THAT YOU DIDN'T EVEN THINK TO ASK MY OPINION FIRST.

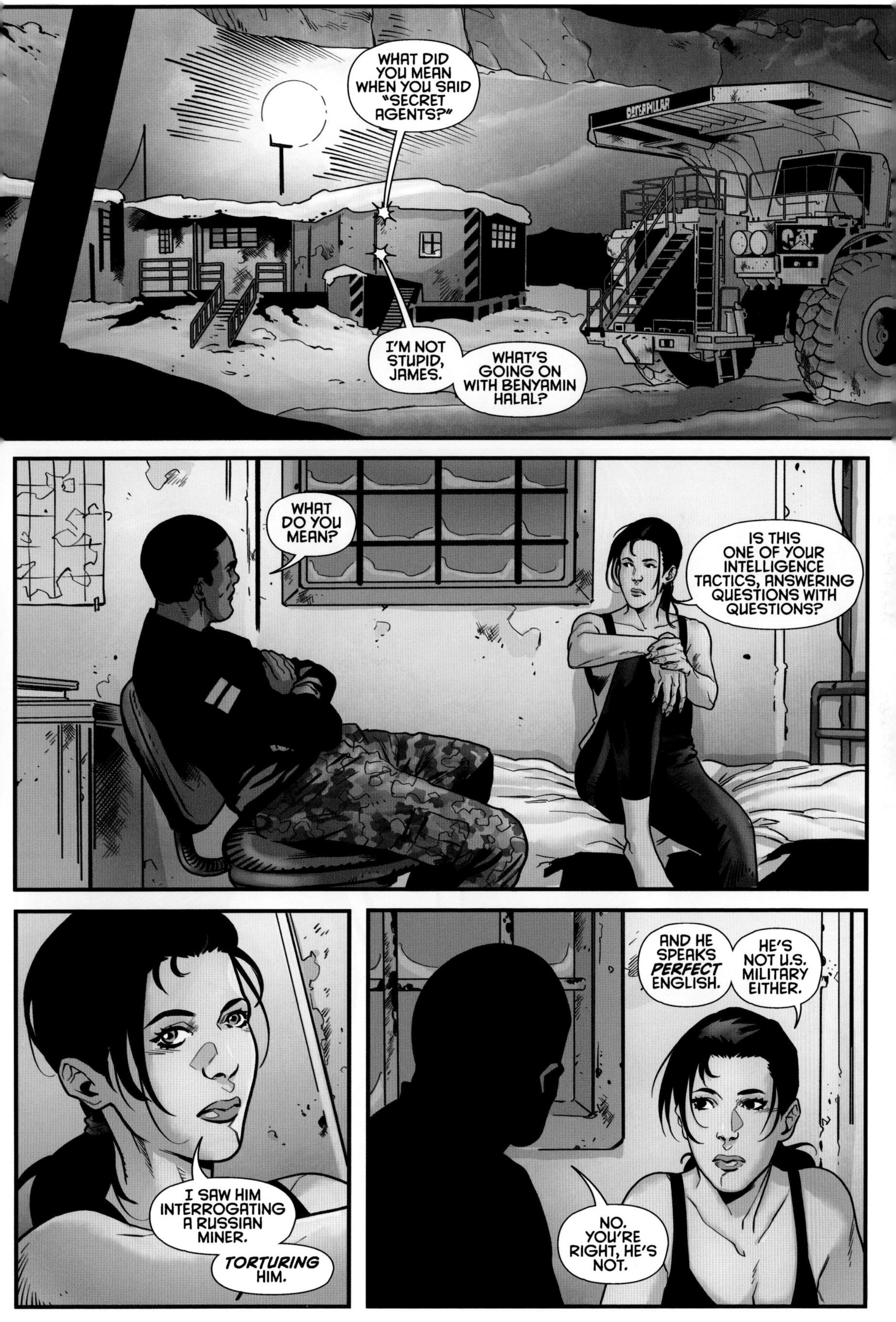

WHAT DID YOU MEAN WHEN YOU SAID "SECRET AGENTS?"
I'M NOT STUPID, JAMES.
WHAT'S GOING ON WITH BENYAMIN HALAL?
WHAT DO YOU MEAN?
IS THIS ONE OF YOUR INTELLIGENCE TACTICS, ANSWERING QUESTIONS WITH QUESTIONS?
I SAW HIM INTERROGATING A RUSSIAN MINER.
TORTURING HIM.
NO. YOU'RE RIGHT, HE'S NOT.
HE'S NOT U.S. MILITARY EITHER.
AND HE SPEAKS *PERFECT* ENGLISH.

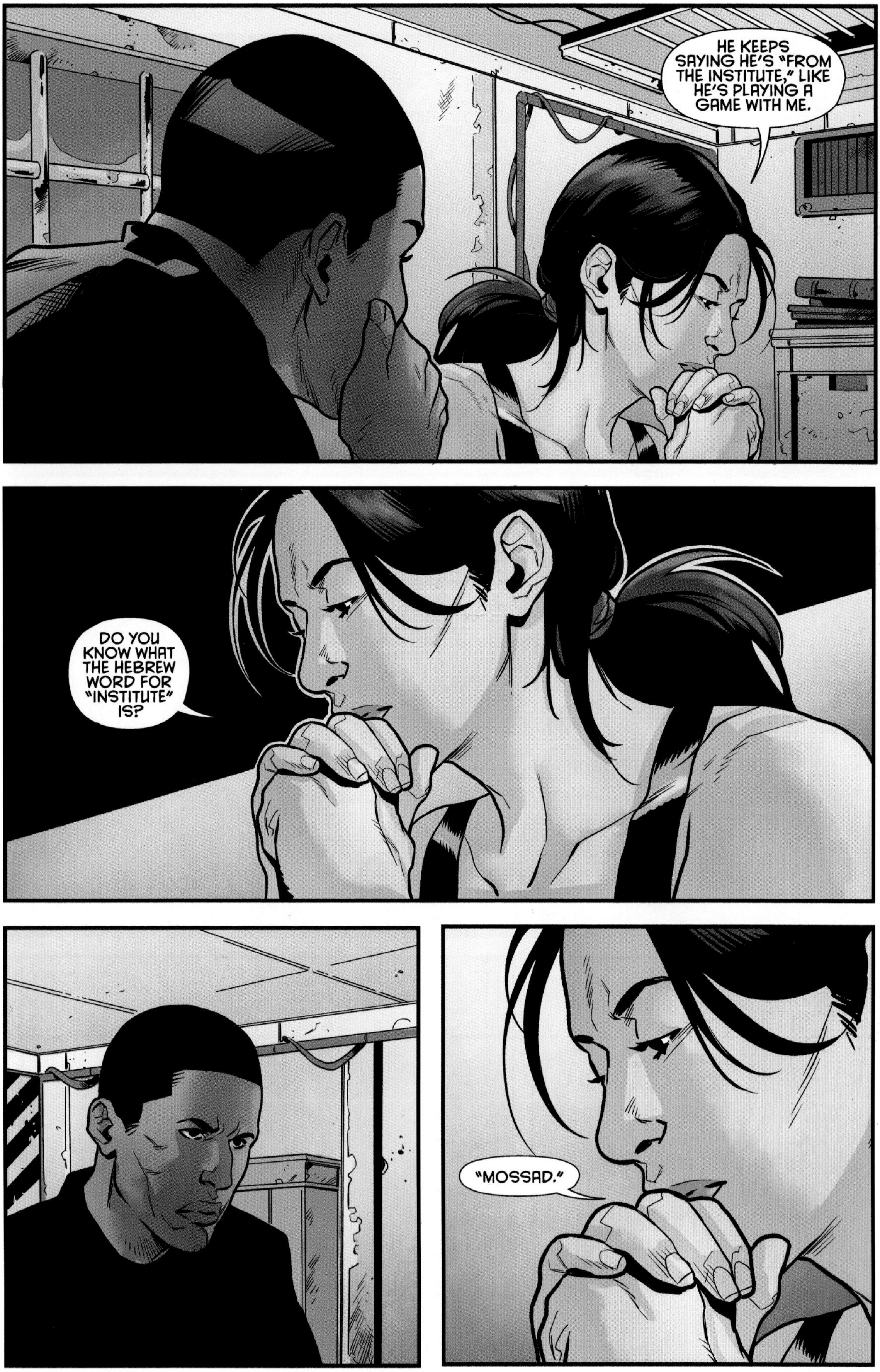
HE KEEPS SAYING HE'S "FROM THE INSTITUTE," LIKE HE'S PLAYING A GAME WITH ME.
DO YOU KNOW WHAT THE HEBREW WORD FOR "INSTITUTE" IS?
"MOSSAD."

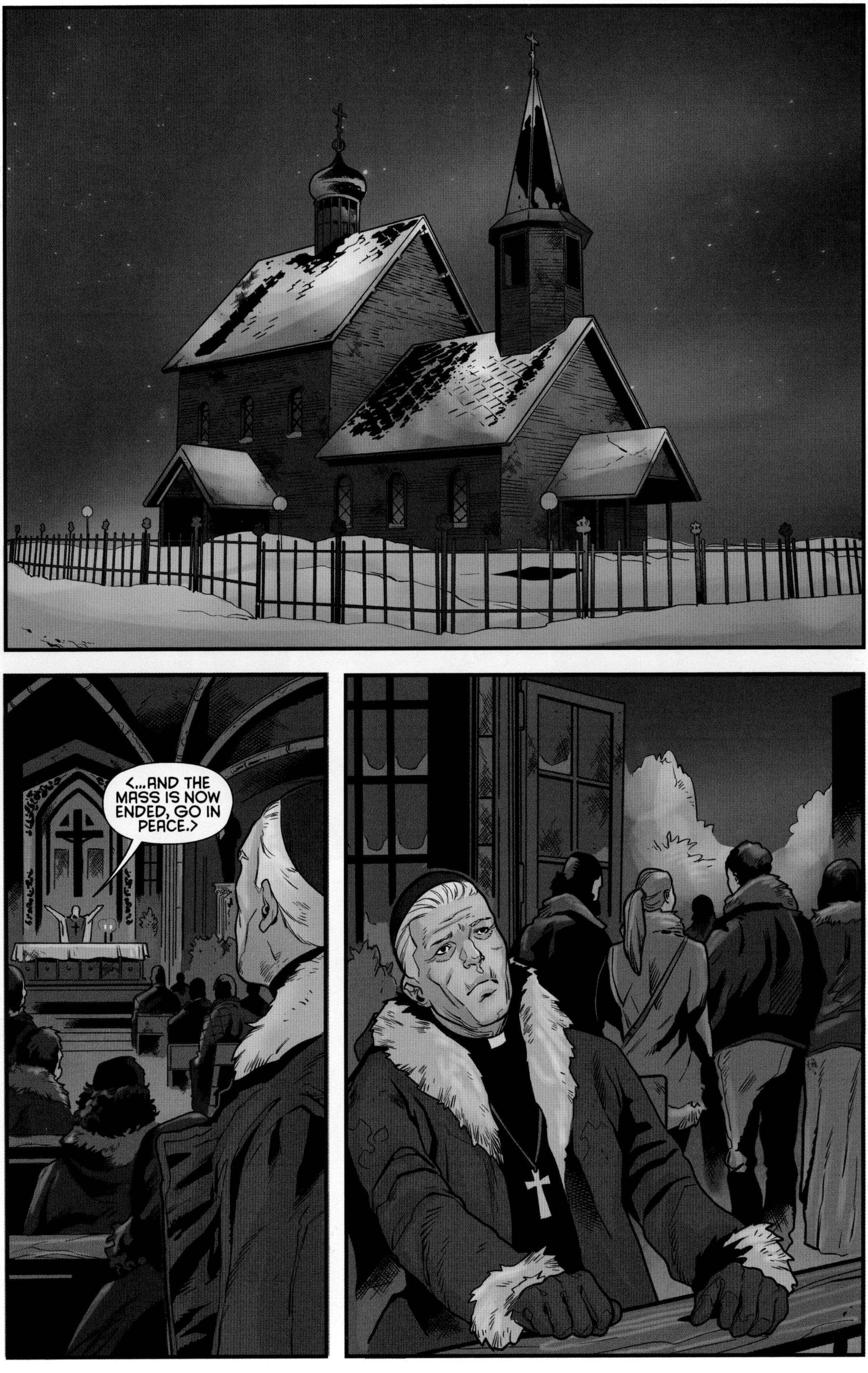
<...AND THE MASS IS NOW ENDED, GO IN PEACE.>

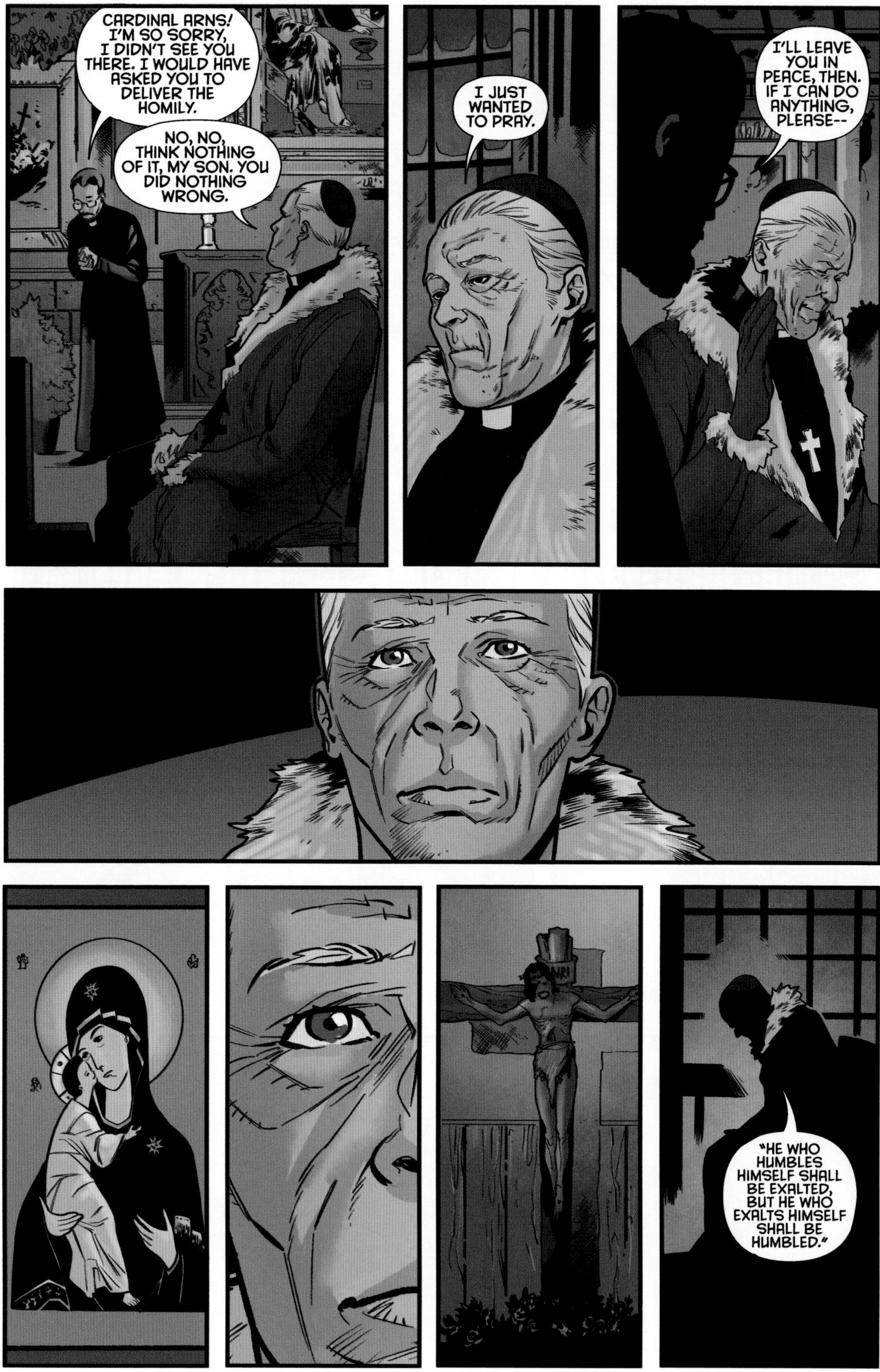
CARDINAL ARNS! I'M SO SORRY, I DIDN'T SEE YOU THERE. I WOULD HAVE ASKED YOU TO DELIVER THE HOMILY.
NO, NO, THINK NOTHING OF IT, MY SON. YOU DID NOTHING WRONG.
I JUST WANTED TO PRAY.
I'LL LEAVE YOU IN PEACE, THEN. IF I CAN DO ANYTHING, PLEASE--
"HE WHO HUMBLES HIMSELF SHALL BE EXALTED, BUT HE WHO EXALTS HIMSELF SHALL BE HUMBLED."

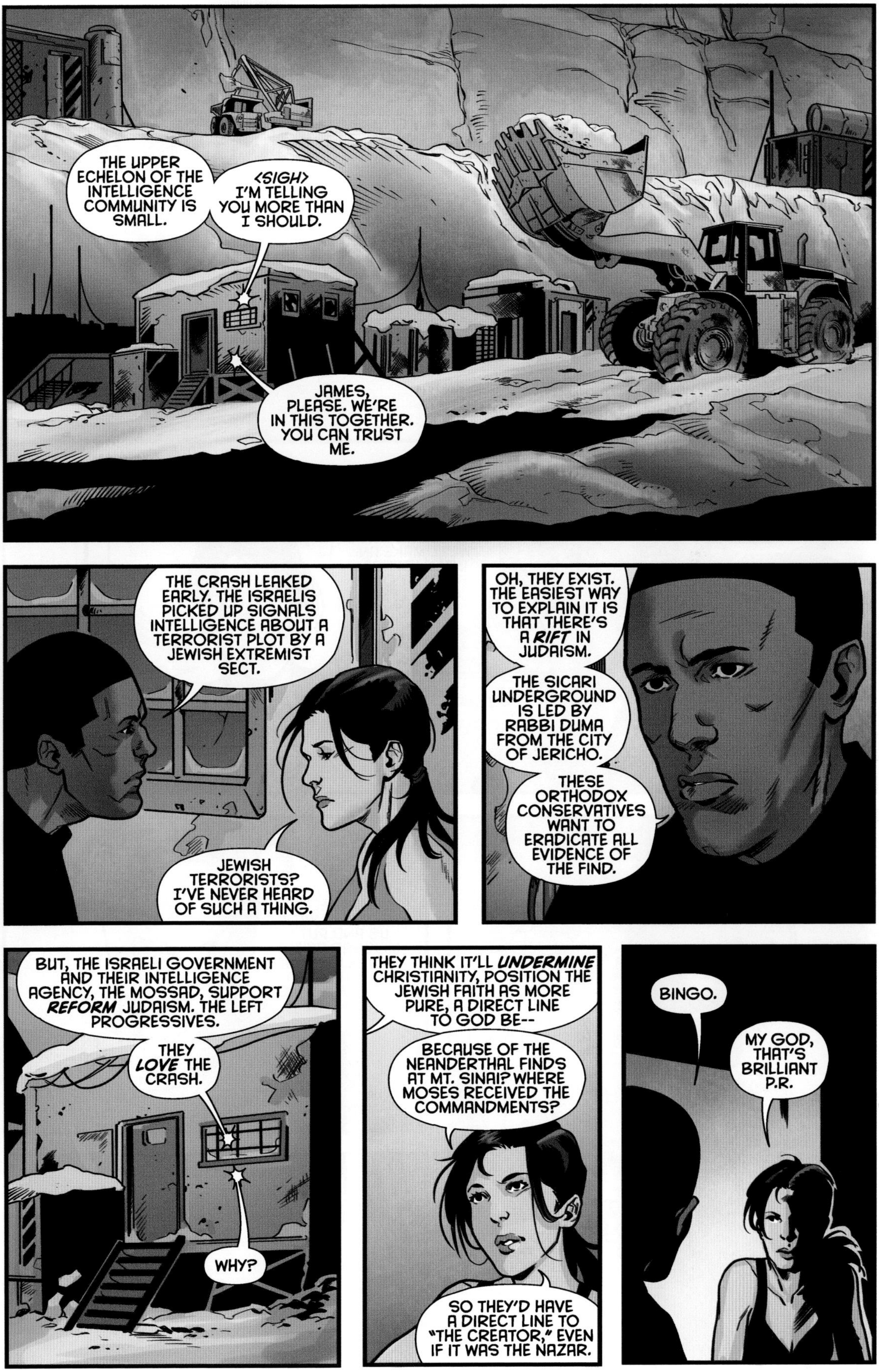
THE UPPER ECHELON OF THE INTELLIGENCE COMMUNITY IS SMALL.
<SIGH> I'M TELLING YOU MORE THAN I SHOULD.
JAMES, PLEASE. WE'RE IN THIS TOGETHER. YOU CAN TRUST ME.
THE CRASH LEAKED EARLY. THE ISRAELIS PICKED UP SIGNALS INTELLIGENCE ABOUT A TERRORIST PLOT BY A JEWISH EXTREMIST SECT.
JEWISH TERRORISTS? I'VE NEVER HEARD OF SUCH A THING.
OH, THEY EXIST. THE EASIEST WAY TO EXPLAIN IT IS THAT THERE'S A *RIFT* IN JUDAISM.
THE SICARI UNDERGROUND IS LED BY RABBI DUMA FROM THE CITY OF JERICHO.
THESE ORTHODOX CONSERVATIVES WANT TO ERADICATE ALL EVIDENCE OF THE FIND.
BUT, THE ISRAELI GOVERNMENT AND THEIR INTELLIGENCE AGENCY, THE MOSSAD, SUPPORT *REFORM* JUDAISM. THE LEFT PROGRESSIVES.
THEY *LOVE* THE CRASH.
WHY?
THEY THINK IT'LL *UNDERMINE* CHRISTIANITY, POSITION THE JEWISH FAITH AS MORE PURE, A DIRECT LINE TO GOD BE--
BECAUSE OF THE NEANDERTHAL FINDS AT MT. SINAI? WHERE MOSES RECEIVED THE COMMANDMENTS?
SO THEY'D HAVE A DIRECT LINE TO "THE CREATOR," EVEN IF IT WAS THE NAZAR.
BINGO.
MY GOD, THAT'S BRILLIANT P.R.

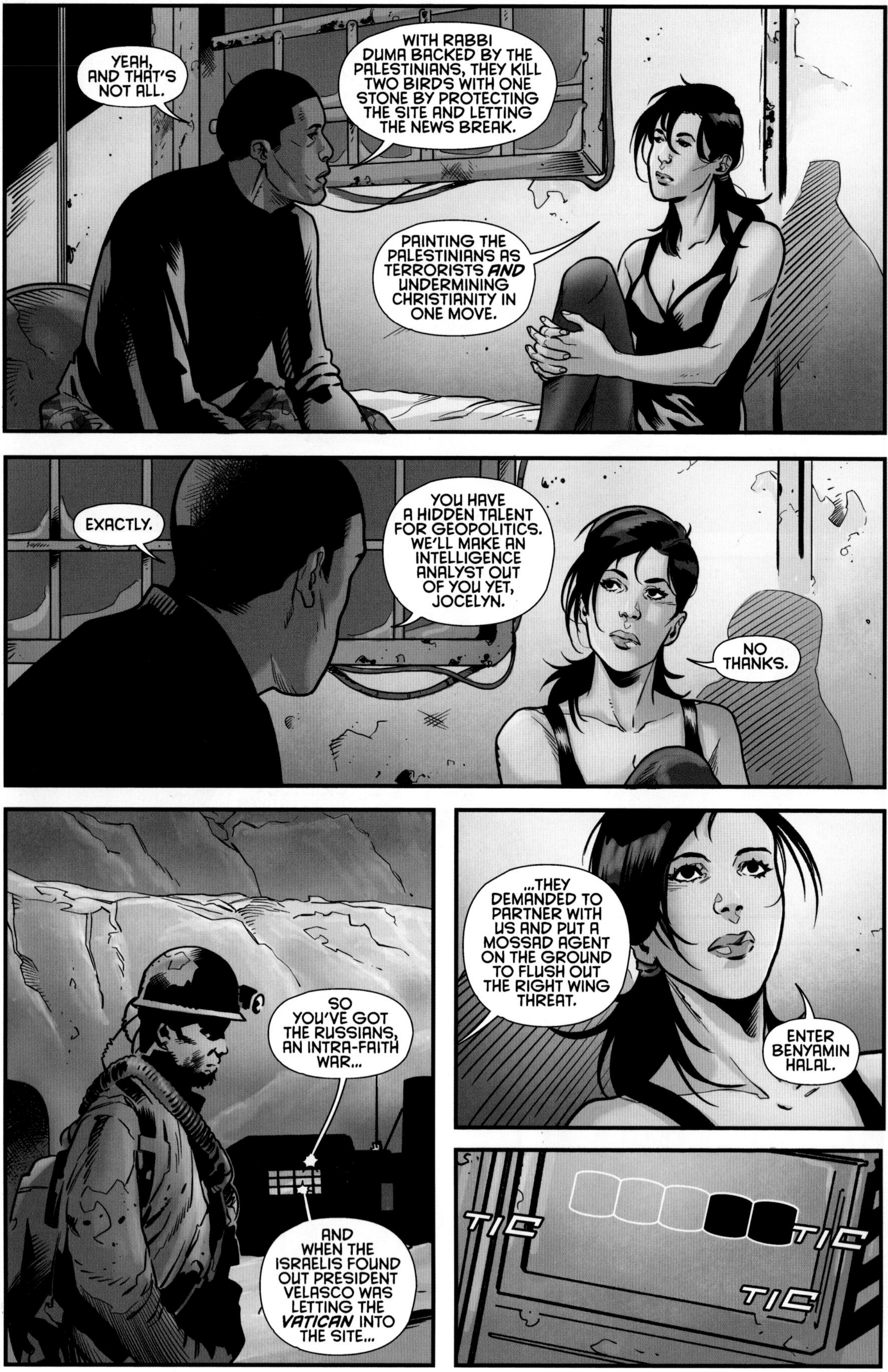
YEAH, AND THAT'S NOT ALL.
WITH RABBI DUMA BACKED BY THE PALESTINIANS, THEY KILL TWO BIRDS WITH ONE STONE BY PROTECTING THE SITE AND LETTING THE NEWS BREAK.
PAINTING THE PALESTINIANS AS TERRORISTS *AND* UNDERMINING CHRISTIANITY IN ONE MOVE.
EXACTLY.
YOU HAVE A HIDDEN TALENT FOR GEOPOLITICS. WE'LL MAKE AN INTELLIGENCE ANALYST OUT OF YOU YET, JOCELYN.
NO THANKS.
SO YOU'VE GOT THE RUSSIANS, AN INTRA-FAITH WAR...
AND WHEN THE ISRAELIS FOUND OUT PRESIDENT VELASCO WAS LETTING THE *VATICAN* INTO THE SITE...
...THEY DEMANDED TO PARTNER WITH US AND PUT A MOSSAD AGENT ON THE GROUND TO FLUSH OUT THE RIGHT WING THREAT.
ENTER BENYAMIN HALAL.
TIC
TIC
TIC

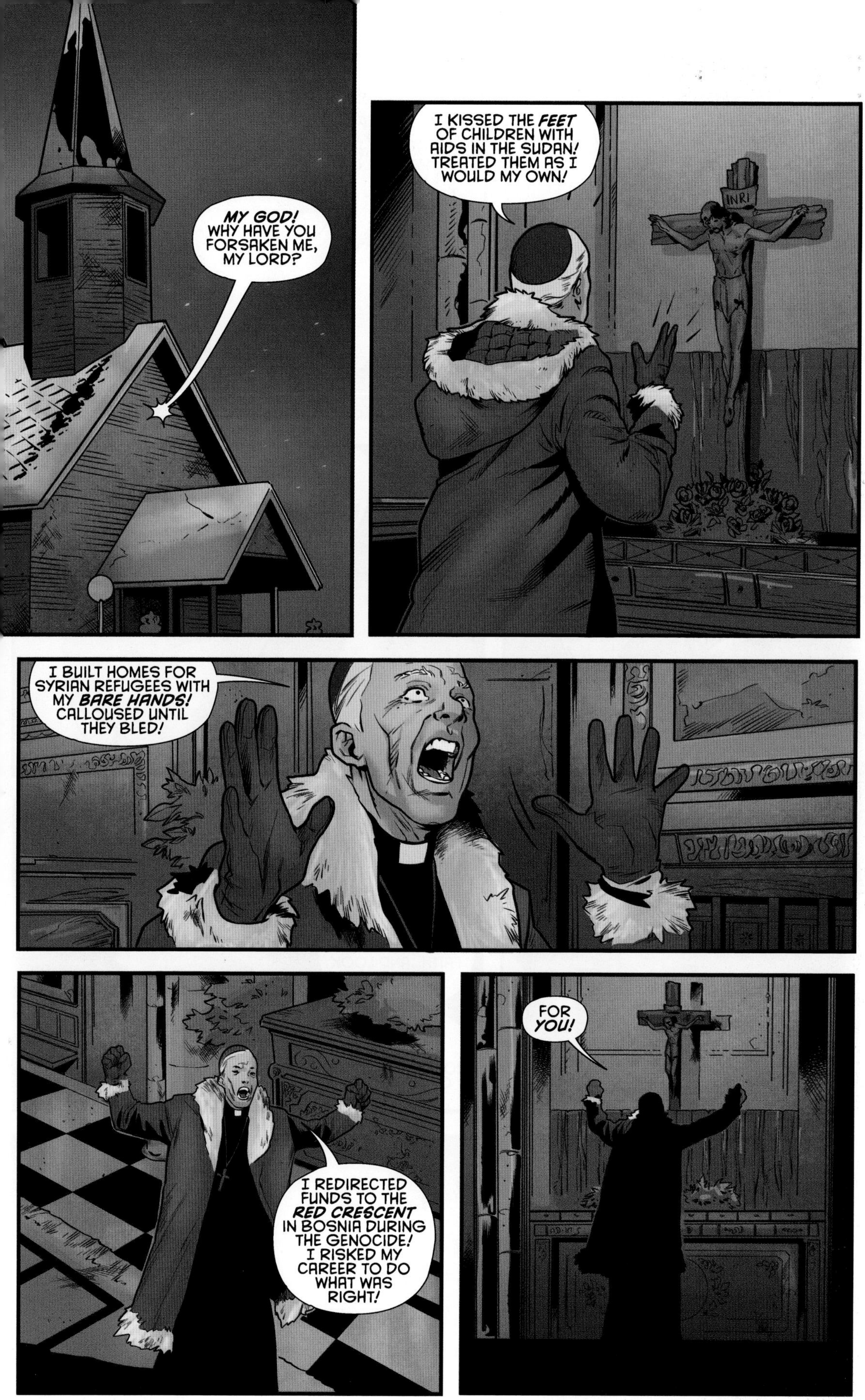
MY GOD! WHY HAVE YOU FORSAKEN ME, MY LORD?
I KISSED THE FEET OF CHILDREN WITH AIDS IN THE SUDAN! TREATED THEM AS I WOULD MY OWN!
INRI
I BUILT HOMES FOR SYRIAN REFUGEES WITH MY BARE HANDS! CALLOUSED UNTIL THEY BLED!
I REDIRECTED FUNDS TO THE RED CRESCENT IN BOSNIA DURING THE GENOCIDE! I RISKED MY CAREER TO DO WHAT WAS RIGHT!
FOR YOU!

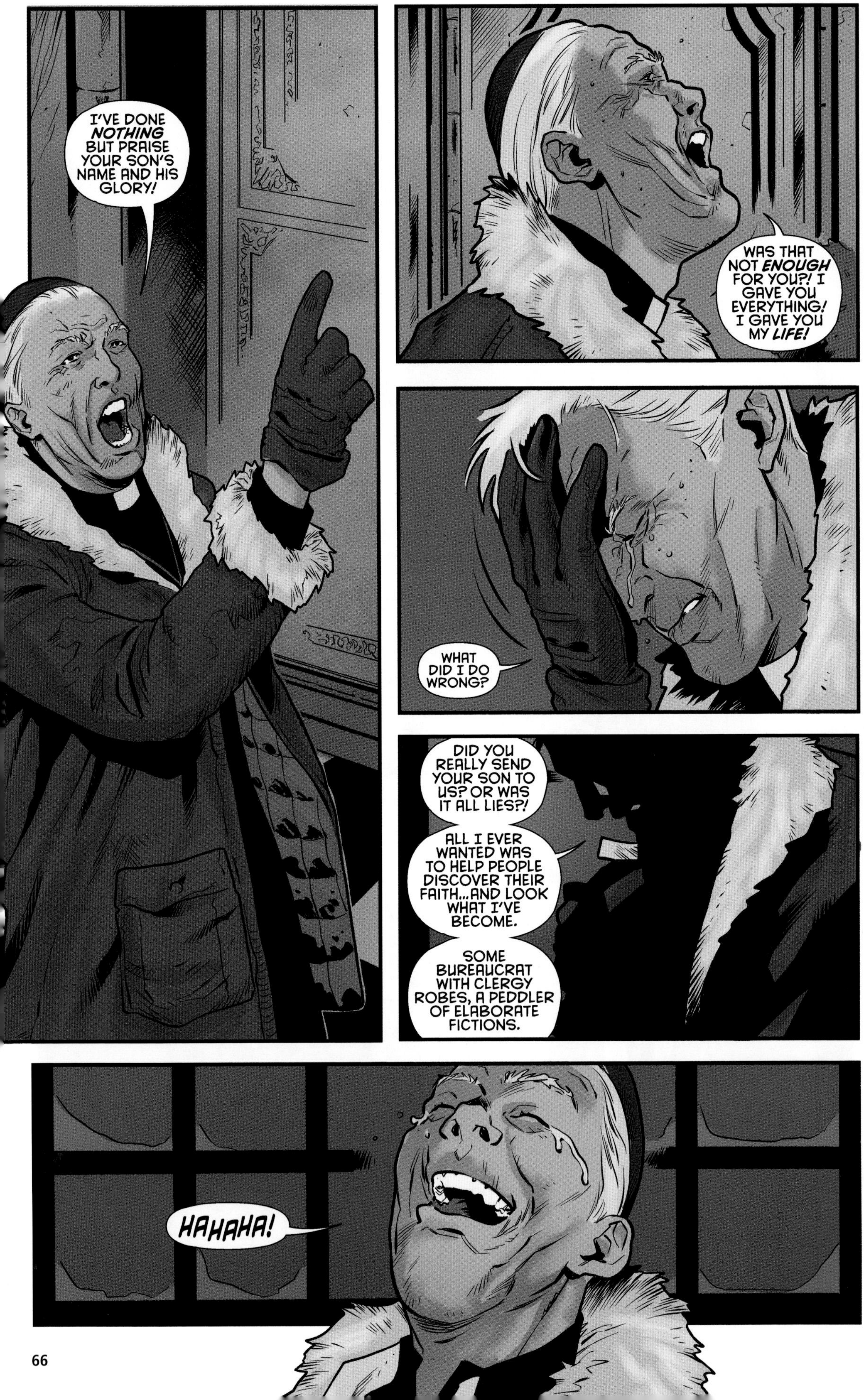

I'VE DONE NOTHING BUT PRAISE YOUR SON'S NAME AND HIS GLORY!
WAS THAT NOT ENOUGH FOR YOU?! I GAVE YOU EVERYTHING! I GAVE YOU MY LIFE!
WHAT DID I DO WRONG?
DID YOU REALLY SEND YOUR SON TO US? OR WAS IT ALL LIES?!
ALL I EVER WANTED WAS TO HELP PEOPLE DISCOVER THEIR FAITH...AND LOOK WHAT I'VE BECOME.
SOME BUREAUCRAT WITH CLERGY ROBES, A PEDDLER OF ELABORATE FICTIONS.
HAHAHA!

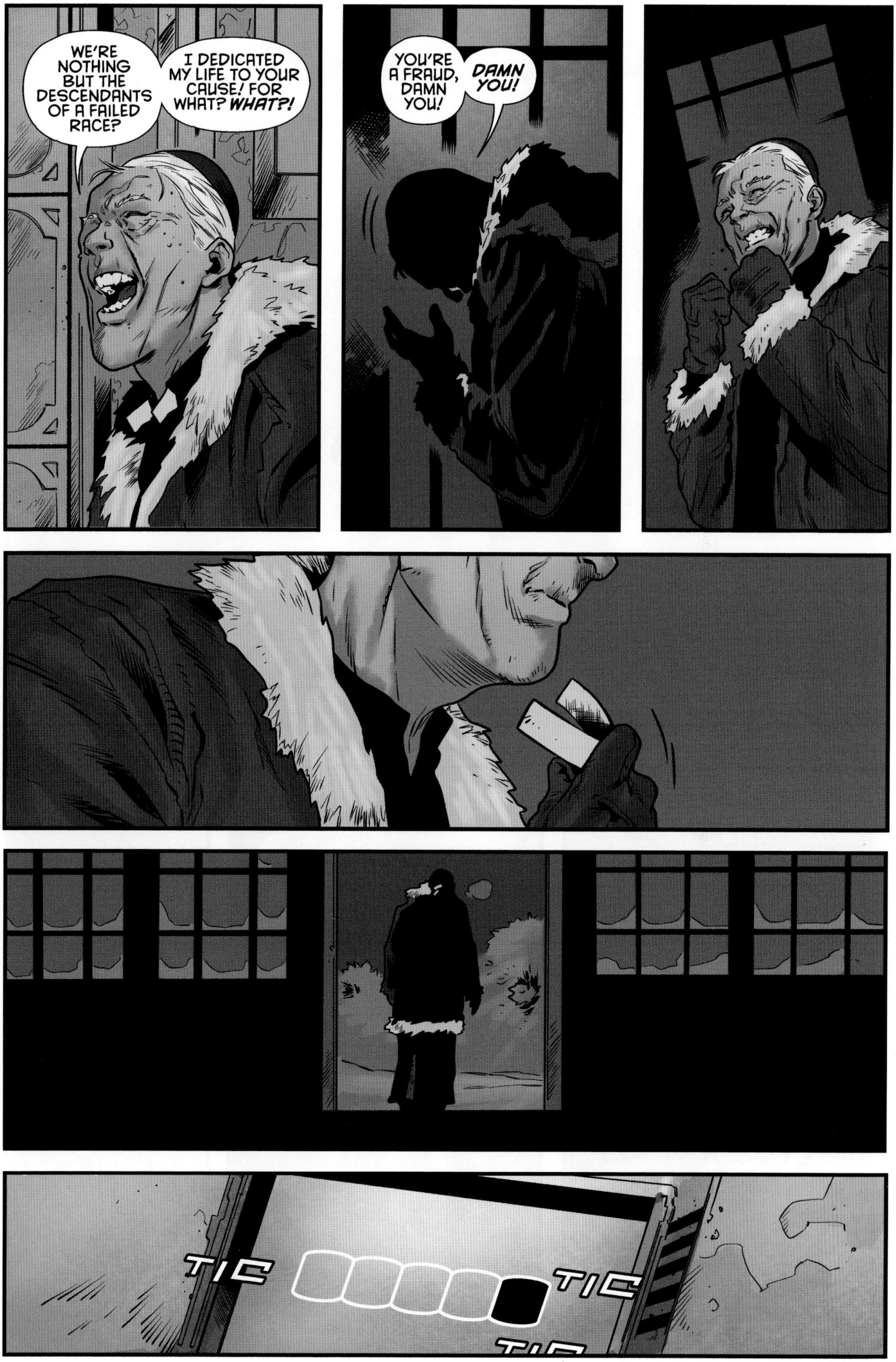
WE'RE NOTHING BUT THE DESCENDANTS OF A FAILED RACE?
I DEDICATED MY LIFE TO YOUR CAUSE! FOR WHAT? WHAT?!
YOU'RE A FRAUD, DAMN YOU!
DAMN YOU!
TIC
TIC

REEET! REEET! REEET!

REEET!

SECURE THE INNER PERIMETER!

DETAIN THE PRESS IN A STAGING AREA, BUT DO NOT FIRE.

I REPEAT, WEAPONS HOLD!

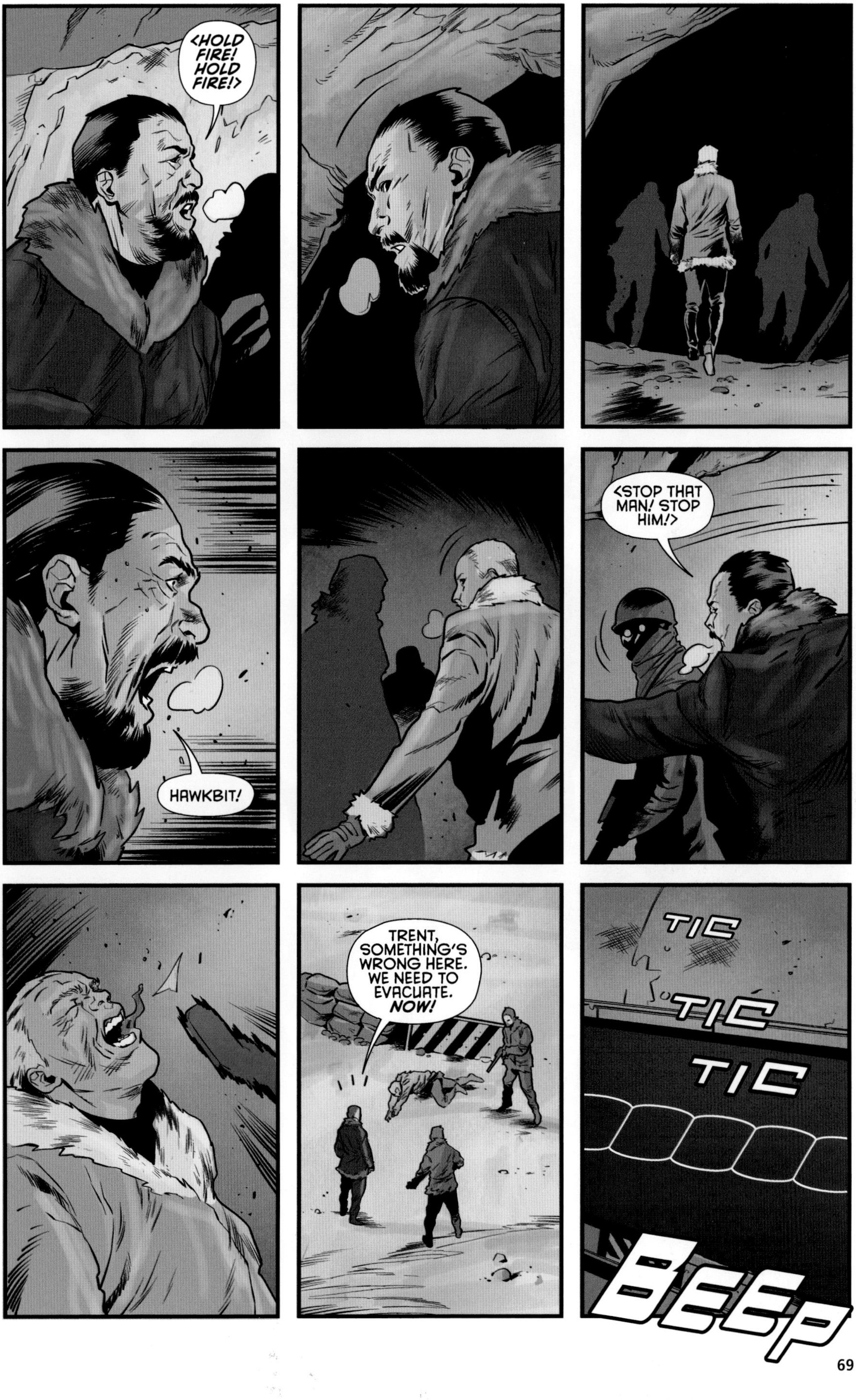
<HOLD FIRE! HOLD FIRE!>
HAWKBIT!
<STOP THAT MAN! STOP HIM!>
TRENT, SOMETHING'S WRONG HERE. WE NEED TO EVACUATE. *NOW!*
TIC
TIC
TIC
BEEP

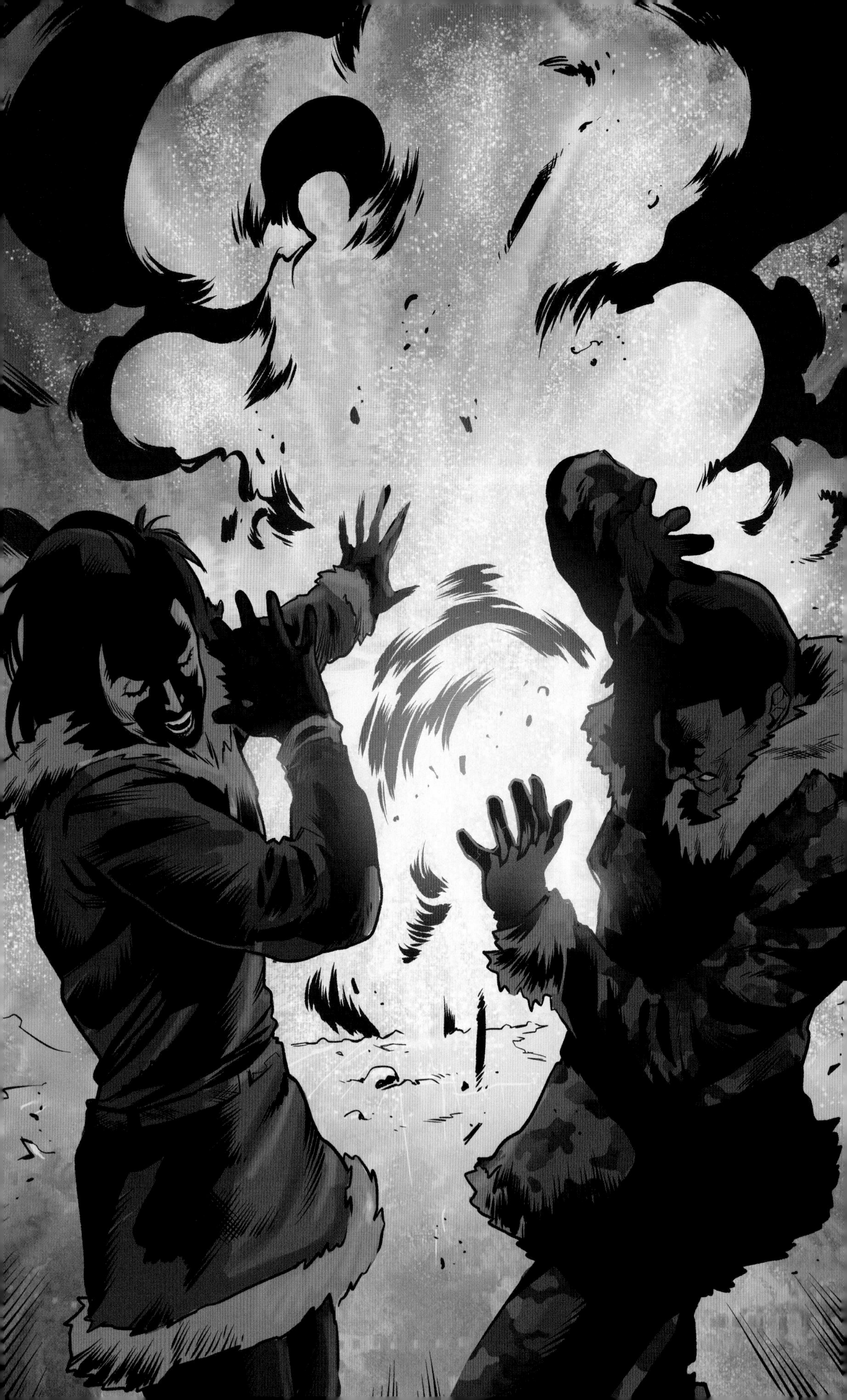

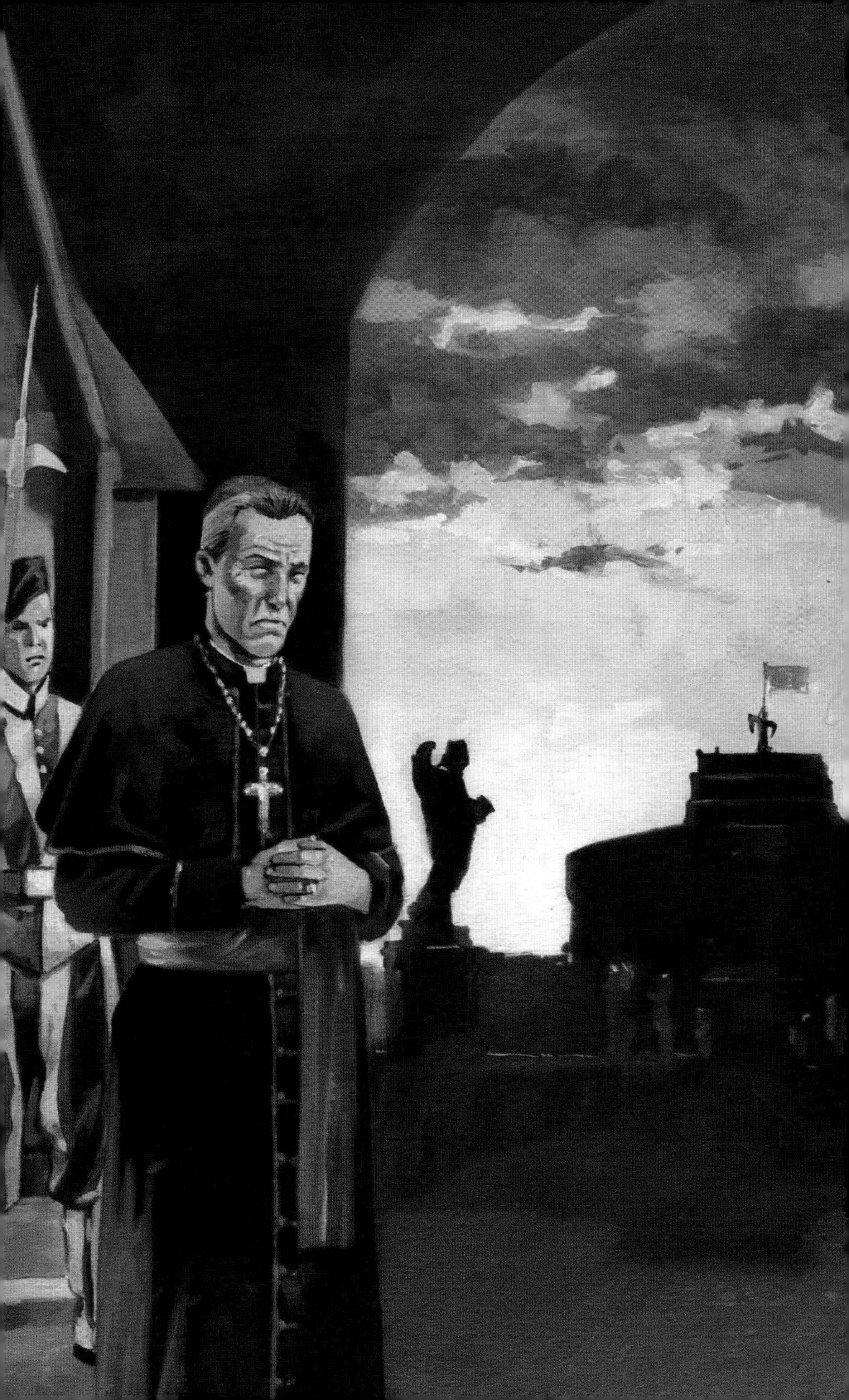

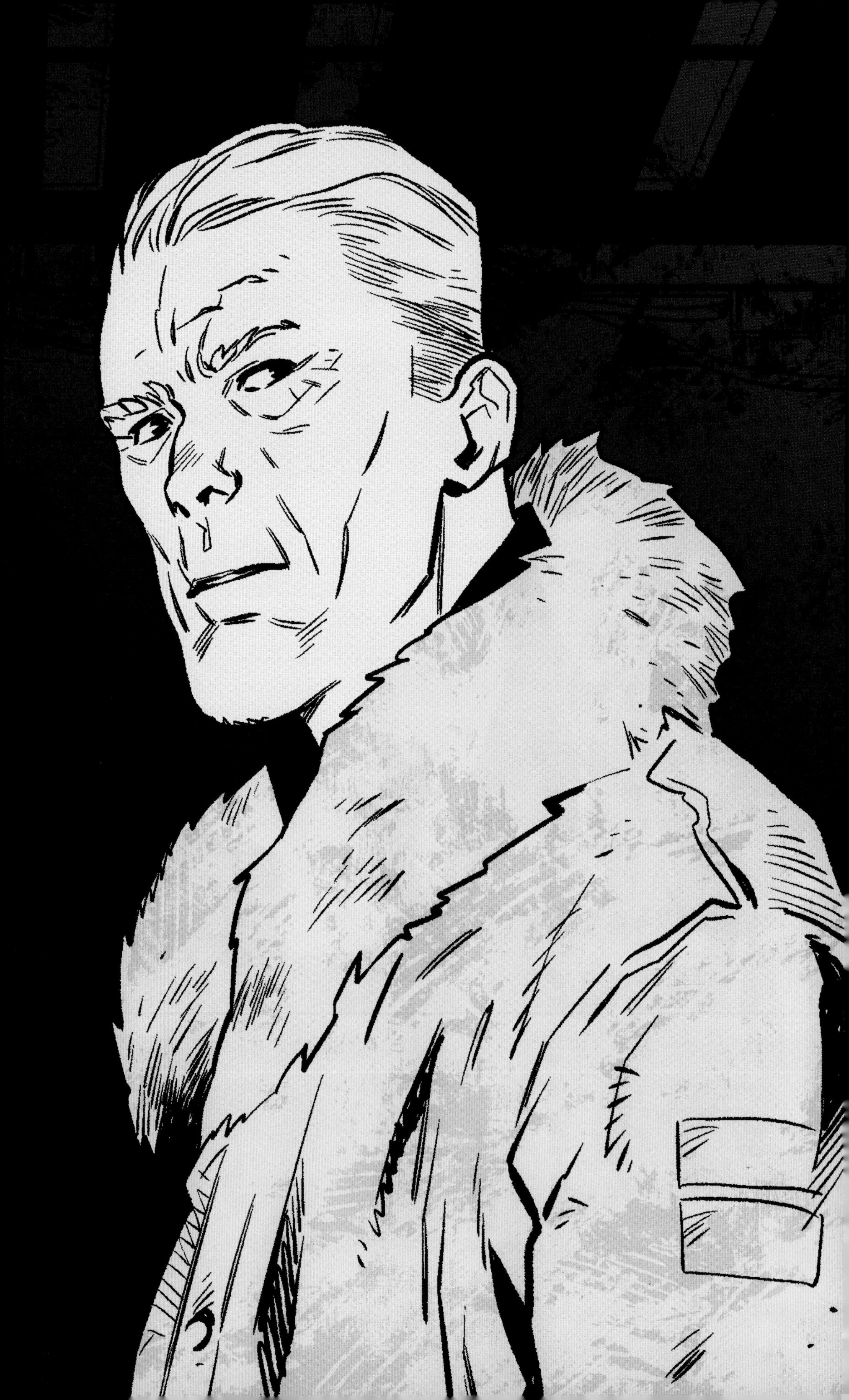

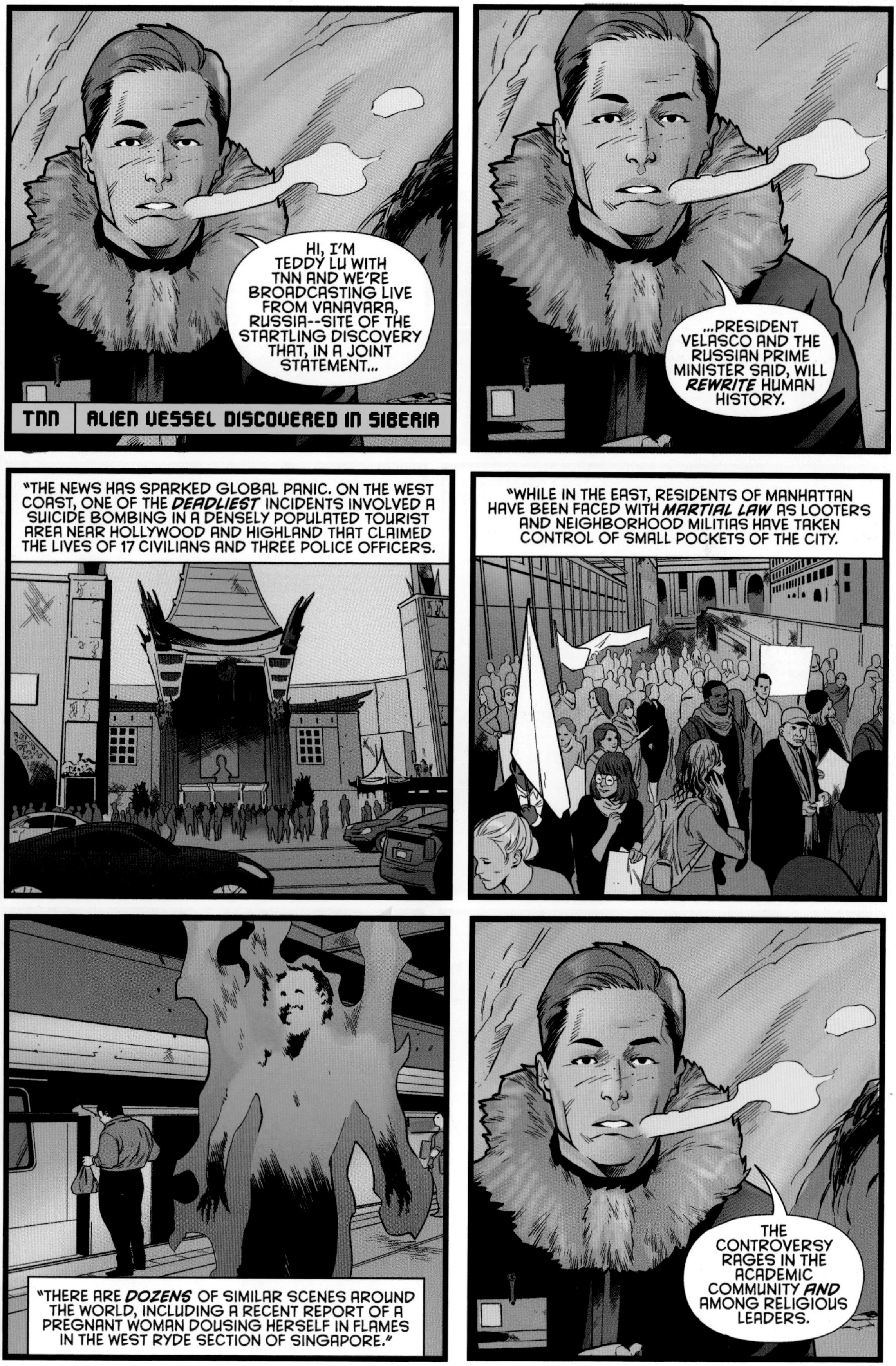
HI, I'M TEDDY LU WITH TNN AND WE'RE BROADCASTING LIVE FROM VANAVARA, RUSSIA--SITE OF THE STARTLING DISCOVERY THAT, IN A JOINT STATEMENT...
TNN
ALIEN VESSEL DISCOVERED IN SIBERIA
...PRESIDENT VELASCO AND THE RUSSIAN PRIME MINISTER SAID, WILL *REWRITE* HUMAN HISTORY.
"THE NEWS HAS SPARKED GLOBAL PANIC. ON THE WEST COAST, ONE OF THE *DEADLIEST* INCIDENTS INVOLVED A SUICIDE BOMBING IN A DENSELY POPULATED TOURIST AREA NEAR HOLLYWOOD AND HIGHLAND THAT CLAIMED THE LIVES OF 17 CIVILIANS AND THREE POLICE OFFICERS.
"WHILE IN THE EAST, RESIDENTS OF MANHATTAN HAVE BEEN FACED WITH *MARTIAL LAW* AS LOOTERS AND NEIGHBORHOOD MILITIAS HAVE TAKEN CONTROL OF SMALL POCKETS OF THE CITY.
"THERE ARE *DOZENS* OF SIMILAR SCENES AROUND THE WORLD, INCLUDING A RECENT REPORT OF A PREGNANT WOMAN DOUSING HERSELF IN FLAMES IN THE WEST RYDE SECTION OF SINGAPORE."
THE CONTROVERSY RAGES IN THE ACADEMIC COMMUNITY *AND* AMONG RELIGIOUS LEADERS.

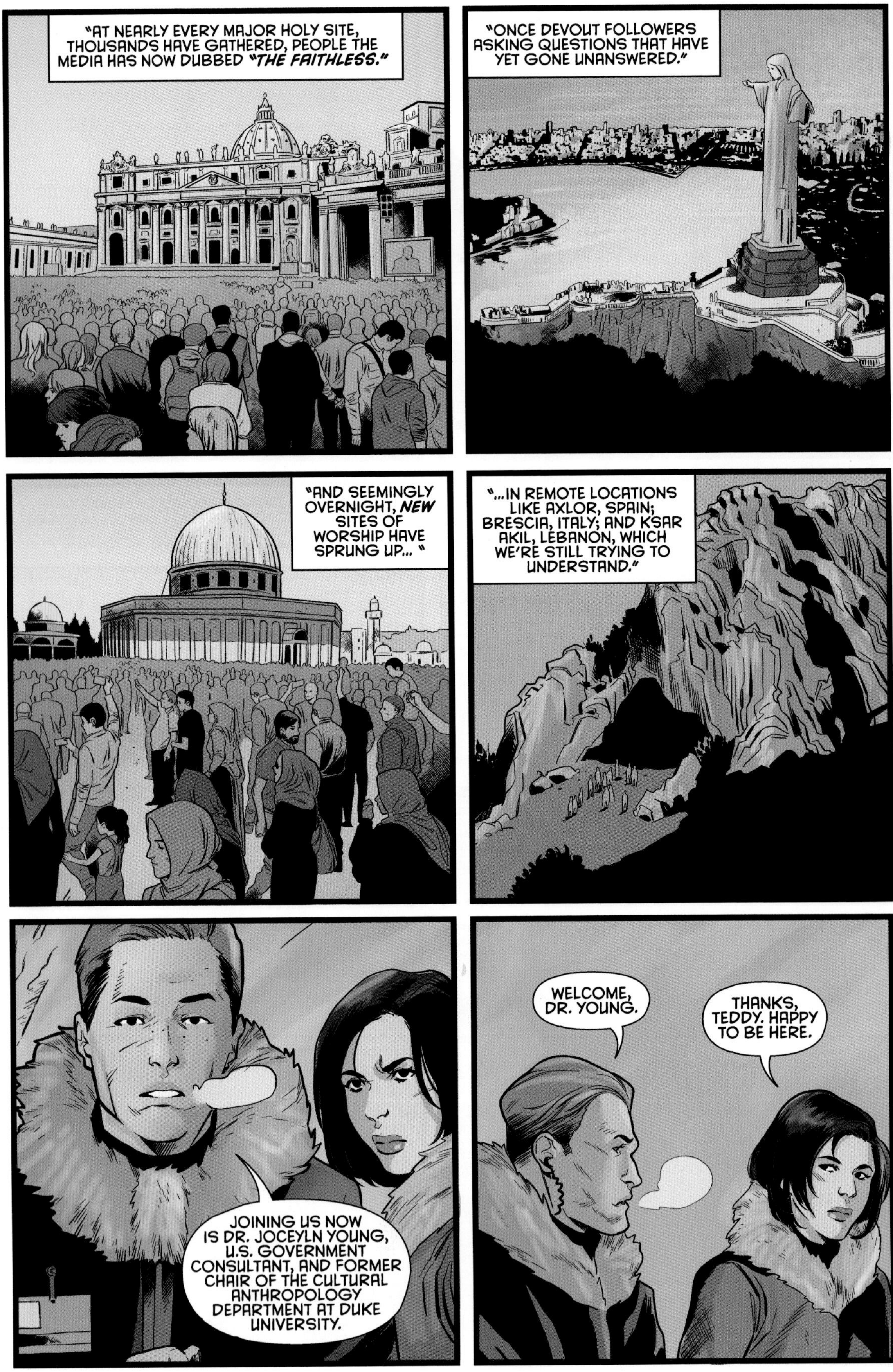
"AT NEARLY EVERY MAJOR HOLY SITE, THOUSANDS HAVE GATHERED, PEOPLE THE MEDIA HAS NOW DUBBED *"THE FAITHLESS."*
"ONCE DEVOUT FOLLOWERS ASKING QUESTIONS THAT HAVE YET GONE UNANSWERED."
"AND SEEMINGLY OVERNIGHT, ***NEW*** SITES OF WORSHIP HAVE SPRUNG UP... "
"...IN REMOTE LOCATIONS LIKE AXLOR, SPAIN; BRESCIA, ITALY; AND KSAR AKIL, LEBANON, WHICH WE'RE STILL TRYING TO UNDERSTAND."
JOINING US NOW IS DR. JOCEYLN YOUNG, U.S. GOVERNMENT CONSULTANT, AND FORMER CHAIR OF THE CULTURAL ANTHROPOLOGY DEPARTMENT AT DUKE UNIVERSITY.
WELCOME, DR. YOUNG.
THANKS, TEDDY. HAPPY TO BE HERE.

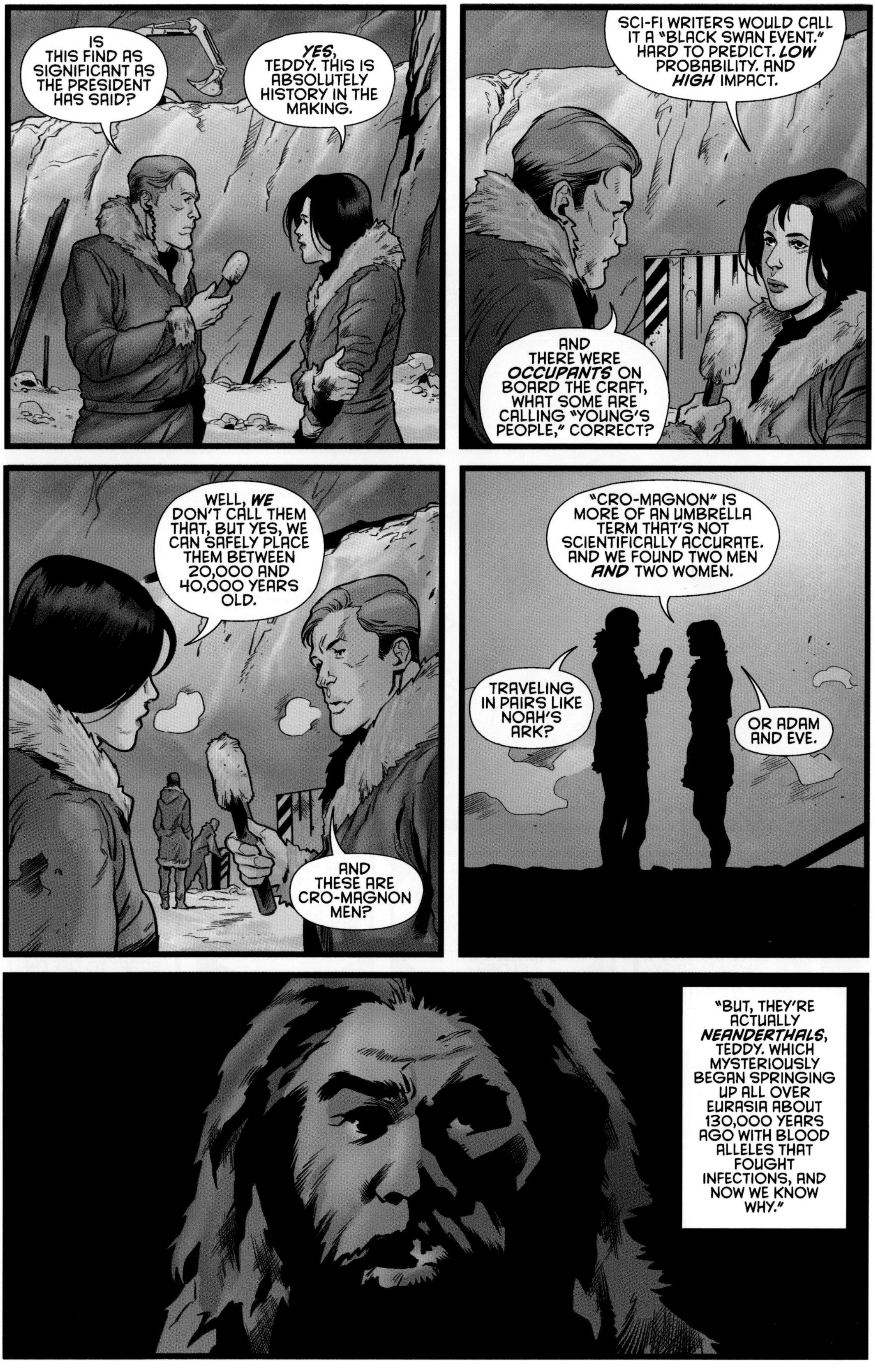
IS THIS FIND AS SIGNIFICANT AS THE PRESIDENT HAS SAID?
YES, TEDDY. THIS IS ABSOLUTELY HISTORY IN THE MAKING.
SCI-FI WRITERS WOULD CALL IT A "BLACK SWAN EVENT." HARD TO PREDICT. LOW PROBABILITY. AND HIGH IMPACT.
AND THERE WERE OCCUPANTS ON BOARD THE CRAFT, WHAT SOME ARE CALLING "YOUNG'S PEOPLE," CORRECT?
WELL, WE DON'T CALL THEM THAT, BUT YES, WE CAN SAFELY PLACE THEM BETWEEN 20,000 AND 40,000 YEARS OLD.
AND THESE ARE CRO-MAGNON MEN?
"CRO-MAGNON" IS MORE OF AN UMBRELLA TERM THAT'S NOT SCIENTIFICALLY ACCURATE. AND WE FOUND TWO MEN AND TWO WOMEN.
TRAVELING IN PAIRS LIKE NOAH'S ARK?
OR ADAM AND EVE.
"BUT, THEY'RE ACTUALLY NEANDERTHALS, TEDDY. WHICH MYSTERIOUSLY BEGAN SPRINGING UP ALL OVER EURASIA ABOUT 130,000 YEARS AGO WITH BLOOD ALLELES THAT FOUGHT INFECTIONS, AND NOW WE KNOW WHY."

THEY TRAVELED TO EARTH FOR THOUSANDS OF YEARS?

WE THINK SO. THE DATES LINE UP WITH DOZENS OF CAVE DRAWINGS DATING BACK TO BEFORE BIBLICAL TIMES.

"THESE WERE USUALLY DISMISSED WITH METEOROLOGICAL OR EVEN PHARMACOLOGICAL EXPLANATIONS."

"SO OUR DISTANT ANCESTORS MAY HAVE KNOWN?"

"THEY LEFT US *PLENTY* OF MESSAGES AND WE DIDN'T WANT TO BELIEVE."

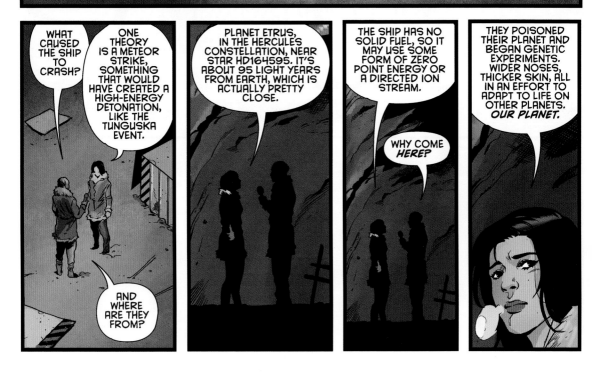

WHAT CAUSED THE SHIP TO CRASH?

ONE THEORY IS A METEOR STRIKE, SOMETHING THAT WOULD HAVE CREATED A HIGH-ENERGY DETONATION, LIKE THE TUNGUSKA EVENT.

AND WHERE ARE THEY FROM?

PLANET ETRUS, IN THE HERCULES CONSTELLATION, NEAR STAR HD164595. IT'S ABOUT 95 LIGHT YEARS FROM EARTH, WHICH IS ACTUALLY PRETTY CLOSE.

THE SHIP HAS NO SOLID FUEL, SO IT MAY USE SOME FORM OF ZERO POINT ENERGY OR A DIRECTED ION STREAM.

WHY COME *HERE?*

THEY POISONED THEIR PLANET AND BEGAN GENETIC EXPERIMENTS. WIDER NOSES, THICKER SKIN, ALL IN AN EFFORT TO ADAPT TO LIFE ON OTHER PLANETS. *OUR PLANET.*

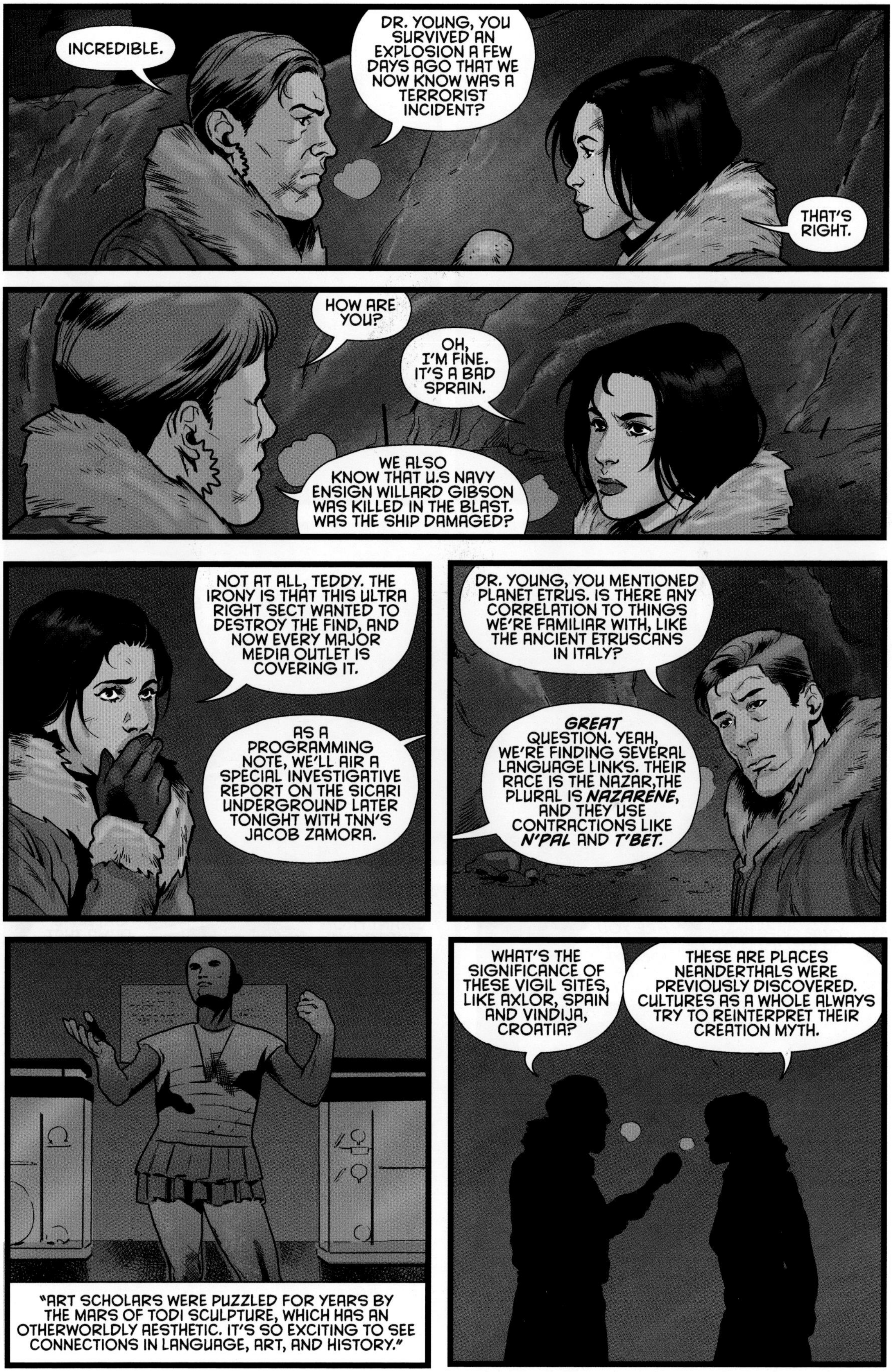
INCREDIBLE.
DR. YOUNG, YOU SURVIVED AN EXPLOSION A FEW DAYS AGO THAT WE NOW KNOW WAS A TERRORIST INCIDENT?
THAT'S RIGHT.
HOW ARE YOU?
OH, I'M FINE. IT'S A BAD SPRAIN.
WE ALSO KNOW THAT U.S NAVY ENSIGN WILLARD GIBSON WAS KILLED IN THE BLAST. WAS THE SHIP DAMAGED?
NOT AT ALL, TEDDY. THE IRONY IS THAT THIS ULTRA RIGHT SECT WANTED TO DESTROY THE FIND, AND NOW EVERY MAJOR MEDIA OUTLET IS COVERING IT.
AS A PROGRAMMING NOTE, WE'LL AIR A SPECIAL INVESTIGATIVE REPORT ON THE SICARI UNDERGROUND LATER TONIGHT WITH TNN'S JACOB ZAMORA.
DR. YOUNG, YOU MENTIONED PLANET ETRUS. IS THERE ANY CORRELATION TO THINGS WE'RE FAMILIAR WITH, LIKE THE ANCIENT ETRUSCANS IN ITALY?
GREAT QUESTION. YEAH, WE'RE FINDING SEVERAL LANGUAGE LINKS. THEIR RACE IS THE NAZAR,THE PLURAL IS *NAZARENE*, AND THEY USE CONTRACTIONS LIKE *N'PAL* AND *T'BET*.
"ART SCHOLARS WERE PUZZLED FOR YEARS BY THE MARS OF TODI SCULPTURE, WHICH HAS AN OTHERWORLDLY AESTHETIC. IT'S SO EXCITING TO SEE CONNECTIONS IN LANGUAGE, ART, AND HISTORY."
WHAT'S THE SIGNIFICANCE OF THESE VIGIL SITES, LIKE AXLOR, SPAIN AND VINDIJA, CROATIA?
THESE ARE PLACES NEANDERTHALS WERE PREVIOUSLY DISCOVERED. CULTURES AS A WHOLE ALWAYS TRY TO REINTERPRET THEIR CREATION MYTH.

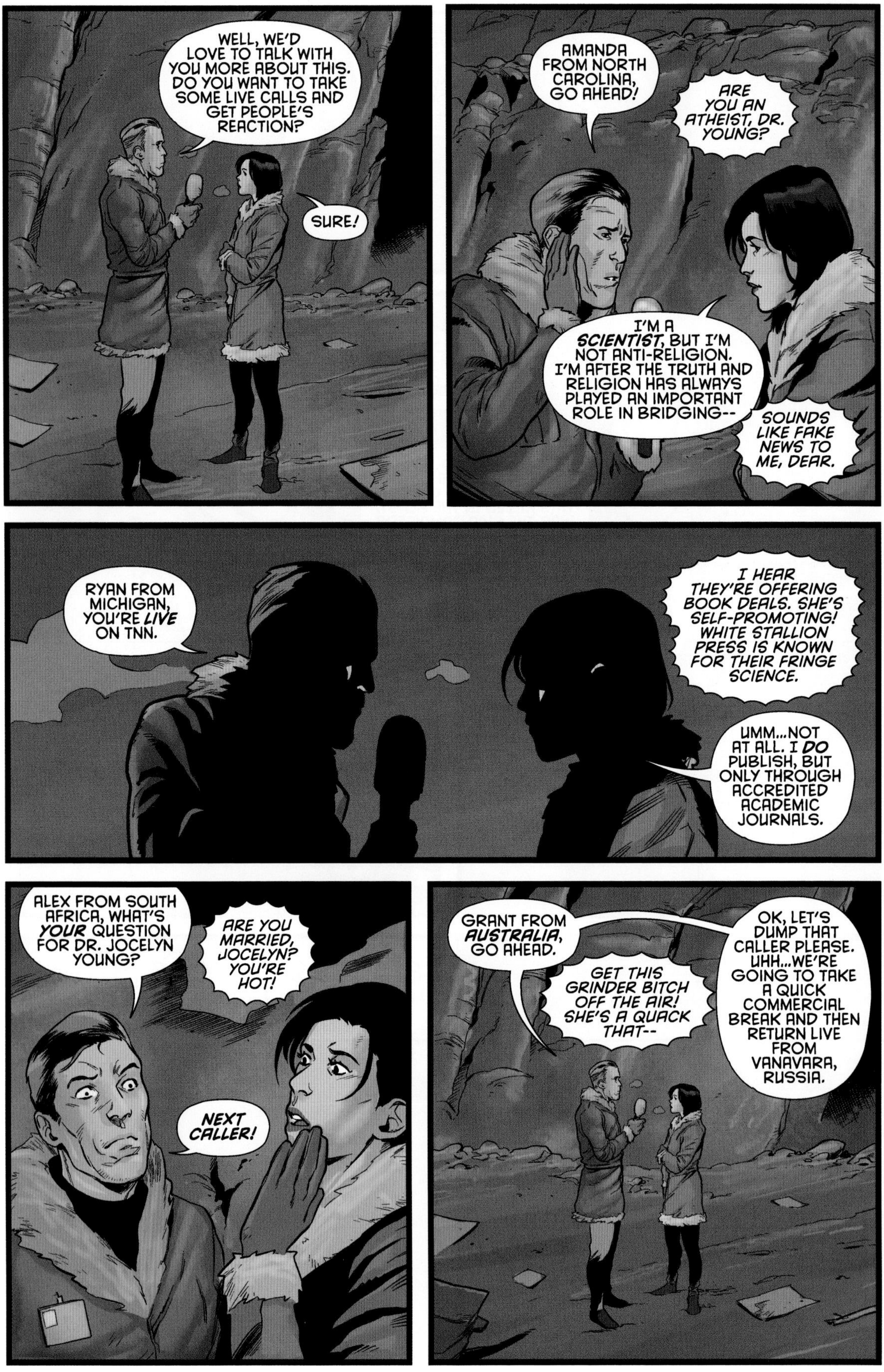
WELL, WE'D LOVE TO TALK WITH YOU MORE ABOUT THIS. DO YOU WANT TO TAKE SOME LIVE CALLS AND GET PEOPLE'S REACTION?
SURE!
AMANDA FROM NORTH CAROLINA, GO AHEAD!
ARE YOU AN ATHEIST, DR. YOUNG?
I'M A SCIENTIST, BUT I'M NOT ANTI-RELIGION. I'M AFTER THE TRUTH AND RELIGION HAS ALWAYS PLAYED AN IMPORTANT ROLE IN BRIDGING--
SOUNDS LIKE FAKE NEWS TO ME, DEAR.
RYAN FROM MICHIGAN, YOU'RE LIVE ON TNN.
I HEAR THEY'RE OFFERING BOOK DEALS. SHE'S SELF-PROMOTING! WHITE STALLION PRESS IS KNOWN FOR THEIR FRINGE SCIENCE.
UMM...NOT AT ALL. I DO PUBLISH, BUT ONLY THROUGH ACCREDITED ACADEMIC JOURNALS.
ALEX FROM SOUTH AFRICA, WHAT'S YOUR QUESTION FOR DR. JOCELYN YOUNG?
ARE YOU MARRIED, JOCELYN? YOU'RE HOT!
NEXT CALLER!
GRANT FROM AUSTRALIA, GO AHEAD.
GET THIS GRINDER BITCH OFF THE AIR! SHE'S A QUACK THAT--
OK, LET'S DUMP THAT CALLER PLEASE. UHH...WE'RE GOING TO TAKE A QUICK COMMERCIAL BREAK AND THEN RETURN LIVE FROM VANAVARA, RUSSIA.

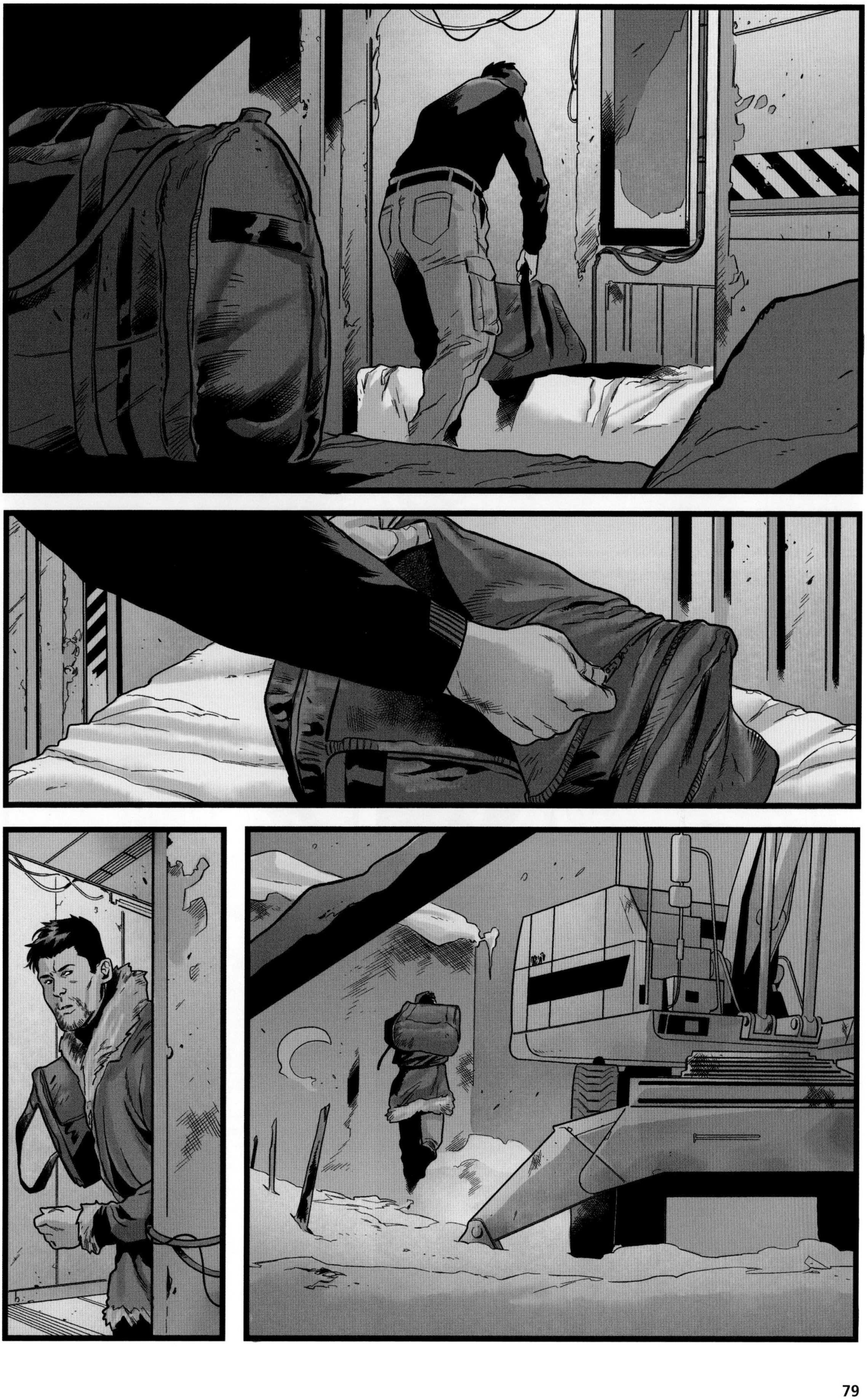

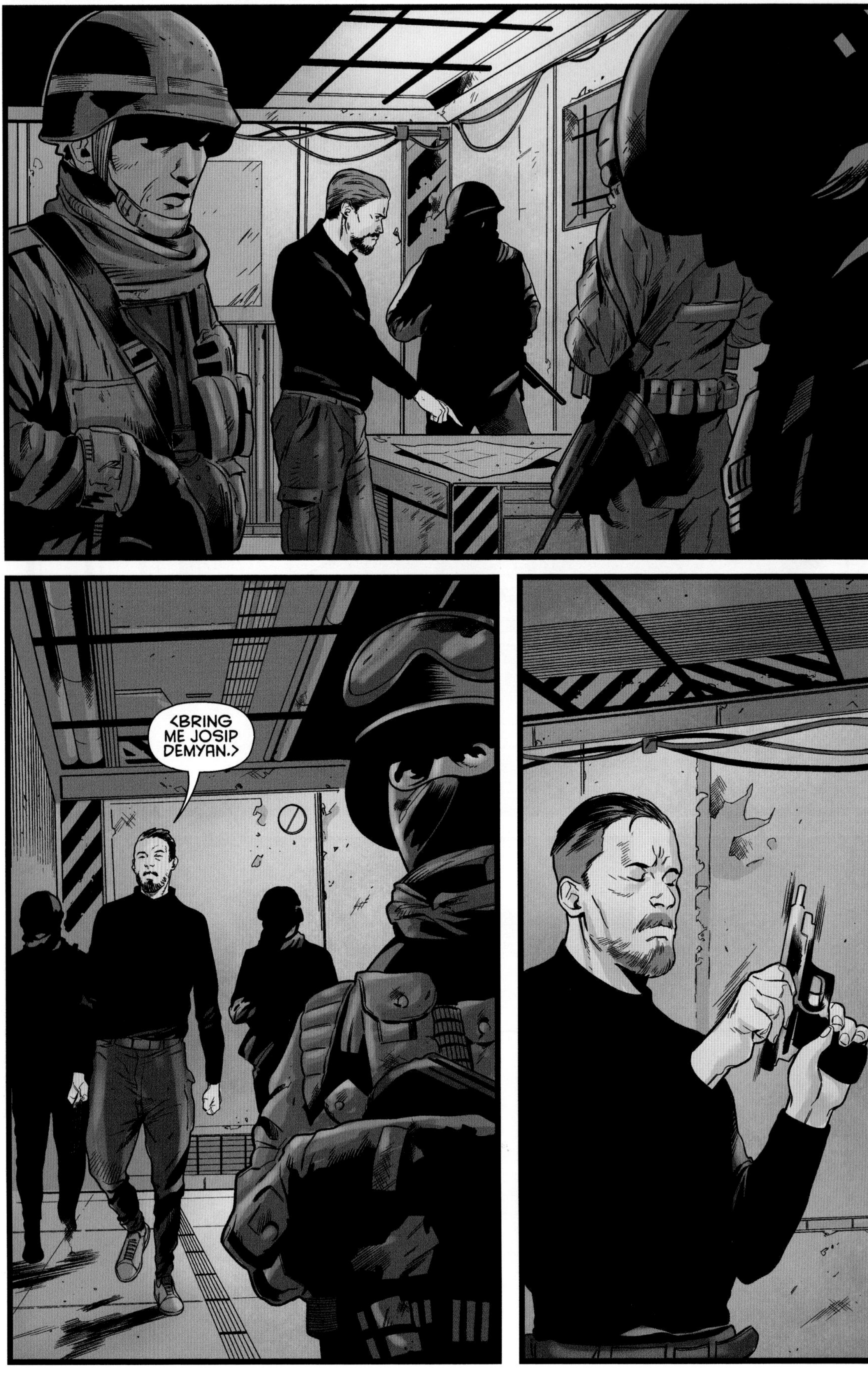
<BRING ME JOSIP DEMYAN.>

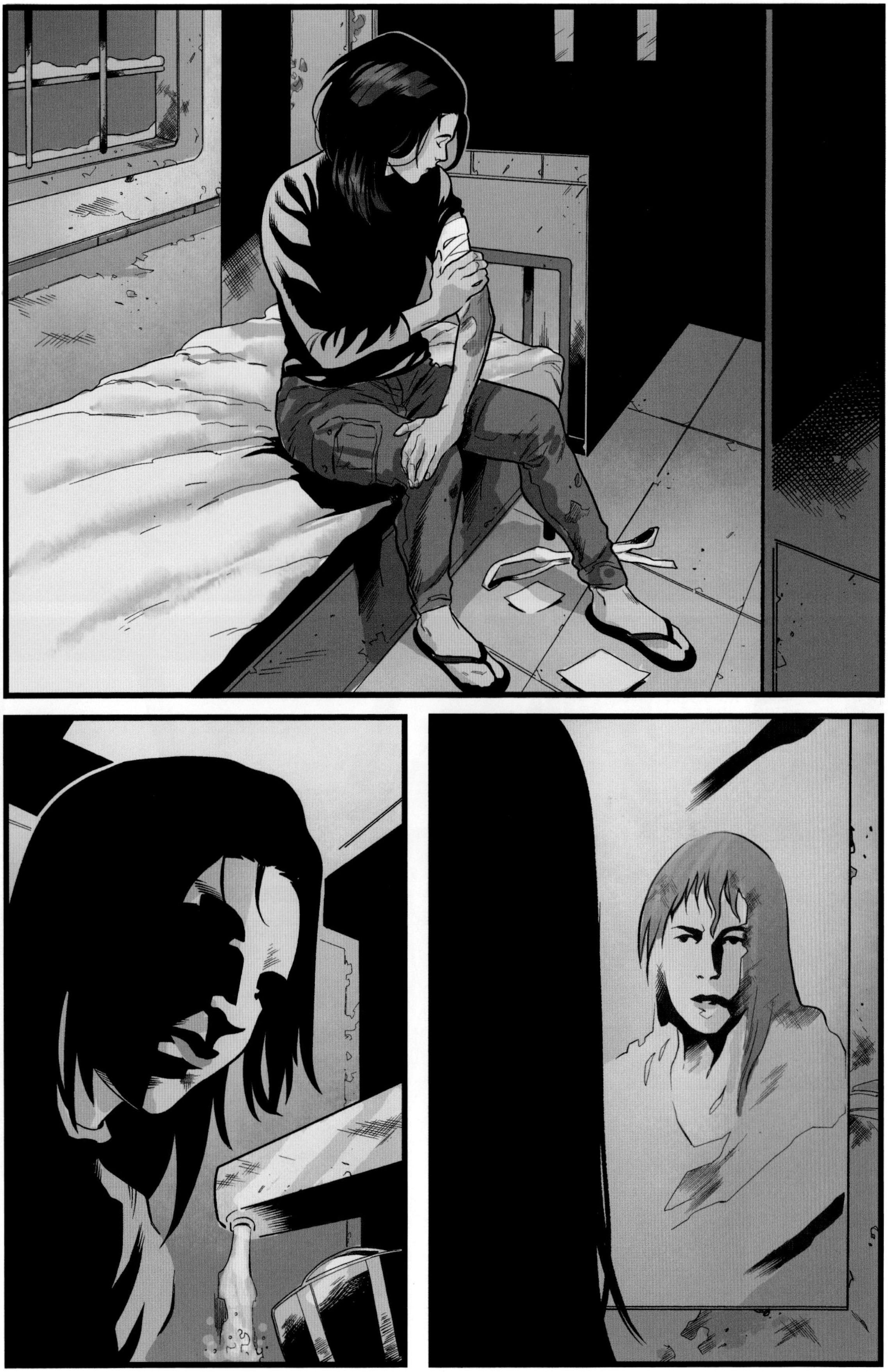

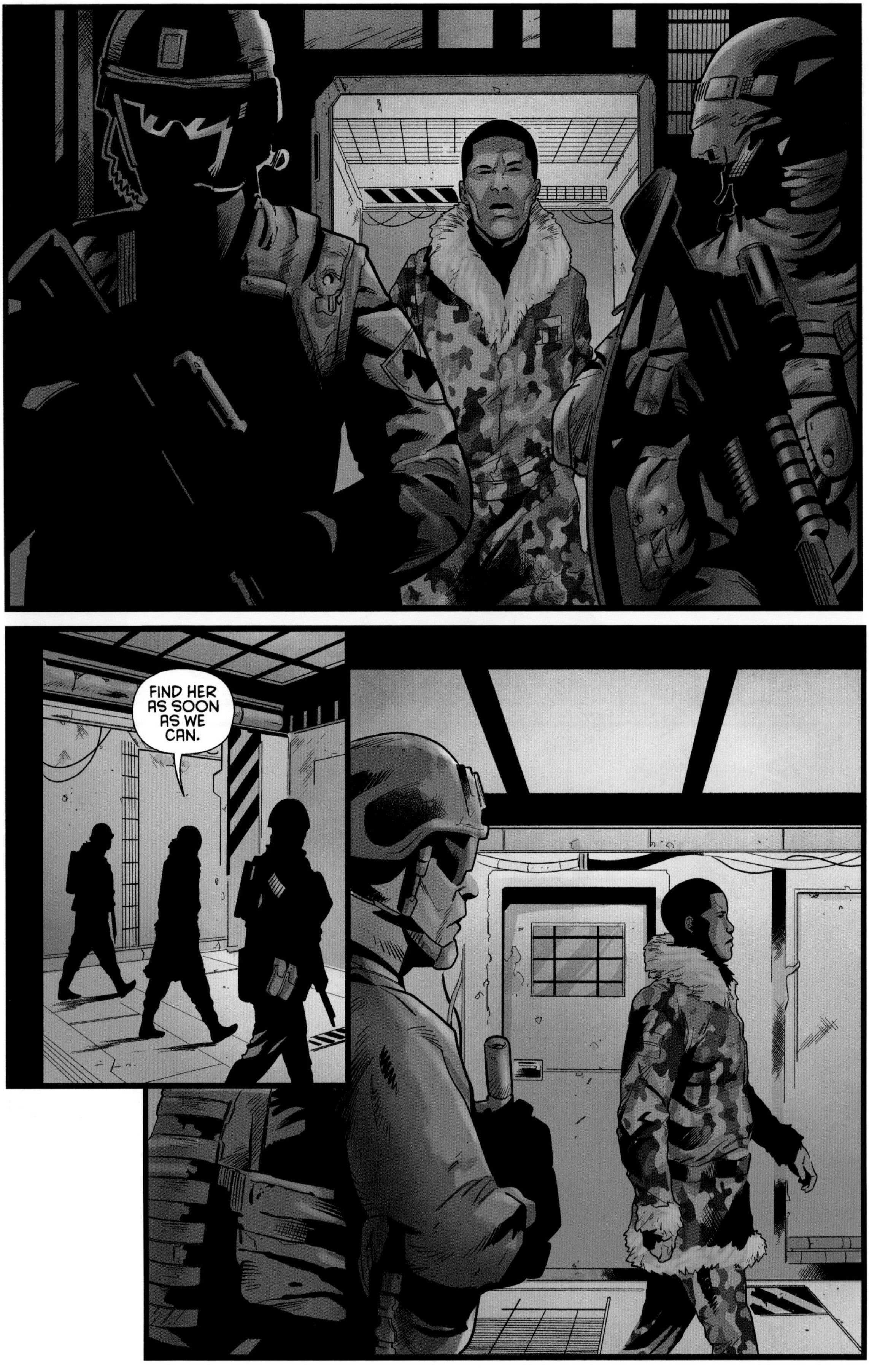
FIND HER AS SOON AS WE CAN.

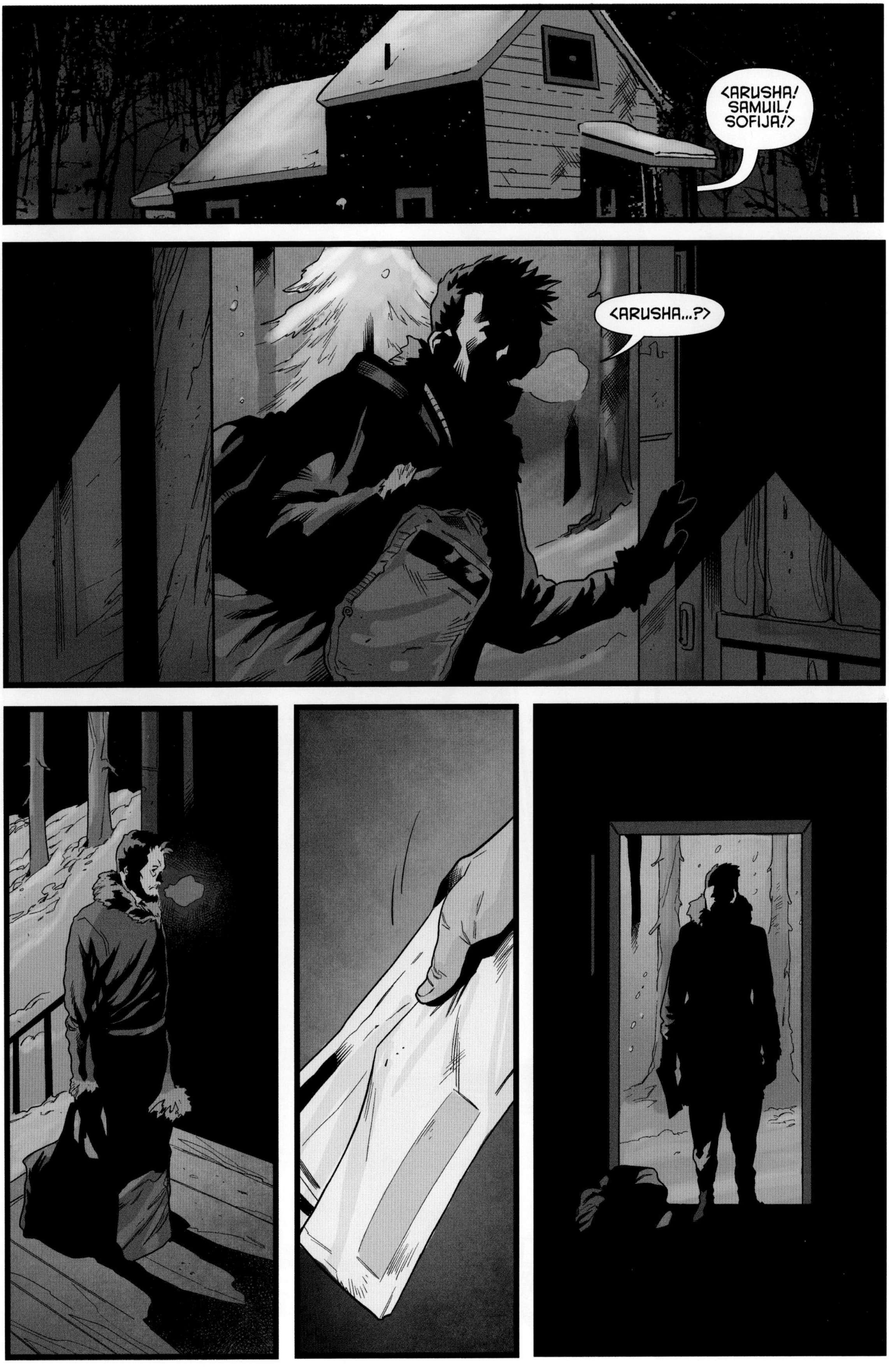
<ARUSHA! SAMUIL! SOFIJA!>
<ARUSHA...?>

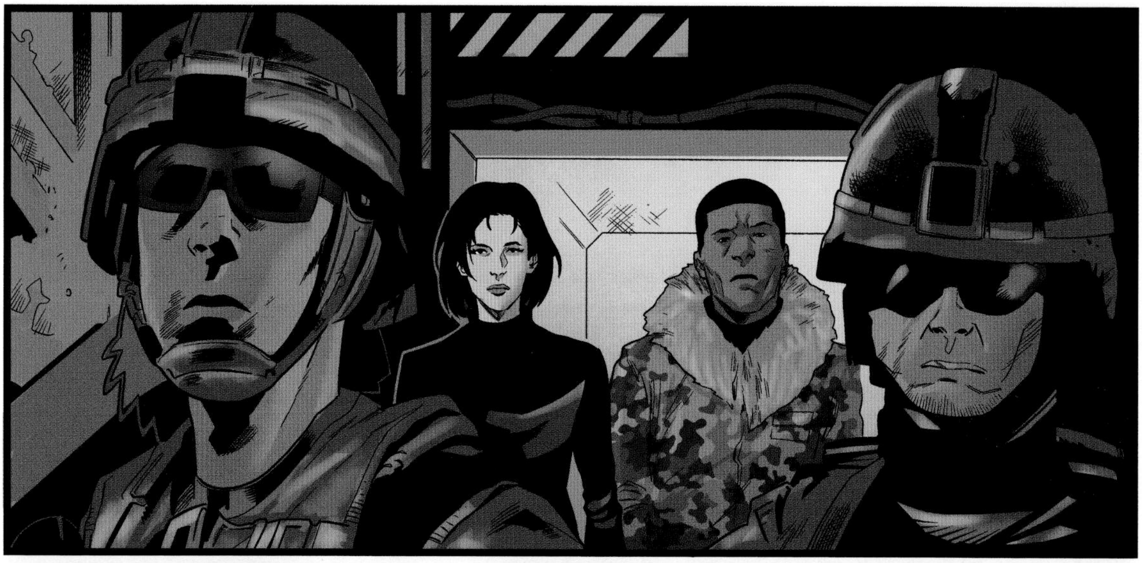

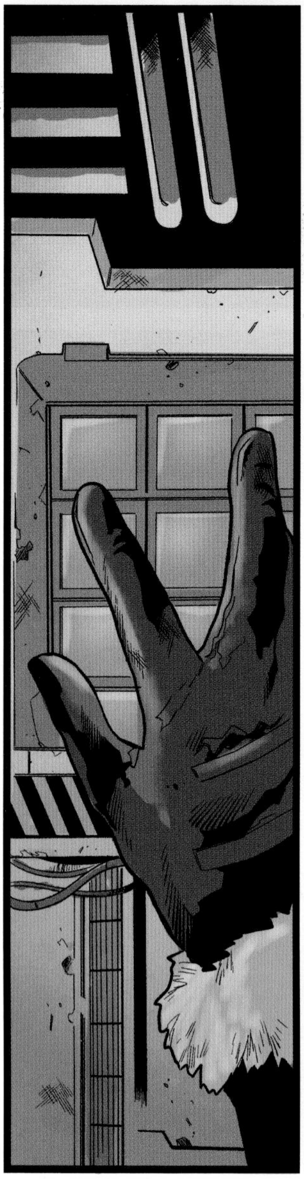

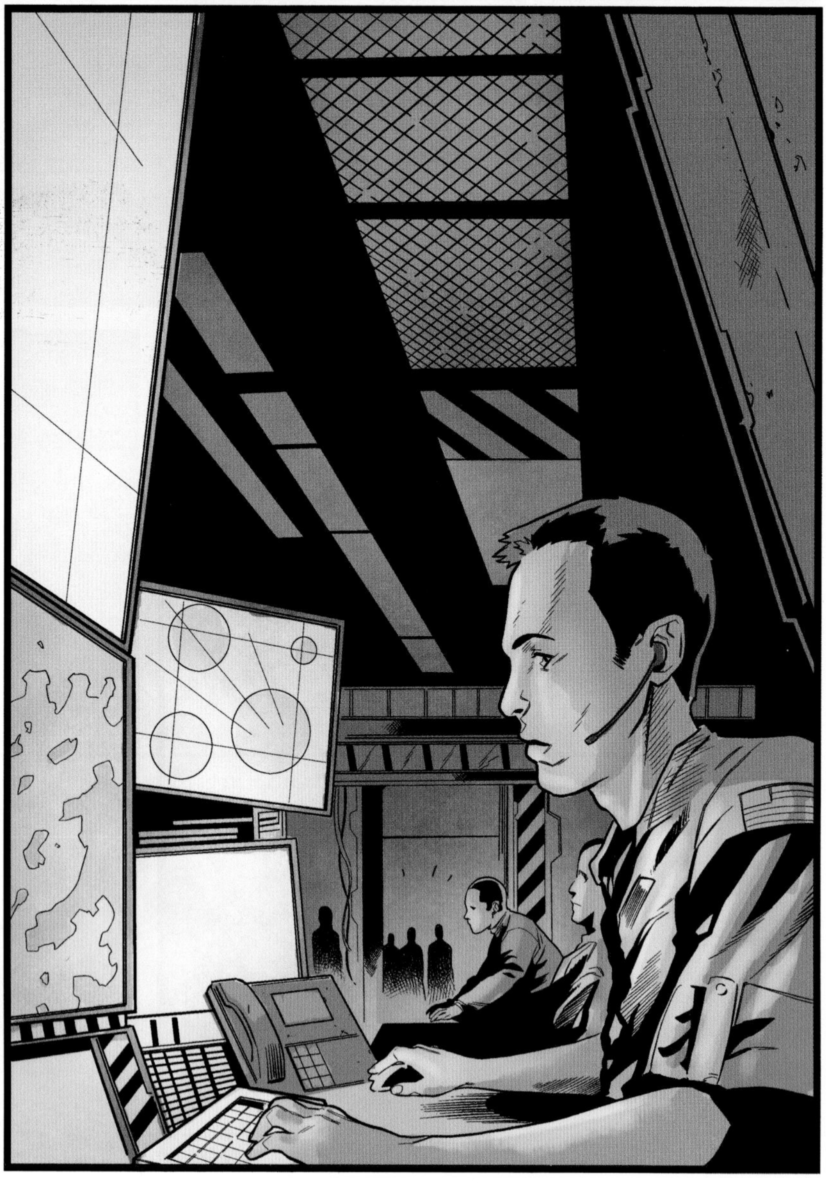

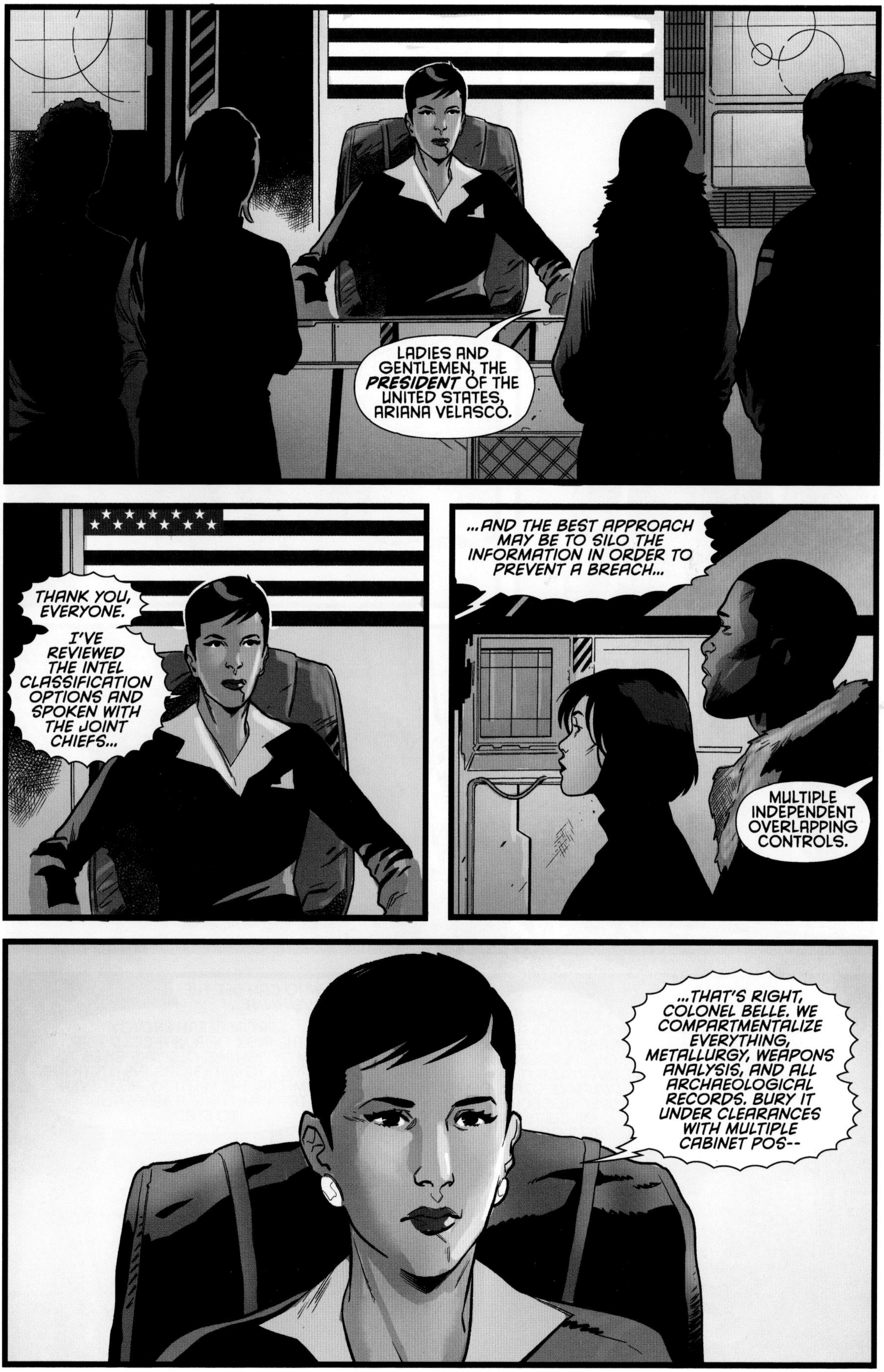
LADIES AND GENTLEMEN, THE *PRESIDENT* OF THE UNITED STATES, ARIANA VELASCO.
THANK YOU, EVERYONE.
I'VE REVIEWED THE INTEL CLASSIFICATION OPTIONS AND SPOKEN WITH THE JOINT CHIEFS...
...AND THE BEST APPROACH MAY BE TO SILO THE INFORMATION IN ORDER TO PREVENT A BREACH...
MULTIPLE INDEPENDENT OVERLAPPING CONTROLS.
...THAT'S RIGHT, COLONEL BELLE. WE COMPARTMENTALIZE EVERYTHING, METALLURGY, WEAPONS ANALYSIS, AND ALL ARCHAEOLOGICAL RECORDS. BURY IT UNDER CLEARANCES WITH MULTIPLE CABINET POS--

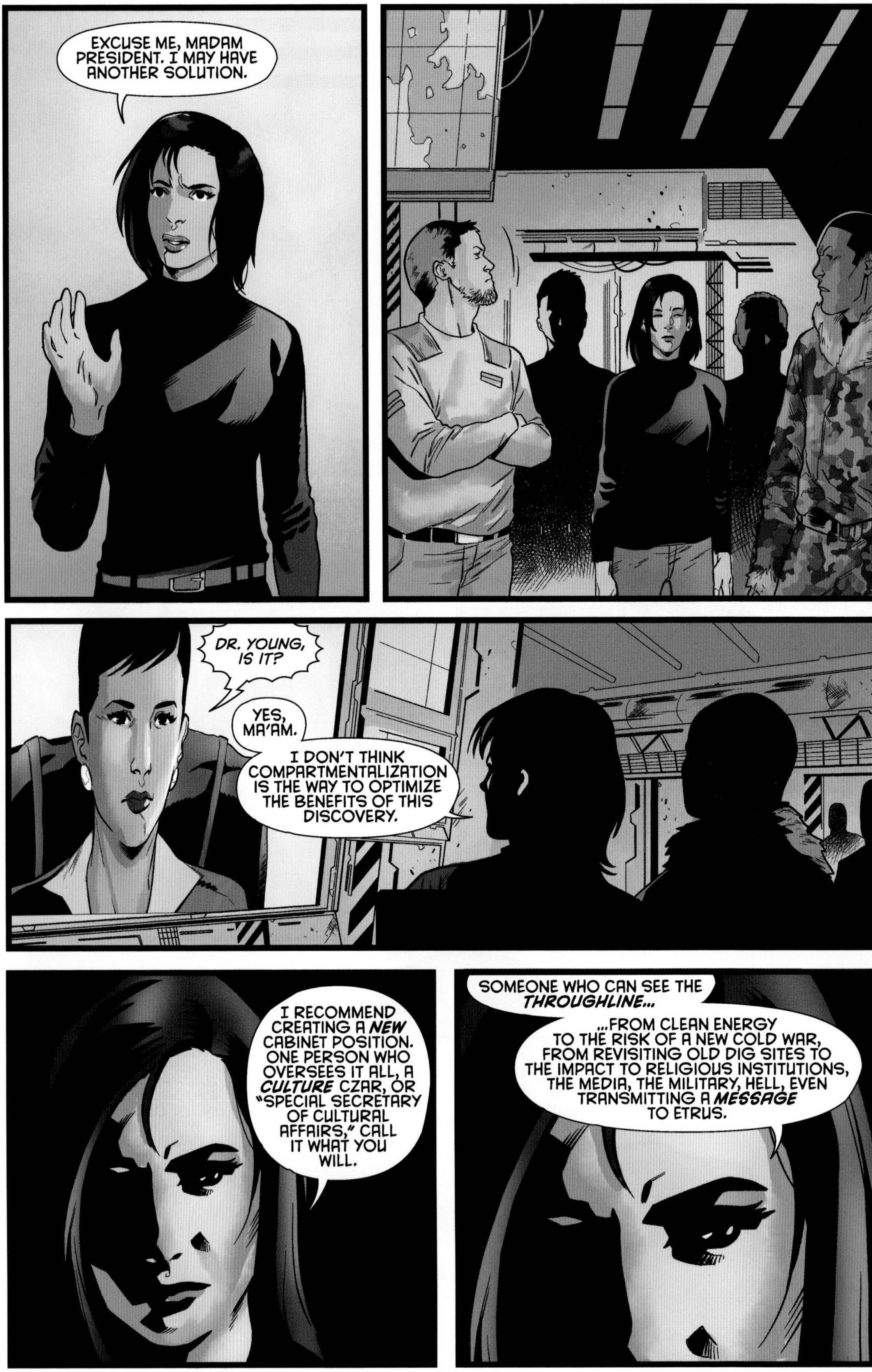
EXCUSE ME, MADAM PRESIDENT. I MAY HAVE ANOTHER SOLUTION.
DR. YOUNG, IS IT?
YES, MA'AM.
I DON'T THINK COMPARTMENTALIZATION IS THE WAY TO OPTIMIZE THE BENEFITS OF THIS DISCOVERY.
I RECOMMEND CREATING A NEW CABINET POSITION. ONE PERSON WHO OVERSEES IT ALL, A CULTURE CZAR, OR "SPECIAL SECRETARY OF CULTURAL AFFAIRS," CALL IT WHAT YOU WILL.
SOMEONE WHO CAN SEE THE THROUGHLINE...
...FROM CLEAN ENERGY TO THE RISK OF A NEW COLD WAR, FROM REVISITING OLD DIG SITES TO THE IMPACT TO RELIGIOUS INSTITUTIONS, THE MEDIA, THE MILITARY, HELL, EVEN TRANSMITTING A MESSAGE TO ETRUS.

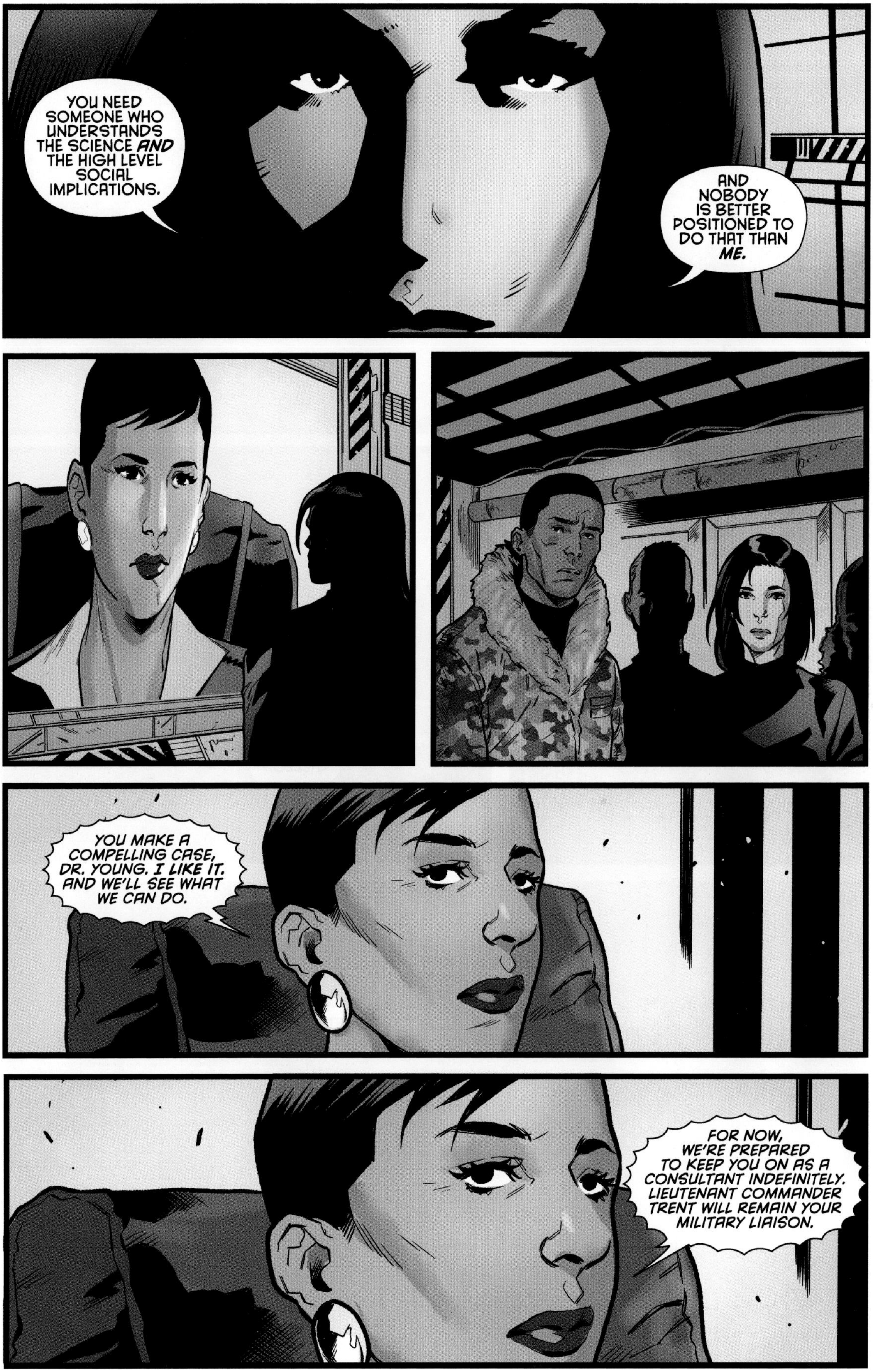
YOU NEED SOMEONE WHO UNDERSTANDS THE SCIENCE *AND* THE HIGH LEVEL SOCIAL IMPLICATIONS.
AND NOBODY IS BETTER POSITIONED TO DO THAT THAN *ME.*
YOU MAKE A COMPELLING CASE, DR. YOUNG. *I LIKE IT.* AND WE'LL SEE WHAT WE CAN DO.
FOR NOW, WE'RE PREPARED TO KEEP YOU ON AS A CONSULTANT INDEFINITELY. LIEUTENANT COMMANDER TRENT WILL REMAIN YOUR MILITARY LIAISON.

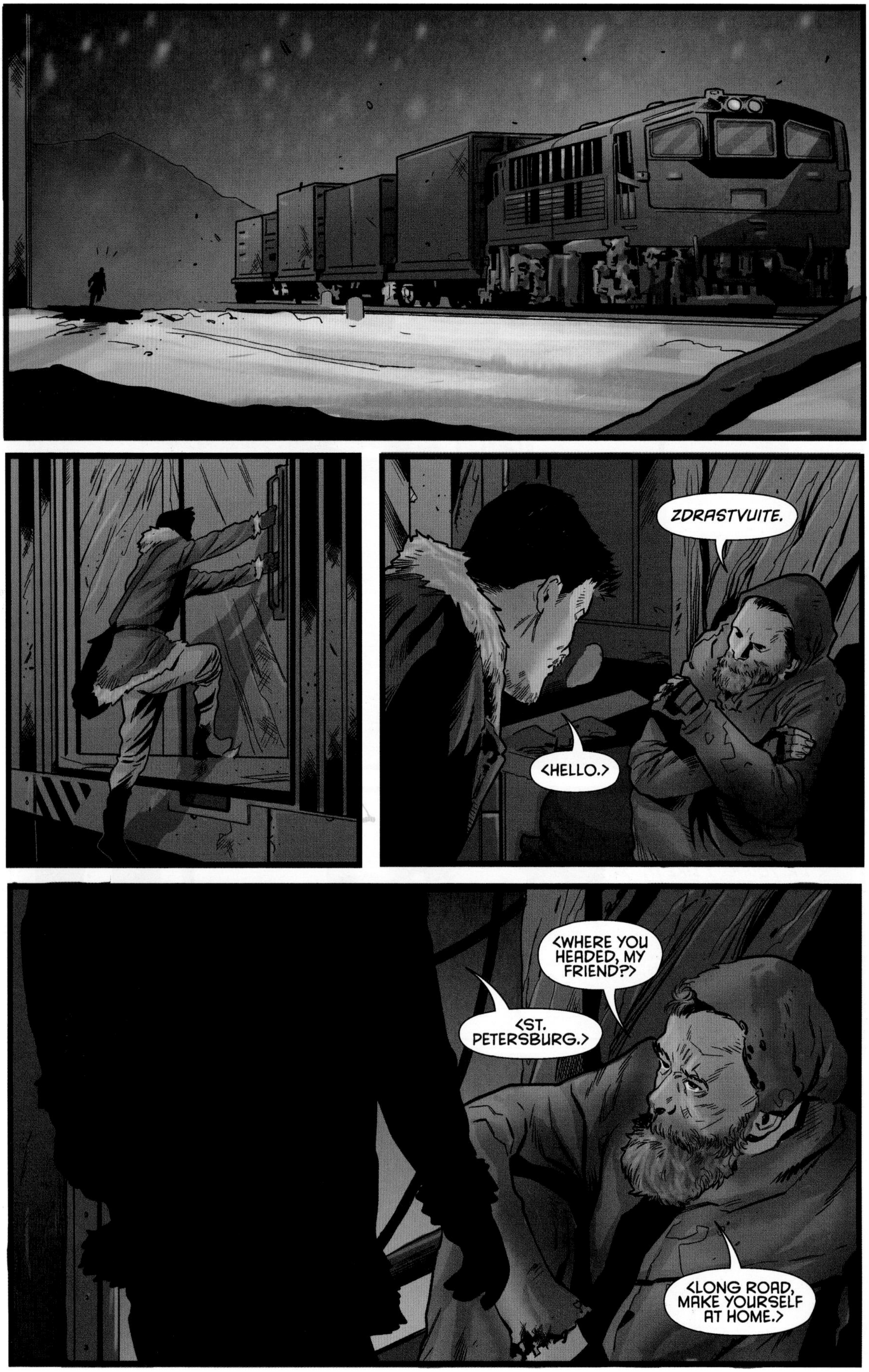
ZDRASTVUITE.
<HELLO.>
<WHERE YOU HEADED, MY FRIEND?>
<ST. PETERSBURG.>
<LONG ROAD, MAKE YOURSELF AT HOME.>

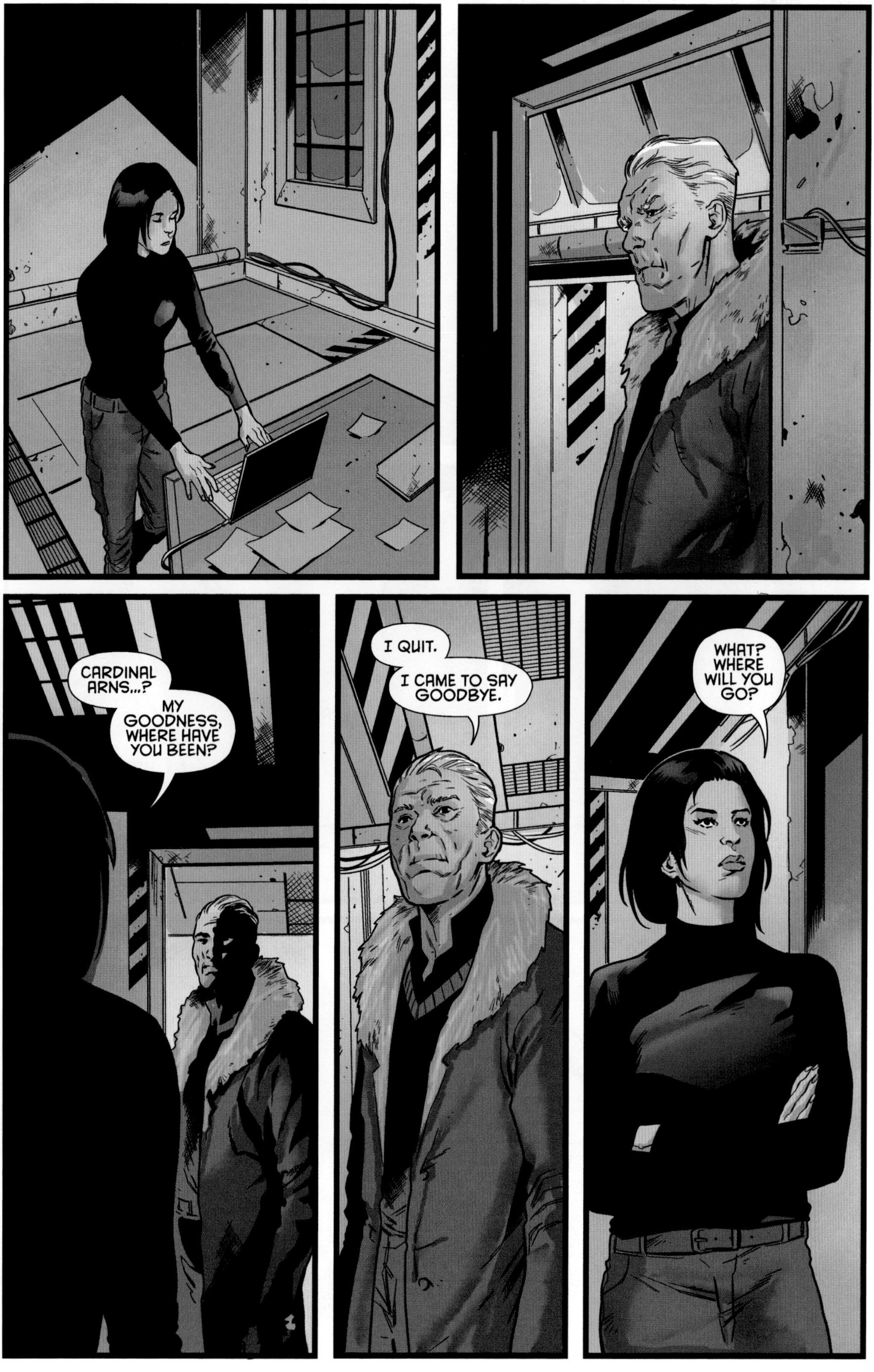
CARDINAL ARNS...?
MY GOODNESS, WHERE HAVE YOU BEEN?
I QUIT.
I CAME TO SAY GOODBYE.
WHAT? WHERE WILL YOU GO?

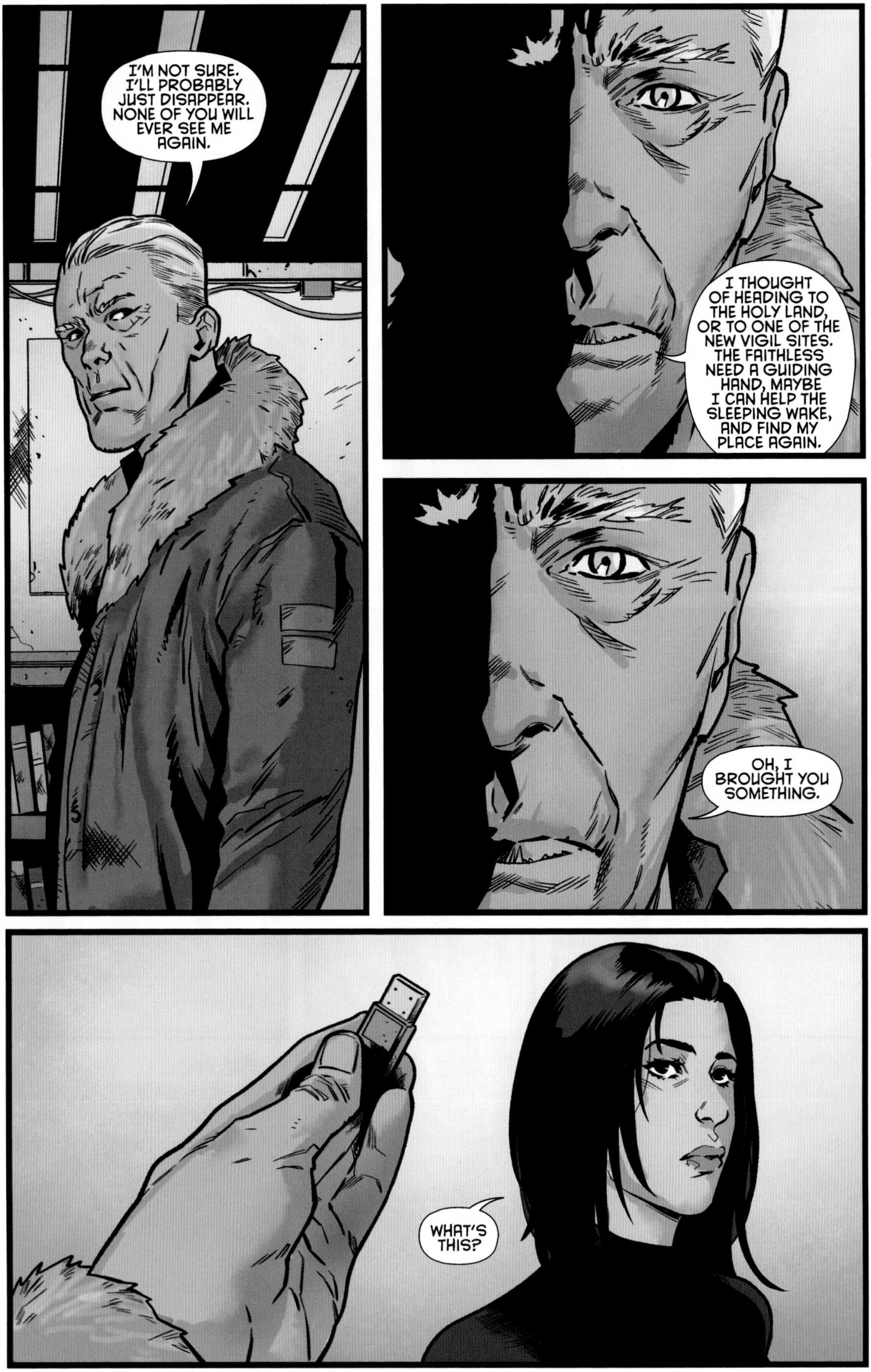
I'M NOT SURE. I'LL PROBABLY JUST DISAPPEAR. NONE OF YOU WILL EVER SEE ME AGAIN.
I THOUGHT OF HEADING TO THE HOLY LAND, OR TO ONE OF THE NEW VIGIL SITES. THE FAITHLESS NEED A GUIDING HAND, MAYBE I CAN HELP THE SLEEPING WAKE, AND FIND MY PLACE AGAIN.
OH, I BROUGHT YOU SOMETHING.
WHAT'S THIS?

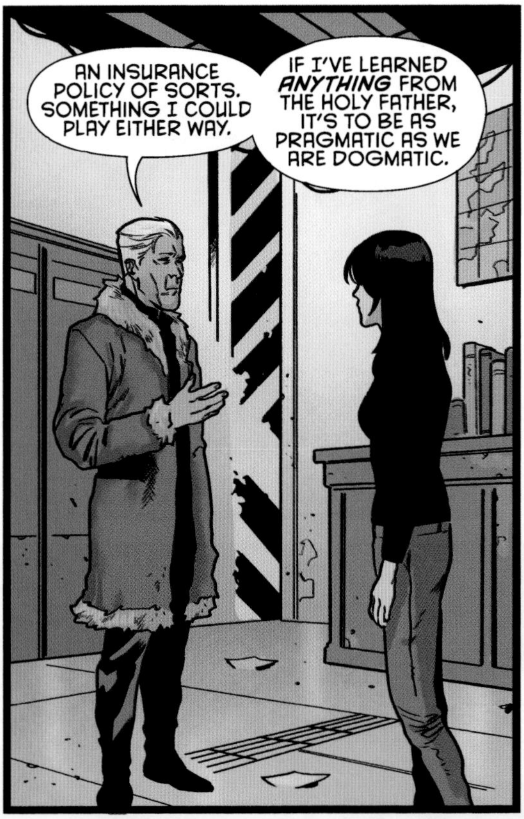
AN INSURANCE POLICY OF SORTS. SOMETHING I COULD PLAY EITHER WAY.
IF I'VE LEARNED *ANYTHING* FROM THE HOLY FATHER, IT'S TO BE AS PRAGMATIC AS WE ARE DOGMATIC.

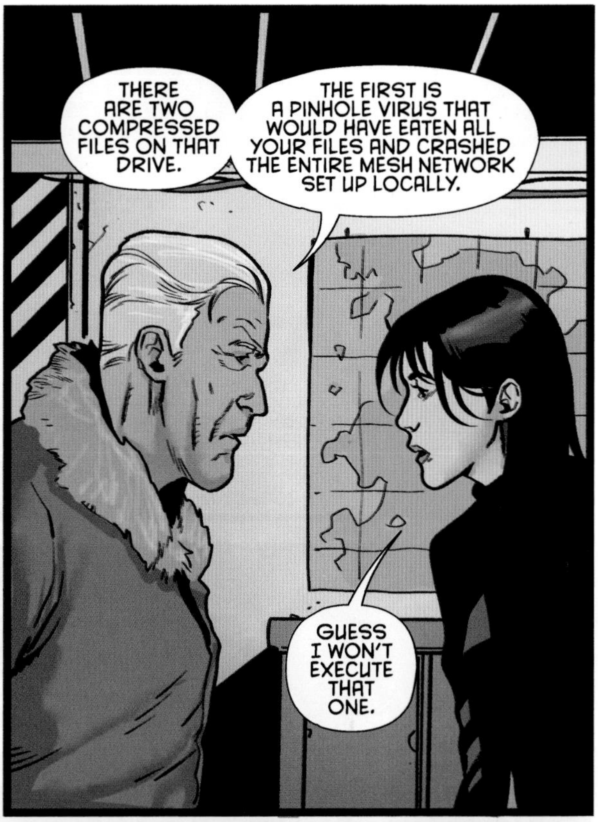
THERE ARE TWO COMPRESSED FILES ON THAT DRIVE.
THE FIRST IS A PINHOLE VIRUS THAT WOULD HAVE EATEN ALL YOUR FILES AND CRASHED THE ENTIRE MESH NETWORK SET UP LOCALLY.
GUESS I WON'T EXECUTE THAT ONE.

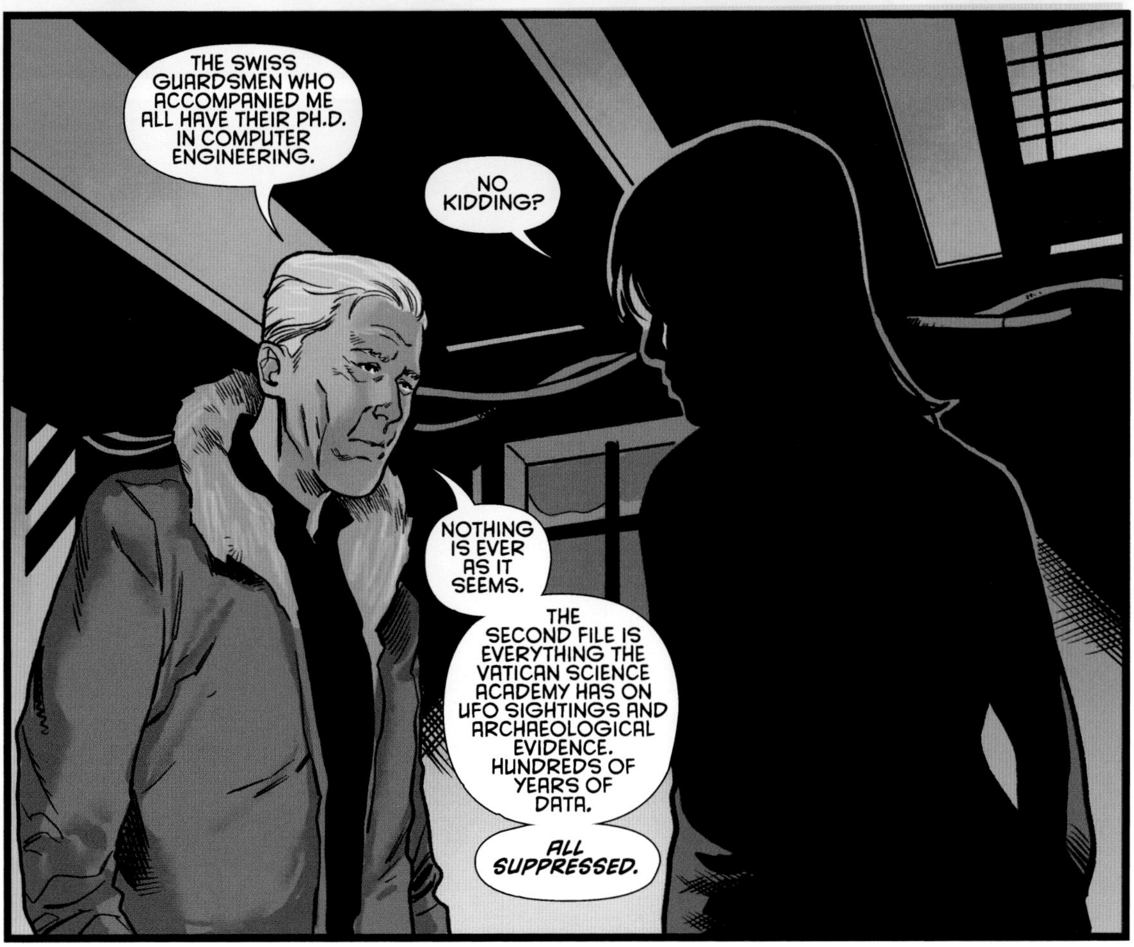
THE SWISS GUARDSMEN WHO ACCOMPANIED ME ALL HAVE THEIR PH.D. IN COMPUTER ENGINEERING.
NO KIDDING?
NOTHING IS EVER AS IT SEEMS.
THE SECOND FILE IS EVERYTHING THE VATICAN SCIENCE ACADEMY HAS ON UFO SIGHTINGS AND ARCHAEOLOGICAL EVIDENCE. HUNDREDS OF YEARS OF DATA.
ALL SUPPRESSED.

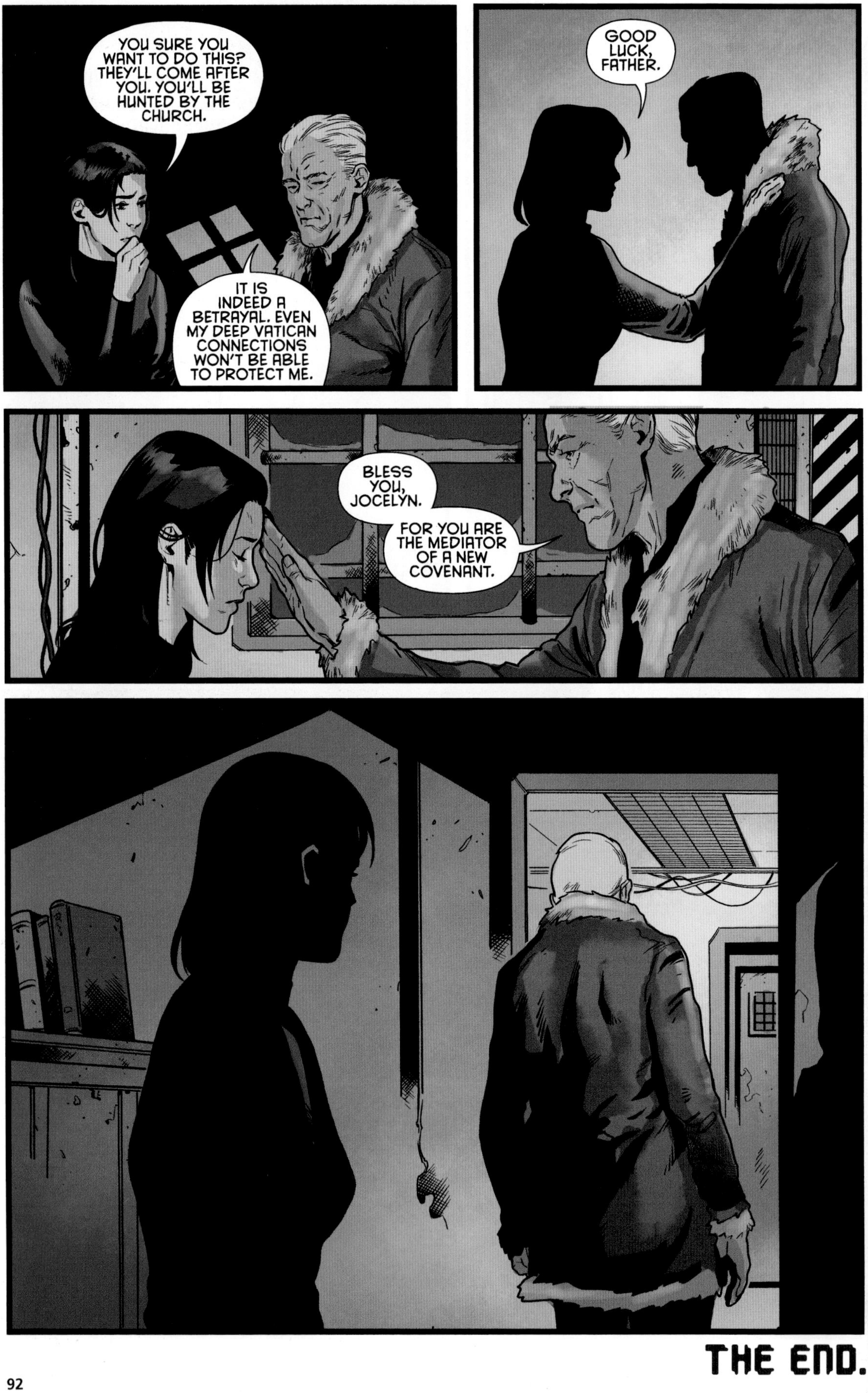
YOU SURE YOU WANT TO DO THIS? THEY'LL COME AFTER YOU. YOU'LL BE HUNTED BY THE CHURCH.
IT IS INDEED A BETRAYAL. EVEN MY DEEP VATICAN CONNECTIONS WON'T BE ABLE TO PROTECT ME.
GOOD LUCK, FATHER.
BLESS YOU, JOCELYN.
FOR YOU ARE THE MEDIATOR OF A NEW COVENANT.

THE END.

Justin Giampaoli, Writer

JUSTIN GIAMPAOLI was a prolific critic at *Thirteen Minutes* and *Comics Bulletin* for over a decade. As a writer, his work includes the self-published crime caper *The Mercy Killing* with artist Tim Goodyear, introductions and bonus content for *New York Times* Bestseller *DMZ* at DC/Vertigo, as well as the alt-history epic *Rome West* and the sci-fi drama *Starship Down*, both with artist Andrea Mutti at Dark Horse. Justin's upcoming work includes a modernization of classic Edgar Allan Poe characters with artist Matthew Southworth for Madefire.

🐦 **@ThirteenMinutes**

Andrea Mutti, Artist

ANDREA MUTTI attended a three-year Visual Arts program directed by Ruben Hector Sosa in Brescia. He started publishing at the beginning of the 1990s, collaborating with various publishers such as Fumettando and Fenix. He then became a part of the HAMMER project and spent about nine years at Sergio Bonelli Editore on the *Nathan Never* series. A continuous collaboration with the French market began when he started making comics with publishers such as Glenat, Dargaud, Soleil, Lombard, Ankama, Casterman, Dupuis, and many others. In 2001, Mutti landed in the US market working with prestigious publishers such as Marvel, DC, Dark Horse, IDW, IMAGE, Top Cow, Vault, Dynamite, BOOM! Studios, Universal, Adaptive, and many more.

🐦 **@andreamutti9**

Vladimir Popov, Colorist

VLADIMIR POPOV is a European-based author who worked for publishers such as Dark Horse, Vault Comics, Top Cow, Image Comics, IDW Publishing, Boom Studios, Dynamite Entertainment, Stela, DoubleTake, Wired Magazine, Soleil, Glenat (French), La Feltrinelli (Italy) and others on high-profile licensed titles such as Clive Barker's *Hellraiser* and *Next Testament*, *Robocop*, *Steed and Mrs. Peel*, *Noir*, *Pathfinder*, Cartoon Network's *Adventure Time* and *Amazing World of Gumball*, *Maze Runner*, and others. He collaborated on creator-owned titles such as *Fearscape*, *Port of Earth*, *Sand + Bone*, *Rome West*, *Control*, *The Returning*, *Darklight*, *Americatown*, *Freelancers*, and others. He is currently on his first year of Ph.D. studies of contemporary art.

🐦 **@VPopov_Artworks**

Sal Cipriano, Letterer

Brooklyn-born **SAL CIPRIANO** is a freelance letterer working with a ride range of publishers and creators. His former comic book experiences include writing, drawing, coloring, editing, and publishing. When not lettering, Sal reviews action figures on YouTube and drinks gallons of coffee. Sal's credits include *The Batman Who Laughs*, *Hellblazer*, *Superman Unchained*, *Invisible Kingdom*, *Rough Riders*, and more!

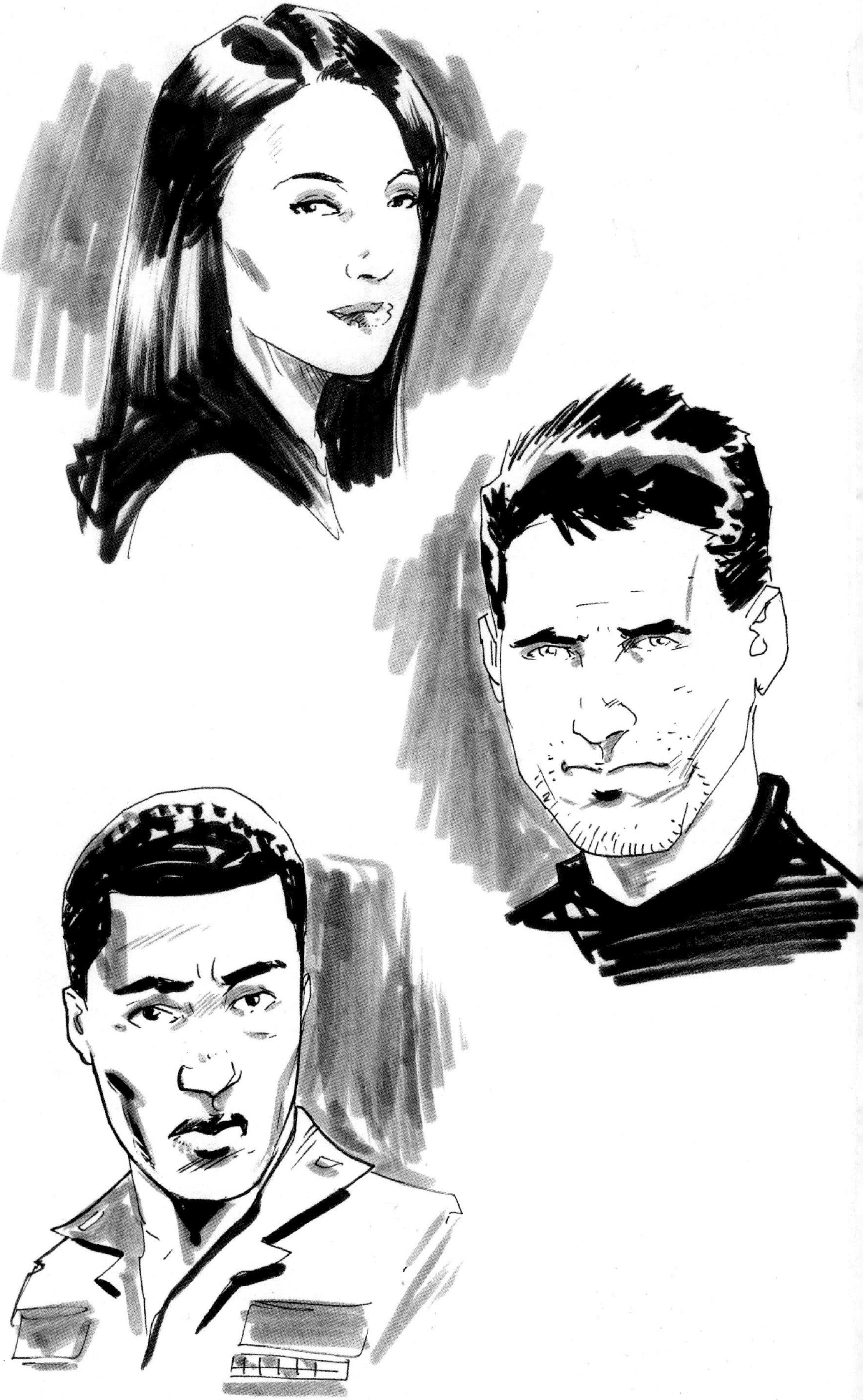

VANAVARA

Alternate Title: "Starship Down"

Pitch Prepared for Spencer Cushing @ Dark Horse

CONCEPT:

Vanavara is a mind-screwing sci-fi drama depicting a startling discovery in the small mining village of Vanavara, Russia. This archaeological find will rewrite human history as we know it, upending our understanding of science, religion, human exceptionalism, and our place in the universe. *Vanavara* is a 5-issue mini-series.

OVERVIEW:

Deep in the Siberian wastes, Vanavara has a population of 3,000 and is notable only for its subzero temperatures, stray cobalt mines, and being the settlement nearest to the 1908 Tunguska Event. It will soon become the most popular locale on Earth. When a long-lost extraterrestrial craft is discovered buried deep in the ice, it definitively chronicles man's origin.

Vanavara is classic science-fiction that begins with a compelling "What If?" premise, and hits the psychological thrills that made *The Twilight Zone* and *The X-Files* into an enduring phenomenon.

SUMMARY:

The series opens with different factions already descending on Vanavara. The Russian government is scrambling to maintain control of the remote crash site, in a contentious debate with US Naval Intelligence, claiming jurisdiction due to the close proximity of an American weather station. We follow a trio of characters grappling with the discovery in their own ways.

Dr. Jocelyn Young is a cultural anthropologist whisked away from Duke University to consult with the military, and is being briefed en route. Her mission is to debunk the find as Russian theatrics, and suppress anything that would upset the status quo and create panic. As a woman of science, she'll become a believer when the data all points to the veracity of the alien find.

Cardinal Dominik Arns is the Archbishop of Eurasia, sent by the Vatican to investigate the happenings at Vanavara. Representing the interests of millions of faithful Roman Catholics around the globe, the church initially embraces the find and tries to spin it as proof of divine intervention, but Arns will experience a deep crisis of faith.

Josip Demyan is a humble family man thrust into the international spotlight, one of the local mining crew who made the find, now hounded by the media, clergy, and government officials.

The shock ending of the first issue is the anachronistic reveal of deceased Neanderthals inside the craft. Holographic evidence divulges the existence of an alien race called the Nazar from the planet Etrus, who once seeded a long-forgotten backwater planet in the Terran system with failed genetic experiments — Earth was an intergalactic garbage dump. *Vanavara* explores our longing for answers and the shockwave of knowledge that ripples through human existence when they finally come. God is Dead. Science is Dead. There is only *Vanavara*.

###

SABERTOOTH SWORDSMAN
Damon Gentry and Aaron Conley
Granted the form of the Sabertooth Swordsman by the Cloud God of Sasquatch Mountain, a simple farmer embarks on a treacherous journey to the Mastodon's fortress!

ISBN 978-1-61655-176-6 | $17.99

PIXU: THE MARK OF EVIL
Gabriel Bá, Becky Cloonan, Vasilis Lolos, and Fábio Moon
This gripping tale of urban horror follows the lives of five lonely strangers who discover a dark mark scrawled on the walls of their building. As the walls come alive, everyone is slowly driven mad, stripped of free will, leaving only confusion, chaos, and eventual death.

ISBN 978-1-61655-813-0 | $14.99

SACRIFICE
Sam Humphries, Dalton Rose, Bryan Lee O'Malley, and others
What happens when a troubled youth is plucked from modern society and sent on a psychedelic journey into the heart of the Aztec civilization—one of the greatest and most bloodthirsty times in human history?

ISBN 978-1-59582-985-6 | $19.99

DE:TALES
Fábio Moon and Gabriel Bá
Brimming with all the details of human life, Moon and Bá's charming stories move from the urban reality of their home in São Paulo to the magical realism of their Latin American background. Named by *Booklist* as one of the 10 Best Graphic Novels of 2010.

ISBN 978-1-59582-557-5 | $19.99

MIND MGMT OMNIBUS
Matt Kindt
This globe-spanning tale of espionage explores the adventures of a journalist investigating the mystery of a commercial flight where everyone aboard loses their memories. Each omnibus volume collects two volumes of the Eisner Award—winning series!

VOLUME 1: THE MANAGER AND THE FUTURIST
ISBN 978-1-50670-460-9 | $24.99

VOLUME 2: THE HOME MAKER AND THE MAGICIAN
ISBN 978-1-50670-461-6 | $24.99

VOLUME 3: THE ERASER AND THE IMMORTALS
ISBN 978-1-50670-462-3 | $24.99